PAUL ROBESON, JR. SPEAKS TO AMERICA

PAUL ROBESON, JR.
S·P·E·A·K·S
TO AMERICA

Paul Robeson, Jr.

Rutgers University Press
New Brunswick, New Jersey

Library of Congress Cataloging-in-Publication Data

Robeson, Paul, Jr.
    Paul Robeson, Jr. speaks to America / Paul Robeson, Jr.
        p.   cm.
    Includes bibliographical references and index.
    ISBN 0-8135-1985-3
    1. Pluralism (Social science)—United States.
    2. United States—Race relations.
    3. Social classes—United States. I. Title
E184.A1R56   1993
305.8'00973—dc20   92-36164
                                                        CIP

British Cataloging-in Publication information available.

For my wife, Marilyn, whose loving patience, steadfast support, and thoughtful counsel helped me to write this book.

CONTENTS

his book of essays presents a personal view of today's American culture as it makes the painful transition from the traditional melting pot to the mosaic of the future. It is about race within the context of the three other central issues of our time—ethnicity, gender, and class—and also about the underlying significance of the ideological conflict between the supporters of the mosaic and the guardians of the melting pot.

American culture and its mass media are still dominated by melting-pot ideology, and, therefore, the struggle between the mosaic and the melting pot is generally misunderstood to be a debate about "cultural diversity" or "the politics of race and gender." My book translates the symbolism of our popular culture into language that reflects the underlying conflicts and contending groups in our society.

Usually, the tension between the mosaic and the melting pot surfaces only indirectly. The media recently reported that Governor Kirk Fordice of Mississippi, speaking at a conference of Republican governors, proclaimed the United States to be "a Christian nation." Governor Carroll A. Campbell, Jr. of South Carolina corrected Fordice by stating that our country is based on the "Judeo-Christian heritage." Fordice retorted that if he had wanted to add the "Judeo" part, he would have done so. This exchange has profound social and political implications, but the reports provided no commentary.

A Christian America which is *not* Judeo-Christian means, in historical context, a *White Anglo-Saxon Protestant America.* The explicit denial of equal status to Jews implies a similar denial to all immigrants who are not Anglo-Saxon Protestants, not to speak of non-Whites. This, it seems to me, accurately describes the traditional melting pot.

The mosaic, which Blacks of slave ancestry have fought for unremittingly and with undying hope since the founding of our Republic, shatters the foundations of the melting pot by treating *everyone,* including Anglo-Saxons, equally as *ethnics,* thus minimizing both racial and ethnic distinctions. We want *everyone* to be accepted as an ethnic American in a *multicultural* society that guarantees the equal rights of every ethnic group and not merely the equal rights of every individual. Then there will be no "them"; there will be only "us." However, until equal *ethnic* rights are guaranteed, African-Americans of all ethnicities are determined to rely on *racial* solidarity to protect their interests.

The great majority of African-Americans are the descendants of southern slaves whose ancestors belonged to the ethnic groups of West and Central Africa who based their common culture on African values that bridged the differences between the different ethnic groups among them. Then they joined this culture with the Judeo-Christian heritage to create an enduring mosaic culture that nourished the radical ethnic integrationism of Rev. Martin Luther King, Jr. Today, this cultural tradition underlies the powerful Black political support of the mosaic trend in White America.

But in addition to creating a common culture, the southern slaves preserved the essential elements of their diverse ethnic (tribal) cultures, and these elements are still present today.

I bring to this book my own life experience as the grandson of a slave whose ancestors belonged to the Ibo tribe of Nigeria, West Africa.

My father was the preeminent cultural figure in America in the 1940s as a world-famous singer and actor, and as a leading spokesman for both Black Americans and liberal White Americans. His record-breaking performance in the lead role of *Othello* on Broadway helped to improve the racial climate in our nation. At the same time, he refused to be exploited as a role model by the White establishment, choosing instead to become a forerunner of both the African awareness and civil rights movements.

Later, as a close aide to my father over a period of twenty years, I learned from him that cultural values are more important than role models in promoting individual growth and the advancement of a people. So, along with the pursuit of my professional careers, I have been a civil rights activist ever since the 1940s.

My experiences have convinced me that there is no contradiction between fighting uncompromisingly for racial equality and building coalitions across racial boundaries. In fact, racial cultures are by definition mosaic in the sense that they include a wide diversity of ethnic (i.e., tribal, clan, national) cultures, and, therefore, race is more inclusive than ethnicity. Consequently, if America has been able to bridge ethnic differences, it is even more possible to bridge racial differences given the political will to do so. The chief obstacle to racial reconciliation lies in American culture's artificial reduction of race to *skin color only*—a reduction which denies the incontrovertible reality of *racial cultures* and confines culture exclusively to ethnicity.

It is the racial culture reflected in the tradition of the southern Black slaves that underlies the positive response of Black voters to President Bill Clinton's message of cultural (ethnic) inclusion across racial boundaries. A united Black vote for the Clinton-Gore ticket in the 1992 presidential election provided 4.5 points out of Clinton's total winning margin of 5.6 points in a 43.0 percent to 37.4 percent victory. The Black vote was also decisive in the pivotal and closely contested midwestern and southern states.

Moreover, Blacks were an integral part of a broad mosaic coalition that propelled Clinton into the White House: 82 percent of the total Black vote; 78 percent of the Jewish vote; 62 percent of Hispanics; a plurality of Catholics; 55 percent of union households, and a plurality of households earning under $50,000 annually. On the other hand, the staunchest defenders of the melting pot were those who voted for George Bush: a strong plurality of White Protestants; 61 percent of born-again White Christians, and, demonstrating that race is not always the primary issue, 55 percent of Asians.

Four seemingly unrelated events—the Anita Hill vs. Clarence Thomas confrontation, the Crown Heights clash between Blacks and Jews, Spike Lee's film *Malcolm X,* and a documentary film about President Lincoln offer evidence that the melting pot is giving way to the mosaic.

As a Black woman, Anita Hill challenged the rules of *both* the Black *and* White male establishments by publicly accusing a Black male Supreme Court nominee of sexual harassment. In doing so, she provided the spark that led to the political unity of Black and White women across the boundary of race. Her courage reminded me of my mother, who was a renaissance *woman* and behaved as a liberated *person* long before the women's movement became popular.

The Crown Heights conflict is primarily an *ethnic* clash between ultra-orthodox Lubavitcher Hasidim and Jamaican West Indians who are often Catholic, rather than a Black-Jewish *racial* confrontation.

White America's acceptance of Spike Lee's film *Malcolm X,* which represents a powerful image of an ethnic Black male, signals our nation's readiness for the beginning of mosaic ethnic integration.

The documentary film *Abraham Lincoln: A New Birth of Freedom,* which was first shown on public television in December 1992, evokes President Lincoln's launching of the nation along the path toward the mosaic culture with his Gettysburg Address. It reminds us that we have come full circle from Lincoln to Clinton—from the progressive WASP president who began the long march toward the mosaic to another progressive WASP president who is destined to complete it. As in Lincoln's time, Black Americans of slave ancestry will play a crucial role, for they constitute the only large ethnic group capable of mobilizing racial solidarity in the service of nonracial, universal goals. This healing capability has been nurtured in different ways by the legacies of Paul Robeson, whose artistry expressed the universality of American slave culture; of Martin Luther King, who achieved the political fruition of this culture; and the latter-day Malcolm X, who gave his life to repudiate the racial nationalism of the Nation of Islam.

ACKNOWLEDGMENTS

he idea for this book originated with Kenneth Arnold, Director of Rutgers University Press, who suggested to me that I write a book about cultural diversity based on a 1991 lecture I had given at Rutgers University. And it was he who provided invaluable assistance during my initial efforts to produce a series of focused but connected essays on diverse cultural topics.

I have benefited greatly from the experience and dedication of editor Judith Martin Waterman whose work on the manuscript helped me to improve the quality of my prose and to sharpen my message.

My thanks also to the cover designer, John Romer, for the imaginative and effective cover.

PAUL ROBESON, JR. SPEAKS TO AMERICA

WHICH CULTURE?
WHOSE DIVERSITY?

he controversy over multiculturalism is not, as many claim, merely a manifestation of the politics of race and gender; rather, it is at the heart of a profound ideological struggle over the values of American culture and the nature of u.s. civilization. Above all, it is a debate about whether the melting-pot culture, which is the foundation of the American way of life and imposes its Anglo-Saxon Protestant values on our society, should be replaced by a mosaic culture incorporating the values of the diverse groups that make up America's population.

I decided to explore in a series of essays the racial, ethnic, gender, and class conflicts that are generated by the monocultural melting-pot model in an increasingly multiethnic, multiracial United States. The issue of *which* culture we should have is linked to the issue of *whose* diversity we are talking about: the diversity of those who peer out at the world from the confines of the monocultural melting pot, or the diversity of those who move comfortably through the spreading multicultural mosaic. Do we support a melting-pot culture that confines diversity to the *recognition* of different individual cultural *styles,* or a mosaic culture that *accepts* the different *values* of group cultures in our society.

The cultural conflict between the supporters of the mosaic and the defenders of the melting pot places in doubt the current distribution of political and economic power, since the Anglo-Saxon Protestant cultural bias of the melting pot translates into long-established racial and ethnic hierarchies in the political and economic spheres. For example, in electoral politics Whites descended from immigrants whom the melting pot accepted are pitted against Blacks whom the melting pot excluded. Peter Vallone, speaker of New York's City Council, used an interview with the *New York Times* (May 20, 1991) on the newly enhanced powers of the City Council to reject Mayor Dinkins's idea of a mosaic: "Forget this mosaic; I like the melting pot."

Additionally, powerful pressures exerted on most Americans by the economic recession in the early 1990s, the crisis in education, the drug-abuse epidemic, increased racial conflict, and a widening income spread between social classes contributed to the rapid growth of racial, ethnic, gender, and class consciousness throughout u.s. society. As a result, an expanding multiculturalist movement resting on strong individual identification with ethnic, racial, and social groups has challenged the melting-pot culture. This challenge by the mosaic alternative raises questions about the foundations of the liberal democracy which the Constitution was designed to establish.

Although the original Constitution explicitly defined a deservedly revered model of human freedom, it implicitly subordinated all those who were not White, male, and middle-class by the restriction of voting rights to White male property owners. It was from this implicit license that the traditional melting pot obtained its mandate to induct successive generations of White male immigrants into American culture while relegating White women and non-Whites to second-class status.

Moreover the ideology expressed in the founding fathers' motto "life, liberty, and the pursuit of happiness" required the expansion of individual rights to a near-absolute maximum at the expense of group rights and community responsibility. The rights of the individual were defined as individual *liberties*, and individuals were defined as *voters*. Since the only voters were White male property owners, they were the only ones entitled to individual liberties. These *liberties* included the right to violate the *freedoms* of those not defined as individuals—e.g., the right to own slaves or to oppress indentured servants—and therefore a distinction was made between *liberty* and *freedom.*

The dictionary definitions of liberty and freedom have similar meanings. Both terms embody two basic concepts: freedom *to do* what a person or group reasonably wishes, and freedom *from* unequal treatment by other persons, groups, or the government. However, U.S. tradition has produced an artificial separation between liberty and freedom by associating liberty primarily with the right of *individuals* to do reasonably as they wish, and associating freedom mainly with the right of *groups* to be protected from unequal treatment. Thus, the White male property owners who wrote the Declaration of Independence and the Constitution spoke of liberty rather than of freedom, whereas Black slaves spoke of freedom but not of liberty.

Consequently, the defense of liberty came to mean the prevention of government interference with majority *individuals'* ability to act according to their will through the exercise of their civil *liberties,* whereas the guarantee of freedom came to rest on the power of the government to protect minority *groups* by enforcing their civil *rights.* And since the enforcement of these minority rights necessarily infringes on the individual liberties of majority-group members, it is not surprising that the majority culture opposes group rights and elevates liberty above freedom.

The melting-pot culture is based on the denial of group rights and a one-sided emphasis on "radical individualism," whereas the mosaic culture affirms group rights along with individual rights and emphasizes a balance between individual liberty and individual responsibility to the community. This difference underlies the conflict between the melting pot and the mosaic over the issues of race, ethnicity, gender, and class, since the melting pot has traditionally used the denial of group rights to subordinate non-Anglo-Saxon White ethnic groups, non-Whites, White women, and those who do not own property (i.e., people who do not belong to the middle or upper classes).

Syndicated columnist Charles Krauthammer described the individualist foundation of the melting pot in a column hailing the joint protest of twenty-four historians, including Arthur Schlesinger Jr., C. Vann Woodward, and Diane Ravitch, against the official 1990 recommendations for the inclusion of multiculturalism in the New York state school curriculum (*The Providence Journal,* August 5, 1990):

> American unity has been built on a tightly federalist politics and a powerful melting-pot culture. America chose to deal with the problem of differentness (ethnicity) by embracing radical individualism and rejecting the notion of group rights.

Note that Mr. Krauthammer identifies "the problem of differentness" solely with "ethnicity," meaning immigrant White ethnic groups, while ignoring the other main differentnesses in American society—race, gender, and class. This omission reflects the exclusion of racial minorities, women, and the so-called underclass from "melting-pot culture," and the rejection of "the notion of group rights" denies these groups any legal protection from unequal treatment.

Thus, *ethnicity,* rather than race, has always served as the foundation of melting-pot culture. Today, ethnicity determines the status of groups *inside* the melting pot, whereas race is used to exclude most Blacks *from* the melting pot.

My ten essays address various aspects of the mosaic challenge to the melting pot's denial of group rights, and to the resulting distortion of racial, ethnic, gender, and class relations in the service of an Anglo-Saxon Protestant dominance. The mosaic rejects the notion of innate Anglo-Saxon cultural superiority by championing the cultural recognition of all *groups,* thus advancing American culture toward the natural combination of its diverse parts in a society where everyone, regardless of ethnicity, race, gender, or class, will be accepted as a culturally endowed American.

THE BOOK COVERS A VARIETY of topics ranging from the artificial manipulation of ethnicity against race by the melting pot to the birth of a new American culture.

The first four chapters provide an overall setting for today's cultural controversies by examining how the ideological struggle between the melting pot and the mosaic is manifested under the surface of an American culture still dominated by the melting pot. The challenges mounted against the melting pot by the advocates of the mosaic are almost invariably cloaked as reforms of the present American culture rather than as proposals for a new one, or else as historical references that have a concealed ideological significance.

Thus, the supporters of the mosaic do not speak of a mosaic but only of inclusion, whereas the defenders of the melting pot argue openly that the melting pot is the only effective barrier against social chaos. Lincoln, who emancipated the slaves and championed group rights, is the special hero of the mosaic, whereas Jefferson, who owned slaves and championed individual liberties, is favored by the melting pot.

The next five chapters address specific controversies in today's American society from a mosaic viewpoint: the "culture wars" on university campuses; cultural diversity in the workplace; the gender conflict; the clash between Jews and Blacks, and divisions within the Black middle class. The concluding chapter discusses the multiculturalist movement as the harbinger of a new, mosaic American culture.

Chapter 1, "Ethnicity versus Race," and chapter 2, "Multiculturalism and the Bush Supreme Court," analyze the interconnected melting-pot principles of denying *ethnic* recognition to racial minorities and outlawing group rights with the effect of excluding these minorities from the melting pot. These two principles underlie melting-pot resistance to the campaign by Blacks for a *group* cultural recognition that is equivalent to *ethnic* status.

This can be seen in historian C. Vann Woodward's sympathetic review of Dinesh D'Souza's book, *Illiberal Education: The Politics of Race and Sex on Campus* (*New York Review of Books*, July 18, 1991):

> In the present crisis the attack on freedom comes from outside as well as inside and is led by minorities, that is, people who speak or claim to speak for groups of students and faculty. Their cause is minority rights and sensitivities. . . .
>
> . . . Increasingly, they have thought of themselves as groups rather than as individuals, and their culture as determined by their race.
>
> One form separatism has taken is an attack upon the

curriculum as an expression of white racial arrogance
and propaganda, an attack accompanied by demands for
a curriculum of their own.

Professor Woodward sees "freedom" in melting-pot society threatened by "minority" rights in general, but the context in which he uses the
terms "minority" and "race" reveals that he is referring mainly to Blacks. His
point seems to be that Blacks must not identify their *culture* with their *race,*
and must think of themselves as Black *individuals* rather than as a Black
racial group having a distinct culture. In other words, Blacks must abandon
their *racial* solidarity in favor of individualism so that there will be no need
for them to demand group *cultural* status.

One is led to wonder whether Professor Woodward would expect
Whites to accept this artificial separation of race from culture and to think
of their culture as *not* "determined by their race." In any case, African-
Americans reject such a detachment of culture from race because our race,
culture, and ethnicity are inseparably connected. We are at one and the
same time *both* Black *and* African-American. Like European-Americans,
Latin-Americans, Asian-Americans, and Native Americans, we are *both*
racial *and* ethnic. We use the term Black to emphasize the common, racial
aspect of our culture, while African-American refers to the diverse, ethnic
aspect.

The mosaic accepts this duality, whereas the melting pot confines
racial terms to the literal meaning of color and so avoids attaching any
cultural significance to them. In today's scholarly style the racial terms
black and white are put in lower case in contrast to the ethnic terms African
and European. Therefore, in keeping with my mosaic outlook, Black and
White take initial capital letters throughout this book in order to underscore the cultural aspect of race.

A White acquaintance of mine who is a product of the melting pot
expressed the opposing view by cutting right through all such subtleties
with a pithy comment about former President Bush's 1991 nomination of
Judge Clarence Thomas to the U.S. Supreme Court: "Good nomination.
He's an *American* black, not one of those African blacks."

Bush's nomination of Judge Thomas, a conservative Republican, to the Supreme Court was designed to be a master stroke in defense of the melting pot. By nominating a Black judge of American slave ancestry who had climbed to success from a poor family in a small southern town and become a staunch defender of the melting pot against group rights, Mr. Bush aimed to split the supporters of the mosaic over the issue of race while placing exclusive rhetorical emphasis on individual liberties. Blacks, White women, and liberals would be forced to oppose a Black man who had risen by dint of melting-pot individualism, while his conservative supporters could focus on attacking group rights.

In a University of Michigan commencement address on May 4, 1991, only two months before his nomination of Judge Thomas, President Bush signaled this line by subordinating the issues of race and gender to the issue of individual liberties versus group rights:

> Ironically, on the 200th anniversary of our Bill of Rights, we find free speech under assault throughout the United States, including on some college campuses. The notion of political correctness has ignited controversy across the land. And although the movement arises from the laudable desire to sweep away the debris of racism and sexism and hatred, it replaces old prejudices with new ones.
>
> ... In their own Orwellian way, crusades that demand correct behavior crush diversity in the name of diversity.

Here the Bill of Rights, which guarantees freedoms to groups as well as to individuals, is turned against group freedoms in order to defend individual freedoms. By charging that the multiculturalists who want to "sweep away racism and sexism" have set out to crush cultural diversity by totalitarian means, Bush misses the point that the diversity he wants defended is the prejudiced behavior of majority-group members. Moreover, Bush's linkage of minority prejudice with the suppression of free speech implies that minorities must forgo protest against biased behavior by the majority in order to safeguard the freedoms of majority individuals.

Mr. Bush also tries to discredit the multiculturalist movement by pinning the political-correctness label on it and perceiving an "Orwellian" threat in minority-group demands for the restriction of majority-individual racist and sexist behavior. The terms "political correctness" and "Orwellian" are Communist-baiting ones: George Orwell's novel *1984* was a searing caricature of Communism, and "political correctness" was used in Stalinist Russia and Maoist China as the basis for cultural censorship.

Chapter 3 is an essay about my father's embodiment of the future mosaic culture. Paul Robeson's challenge to the melting pot is encapsulated by his 1920s pride in "the culture of ancient Africa" and his 1940s determination to "strike at the complete liberation of the Negro people in our time."

Because of the close identification of American culture with our governmental system, the expression of loyalty to a racial-minority group by a national figure from that group has usually been perceived as subversive by both the cultural infrastructure and the government. Paul Robeson was a classic example of this. My late father was among the 123 charter members inducted into the U.S. Theater Hall of Fame established in New York City's Uris Theater on October 22, 1972. He was also one of the greatest scholar-athletes in U.S. college history, a world-famous concert singer, and a pioneer Black actor in American film. After he emerged from the melting pot into which he had been recruited because of his extraordinary talents and commanding personality, his increasing dedication to his African-American cultural traditions led him to combat the stereotypes of American culture and to become one of the most censored and persecuted artists in American history when he dared to express his political opinions.

Robeson left the commercial film industry in 1938 at the height of a lucrative film career, attacking Hollywood not only for its anti-Black stereotypes but also for its caricaturing of other groups in society and for its cultural banality:

> I thought I could do something for the Negro race in films—show the truth about them and about other people too; I used to go away feeling satisfied—thought everything was O.K. Well, it wasn't. The industry is not prepared to permit me to portray the life or express the

> living interests, hopes, and aspirations of the struggling
> people from whom I come. . . .
>   . . . I am no longer willing to identify myself with an
> organization that has no regard for reality—an organi-
> zation that attempts to nullify public intelligence, falsify
> life, and entirely ignore the many dynamic forces in the
> world today. . . .
>   . . . You bet they will never let me play a part in a film
> in which a Negro is on top.

Based on his Afrocentric world view and his extensive contacts with European, African, and Eastern cultures, Paul Robeson learned to empathize with the worldwide mosaic of ethnic identifications. By translating this empathy into his artistry, he was able to affect the individuals in his audiences across the boundaries of the melting pot. The gray pictures and muted sounds of the melting-pot culture were replaced with the multicolored images and boundless music of the mosaic culture.

The late James Baldwin commented insightfully on the manner in which the melting-pot culture responded to Paul Robeson's legacy:

> The popular culture is designed to make money. There-
> fore the popular culture confronted with Paul Robeson
> has to find a way to make him moving, charming, noble,
> innocent, and, above all, irrelevant. It wants to present
> him as a kind of chocolate John Wayne.

The fourth chapter, "Black and White History," views the American past through the contrasting lenses of the melting pot and the mosaic, rather than in the traditional liberal-versus-conservative context. A central feature of this approach is a critique of the close link between the melting-pot culture and liberal democracy as a political system.

Liberal democracy has difficulty accommodating the combination of multiculturalism with sharp divisions on social issues, and the present two-party system is already splintering under the pressures generated by such issues as abortion, race, and economic fairness. In the election year of 1992, the Republican party's anti-abortion stand turned many Republican women against Republican candidates, while the failure of the liberal Democratic leadership to support the economic agenda of African-Americans created serious tensions in the Democratic party.

✗ This vulnerability is what American historian Barrington Moore, Jr. had in mind when he laid down the essential conditions for a successful liberal democracy such as that of the United States in the First Annual W. Averell Harriman Lecture (Columbia University, November 15, 1989):

> 1. A homogeneous population in which the same culture is widely shared. One can turn this around by asserting that strong religious differences and ethnic loyalties make trouble for liberal democracies. . . .
> 2. Political issues in a [liberal] democracy cannot be too highly charged or too divisive. They cannot become matters of life and death or, more accurately, matters that arouse intense moral passion.

Moore then went on to define the purpose of liberal democracy:

> Democracy has been a weapon of the poor and the many against the few and the well-to-do ever since it surfaced in ancient Athens. The liberal component, where it has existed, was an attempt to gain protection against arbitrary acts by *either* the poor and many, or the dominant few.

✗ The political system of ancient Greece, the cradle of Western civilization, was based on popular democracy ("the weapon of the poor and the many against the few and the well-to-do") rather than on liberal democracy. This sheds light on one of the reasons for liberal hostility toward multiculturalism: to the extent that this movement links the issues of race and gender to the issue of class, it tends to unite the poor and the many to a degree that threatens liberalism.

Professor Moore acknowledges the importance of the class issue by identifying the wide diffusion of property among the population as the most vital condition for a successful liberal democracy:

This wide diffusion is important because it provides a social base for independence from the government, as well as from other organized groups in the society. Merely to mention this condition at this point in history leads to somewhat pessimistic conclusions because this precondition has largely disappeared. The rise of modern industry and big government has greatly narrowed the diffusion of property in almost all of the advanced areas of the world. Industrial workers have jobs rather than property. So do white-collar workers and even an increasing number of professionals such as lawyers, doctors, and natural scientists who work in and for large firms or the government. To some extent skill has replaced property as a source of independence.

The narrower distribution of property reflects the correspondingly greater concentration of property in the hands of the wealthy at the expense of the working class, middle class, and professionals. But Moore neglects to mention the disproportionate lack of wealth, including property, suffered by Blacks: the average wealth (i.e., net worth) of a Black family is one-tenth the average wealth of a White family, so for Blacks the acquisition of marketable skills is the only realistic means of achieving a degree of economic viability. The result is that the educational system has become a racial battleground on which a struggle is being waged with increasing intensity over the demand of Blacks for equal educational opportunity.

Professor Moore makes another basic point when he refers to the reason why widespread ownership of property is so important: it provides "a social base for independence from the government, as well as from other organized groups." Therefore it follows that the severe deficit of Black property ownership has created an increased individual dependence on government and on groups. Such a condition runs counter to the requirements of radical individualism and leads to heightened Black racial identification.

It is therefore not surprising that Blacks view African-American history differently than do the liberal historians who currently dominate this field. Moreover, a majority of Blacks have always rejected liberal ideology concerning race because of liberals' adherence to the two main precepts of the melting pot: 1. the primacy of individualism over group rights; and 2. the artificial separation of culture (ethnicity) from race.

Chapter 5 centers on a discussion of the controversial book *Illiberal Education: The Politics of Race and Sex on Campus* by Dinesh D'Souza, in the context of the struggle between the melting pot and the mosaic on university campuses. The setting for this essay is the debate among university scholars and administrators that presents the ideologies of both sides along with the issues they stress.

The Op-Ed page of the May 4, 1991, issue of the *New York Times* carried a defense of the melting pot by Dean Donald Kagan of Yale University, and an argument for the mosaic by Professor Henry Louis Gates, Jr. of Harvard University. Their discussion is especially useful because it ignores the most publicized but less fundamental issues of political correctness and affirmative action and concentrates on the three themes that are central to the multiculturalism discussion: 1. the conversion of the melting pot from a system that excludes racial minorities and women to a mosaic that includes them; 2. the individual and the group as viewed from the contrasting positions of the melting pot and the mosaic; and 3. the nature of American culture.

In his treatment of the first theme, Dean Kagan promotes the inclusivity of today's melting pot by extolling ethnic self-identification: "Take pride in your family and in the culture they and your forebears have brought to our shores. Learn as much as you can about that culture." But in return for the right to enter the melting pot, "minorities" are called upon to accept the centrality of Western civilization and to assimilate into an American culture based on radical individualism. Failure to place Western values at the center of the curriculum, says Kagan, would imperil "our students, country and the hopes for a democratic, liberal society."

In presenting his opposing view, Professor Gates advocates a universal core multicultural curriculum on the ground that u.s. society cannot survive without a degree of cultural tolerance attainable solely through cultural understanding. Noting American culture's lack of neutrality in matters of race and gender, Gates rejects the idea of *assimilation* into American culture:

> One's public treatment, and public behavior, are shaped in large part by one's perceived ethnic identity, just as by one's gender. To demand that Americans shuck their cultural heritage and homogenize themselves into a "universal" WASP culture is to dream of an America in cultural white face, and that just won't do.

Clearly, Gates is rejecting the melting pot.

In his discussion of the second theme—the radical individualism which underlies the opposition to multiculturalism, Dean Kagan counterposes individual freedom to group identification: "Western heritage" has created both "a realm of privacy" for the individual and "a free and safe place for the individual conscience." These "great gifts of Western civilization" are threatened by students' identification with groups and by pressure exerted on them to subject themselves to group discipline. He proposes to combat this "threat" by detaching minority students from their group identifications, claiming that "a liberal education needs to bring about a challenge to the ideas, habits and attitudes students bring with them."

Although the idea of such a challenge is a valid one in the general sense, Dean Kagan's application of it here suggests that the university's liberal education should be used to break down minority students' group identifications so as to transform them into "free individuals" who can *assimilate* into American culture. Although their self-identification will remain the same as that of other individuals in their group, the university melting pot will transform their group identification to that of "American" individuals.

The foundation of Professor Gates's opposition to Dean Kagan's melting pot is expressed in his assertion that powerful cultural group identifications are present among minorities in American society and must be recognized formally. He refutes fears that cultural "pluralism" will preclude a "communal 'American' identity" and lead to "fragmentation," pointing out that the multiculturalist movement is partly the *result* of the melting pot's "fragmentation of society by ethnicity, class, and gender." By linking cultural pluralism to societal causes and describing the American identity as "communal" (i.e., made up of a mosaic of *groups*) rather than "common," Gates disputes the central pillar of radical individualism—a homogeneous national culture based on suppression of individual identification with culturally distinct groups.

Dean Kagan, following the practice of those who oppose multiculturalism, ignores the linkage between discrimination against minority individuals and the refusal to recognize the rights of minority groups. Professor Gates, however, begins his piece with a dramatic example of this linkage:

> I recently asked the dean of a prestigious liberal arts college if his school would ever have, as Berkeley has, a 70 percent nonwhite enrollment. "Never," he replied. "That would completely alter our identity as a center of the liberal arts."

In other words, the mere presence of "too many" Asians is a political liability that would cost the college its "liberal" status. Moreover, the Berkeley example is important because Asian students have become preponderant there as a result of their superior entrance-test scores—that is, on the basis of individual merit. Yet the dean would impose group quotas restricting Asian enrollment, thus indirectly violating the rights of Asian individuals. Only the recognition of *group* rights would render such obvious unfairness impossible, since *direct* violation of individual rights would be difficult to prove.

The issue of group rights is similarly at the heart of Professor Gates's insistence that the issue of curriculum changes be separated from the ethnic and gender composition of the student body. In his opinion, the attempts of both right and left to make inclusion of "various ethnic identities" in university studies an issue of "political representation" and to link academic change to population shifts are "wrongheaded." Gates is saying that representation of the cultures of minority *groups*, as distinct from the mention of outstanding minority *individuals*, is a right of minority groups and therefore not subject to political contention. *All* curricula for *all* student bodies should be multicultural.

Finally, the definitions of American culture offered by Dean Kagan and Professor Gates differ widely, the central point of contention being the culture's claim to both universality and superiority.

Dean Kagan defines the shared U.S. culture as "a system of laws and beliefs that shaped the establishment of the country, a system developed within the context of Western civilization":

> More than any other, it has asserted the claims of the individual against those of the state, limiting its power and creating a realm of privacy into which it cannot penetrate.
>
> . . . It has produced the theory and practice of the separation of church from state, protecting each from the other and creating a free and safe place for the individual conscience. At its core is a tolerance and respect for diversity unknown in most cultures. . . .
>
> Western culture and institutions are the most powerful paradigm in the world.

Kagan's use of the term "Western" rather than "European" suggests that he has in mind the Anglo-Saxon tradition of the United States and northwest Europe instead of the culturally diverse traditions of the entire European continent which stretches east as far as Russia's Ural Mountains. This Anglo-Saxon culture marginalizes the Greek, Italian, and Egyptian cultures which are descended from the ancient multicultural Greek, Roman, and Egyptian civilizations.

Professor Gates challenges the notion of a universal, superior Western culture:

> What has passed as "common culture" has been an Anglo-American regional culture, masking itself as universal. Significantly different cultures sought refuge underground. . . .

> ... A curriculum that reflects the achievement of the
> world's great cultures, not merely the West's, is not
> "politicized"; rather it situates the West as one of a
> community of civilizations. After all, culture is always a
> conversation among different voices.

First, Gates exposes the narrow, Anglo-Saxon Protestant basis of American culture. Second, he extends the mosaic metaphor to the world's cultures in the form of a "community of civilizations" where Western civilization is one of several "great cultures."

Taken as a whole, the Kagan-Gates "debate" is important because it confirms the proposition that the controversy about multiculturalism arises from deep ideological and political divisions in our country—divisions that will shape future politics. And as this struggle between the melting pot and the mosaic intensifies, America will face the even more fundamental issue of a wider distribution of political power—of liberal democracy versus popular (social) democracy.

The sixth chapter addresses the thorny issue of affirmative action under the title: "Cultural Diversity in the Workplace." Here the employment of minorities is discussed in light of the melting-pot's rationale for discrimination against Blacks—the double fiction according to which u.s. institutions are alleged to be color-blind and governed by laws, not men. The result is the denial of institutional discrimination against groups and the definition of race or gender bias as discrimination practiced by an *individual* who happens to be a bigot against an *individual* who happens to be a member of a minority group.

The melting-pot system of publicized affirmative action counterbalanced by secret quotas rests on this denial of group rights and has always been used to reward qualified minority individuals who have met the melting-pot standards of group nonidentification. The real quotas have always been secret and have been applied mostly to White males, qualified or unqualified, for the purpose of guaranteeing their entry into the melting-pot. For example, the discriminatory quota of ten percent which for decades restricted the *maximum* number of qualified Jewish men at Yale University illustrates this unacknowledged form of *group* integration benefiting White males only. However, when racial minorities and women demand exactly the same consideration to redress past discriminatory practices, vehement objections are raised on the ground that the principles of radical individualism are being violated; only *individual* integration is legitimate.

This double standard caused the liberal Democratic congressional leadership to water down the 1991 Civil Rights Bill in such a way that the punitive damages which could be sued for by female victims of discrimination were limited, whereas no limit was placed on the punitive damages which could be won by White males in reverse-discrimination suits.

A fundamental question arises here: which individualism are we to support—the uniform radical individualism of assimilation, or the diverse individualism associated with group identification; the individualism of those who have merged into the melting-pot culture, or the individualism of those whose self-image stems from their mosaic ancestral culture? It is the conflict between these two different notions of individualism that contributes to social fragmentation.

Chapter 7, "Gender and the Minority Fixation," focuses on the manner in which the common problem of discrimination has combined with a strengthened group identification to unite women as a group with African-Americans in a promosaic political coalition. A May 5, 1991, *New York Times* review of *Feminism Without Illusions: A Critique of Individualism* by historian Elizabeth Fox-Genovese reported that Professor Fox-Genovese opposed feminism's acceptance of an individualism "that replaces the early and glorious recognition of the claims of the individual against the state with the celebration of egotism and the denial or indefensible reduction of the just claims of the community." The review was accompanied by a quotation from the book which read, in part:

> Race and gender should, in fact, enjoy privileged positions in our understanding of American culture, for they lie at the core of any sense of self. The incalculable advantage of the dominant culture has been to deny their significance, to define the individual as not black and not female. Yet that very negative betrays the centrality of

race and gender to any conception of the American self. American culture has developed as a celebration of freedom and individualism, as a repudiation of inequality. The measure of its success—its hegemony—can be seen in its ability to promote the ideal of American exceptionalism, to deny the existence of systematic or structural inequalities. Above all, its success has consisted in its ability to conflate the subjective notion of the self with the objective notion of national identity and thereby to exclude those who do not fit the subjective model. . . .

Our culture can permit different individuals to claim it as their own—not necessarily as an expression of their immediate personal experience but as an affirmation of their national identity.

This view helps to explain the impact of American culture on individual behavior. The melting pot denies the significance of race and gender in defining the national identity ("the national self"), so that the ideal American individual identifies with the values of the White male middle class and behaves accordingly. Individuals who identify as Black or female strongly enough to identify with their *group* are either disadvantaged by the melting-pot culture or are treated as exotic exceptions.

The eighth and ninth chapters, "Jews and Blacks" and "The Black Middle Class," analyze the important roles played by ethnicity (culture) and class in the Black-Jewish relationship and within the Black community. These roles are widely ignored or misunderstood because they are obscured by the almost exclusive focus on the important role played by race.

For example, communication between Jews and African-Americans is often faulty because of *cultural* differences, rather than as a result of *racial* friction. Blacks are more than satisfied if Whites are neutral toward them, whereas Jews are nervous if non-Jews don't express a liking for them. Most Blacks are more race-conscious than ethnicity-conscious; for most Jews the reverse is true. A low level of White racism is of little concern to Blacks, but any anti-Jewish stereotyping produces extreme anxiety among Jews.

The combination of these cultural differences means that a discussion of anti-Semitism and racism between average groups of Jews and Blacks without the presence of a cultural translator is automatically doomed to failure. Moreover, Black and Jewish leaders who *can* communicate effectively are trapped by the mutual misperceptions of their respective constituencies. Nevertheless, the common political interests of the two groups make a split most unlikely despite serious tensions.

In the case of the Black middle class, racial solidarity prevents most "outsiders" from perceiving the severe strains imposed by the melting-pot culture. The successful entry of this middle class into the melting pot as a result of affirmative action; the especially rapid advancement of middle-class Black women; the continued exclusion of the majority of Blacks—the underclass and the low-skilled working class—from the melting pot; and the increasingly strident voices of Black nationalism have produced class, gender, ethnic, and ideological conflicts within the Black community. These conflicts and their political implications are treated within the framework of the mosaic-versus-melting-pot undercurrent in the 1992 presidential election.

The tenth and last chapter looks toward the mosaic future under the title "The Birth of a New American Culture."

The subservience of the melting-pot culture to the political and economic state system stunts the free development of literature, art, music, and journalism. In their attempts to universalize radical individualism, the opponents of multiculturalism have labeled it un-American and subversive. At the same time, they have politicized and commercialized American culture by identifying it with the political credo of liberal democracy rather than with liberal education, and with the free market rather than with artistic excellence. This is why, it seems to me, the defenders of the melting pot speak of Western civilization but do not dare to discuss American *culture*.

Yet the supporters of multiculturalism who pose the current debate in terms of Eurocentric culture *versus* multiculturalism are likewise misguided. They ignore the fact that the foundations of European culture offer a rich diversity. The ancient Greek and Roman civilizations upon which Western civilization was built derived from an ancient Egyptian culture having deep African roots, and all the ancient European cultures reflect this connection. Thus, one can place the true European civilization at the center of one's studies while refusing to be assimilated into American culture. This is precisely what the greatest African-American intellectuals have done; W.E.B. Du Bois and Paul Robeson are only two of many who have acted on their conviction that Western, and specifically Anglo-Saxon, high culture is one of the gateways to the best in all cultures.

The American cultural experience has demonstrated that the tyranny of unmoderated radical individualism has features in common with the tyranny of unbridled collectivism: the denial of group rights parallels the denial of individual liberties. For this reason, these two essential ingredients of true freedom should be balanced by embracing both multiculturalism and elements of popular (social) democracy.

The era of world multiculturalism is upon us and will not be denied. As for America's diverse cultural identifications, they abound in our contemporary culture if we but acknowledge them. Walt Whitman sang of these identifications in two inspiring poems which explore individuality in unity and universality in diversity.

ONE'S-SELF I SING

ONE'S-SELF I sing, a simple separate person,
Yet utter the word Democratic, the word En-Masse.

Of physiology from top to toe I sing,
Not physiognomy alone or brain alone is worthy for the Muse,

I say the Form complete is worthier far,
The Female equally with the Male I sing.

Of Life immense in passion, pulse, and power,
Cheerful, for freest action form'd under the laws divine,
The Modern Man I sing.

SONG OF MYSELF

. . . .

A child said, *What is the grass?* fetching it to me with full hands;
How could I answer the child? I do not know what it is any more
    than he.

I guess it must be the flag of my disposition, out of hopeful
    green stuff woven.

Or I guess it is the handkerchief of the Lord,
A scented gift and remembrancer designedly dropt,
Bearing the owner's name someway in the corner, that we may see
    and remark, and say *Whose?*

Or I guess the grass is itself a child,
    the produced babe of the vegetation.

Or I guess it is a uniform hieroglyphic,
And it means, Sprouting alike in broad zones and narrow zones,
Growing among black folks as among white,
Kanuck, Tuckahoe, Congressman, Cuff, I give them the same, I
    receive them the same. . . .

I

ETHNICITY VERSUS RACE

he melting-pot system has always pitted ethnic minorities against racial minorities in order to perpetuate the dominance of the White Anglo-Saxon Protestant (WASP) majority that has ruled America since our Republic was founded. The very term for this elite illustrates the artificial separation between ethnicity and race that results in the alignment of immigrants of all colors, but especially White immigrants, against Blacks of U.S.-slave ancestry (native Blacks). The racial classification White in White Anglo-Saxon is redundant, since Anglo-Saxon already encompasses White. This redundancy *separates* the racial classification of Whites from their ethnic classification of Anglo-Saxon.

This separation is arbitrary and artificial, since the accepted experiential and dictionary definitions of race and ethnicity are closely interlinked: the former is simply a less pronounced genetic and cultural similarity between individuals than the latter. Race is a broader, more inclusive version of the tribal or clan relationships represented by ethnicity.

A race is defined as a *diverse* group of individuals who share distinctive genetic and cultural similarities along with wide genetic and cultural differences. For example, people of the same race often have markedly different facial and body structures although their color is virtually the same; conversely, their facial and body structures may be similar, but their shades of color may vary. Moreover, their languages may differ though their social customs and music exhibit a similarity, and vice versa.

An ethnic group is defined as a relatively homogeneous community of individuals having closely matched genetic and cultural characteristics, in which significant differences are those of individuals rather than of subgroups. Typically, ethnic groups share the same language, music, and social customs; they often tend to be exclusionary and to express a them-and-us attitude of varying hostility toward, or difference from, other groups. Occasionally a large, uniform ethnic group constituting a powerful nation claims to be a superior *race*, as in the case of Nazi Germany. This serves to underscore the linkage and continuity between the concepts of race and ethnicity.

The use of racial labels that restrict the definition of race to *color only* ignore the cultural component of race: the noncultural terms white, black, yellow, red, brown replace more representative terms such as European, African, North Asian, American Indian, South Asian which encompasses both ethnicity and race.

The official u.s. government separation of race from ethnicity is confined to native Blacks by attaching the color label to them, since all other Americans, including Blacks descended from immigrants or Whites descended from the European (predominantly Anglo-Saxon) settlers of America, automatically have ethnic status *separate* from their race on the basis of their links to a specific modern nation other than the u.s. and to a language other than u.s. English. Native Blacks lack both of these links, and therefore the ethnic term African-American provides the substantive cultural status that the term black (with a lower case b) denies.

The Black quest for ethnic (i.e., cultural) recognition explains past and current controversies over racial labels. In the past the term colored had no cultural meaning, whereas the term Negro (with a capital N) did. Today the extensive use of the term African-American has muted the previous controversy over whether to spell Black with a capital B in order to invest the term with a cultural component.

Historically, the melting pot counterposed *ethnicity,* which was identified with Whiteness and superiority, to *race,* which meant non-Whiteness and inferiority. Foreign immigrants were welcomed into the melting pot and pitted against native Blacks who were excluded. Native Europeans (WASPs) occupied the top position in America's social hierarchy, whereas native Blacks were banished to the bottom position along with American Indians who are the true Native Americans. Immigrants occupied an ethnically determined hierarchy of intermediate positions with West Europeans at the top and non-Europeans at the bottom. And America as a nation was declared to be multiethnic in recognition of the status of ethnicity, but *not* multiracial in recognition of the status of race.

A mosaic society requires a community of ethnic groups belonging to all the races and enjoying equal status, and, therefore, in one stroke it eliminates both the separation of race from ethnicity and the hierarchy of ethnic groups dominated by Anglo-Saxons. The dominant WASP group would separate into its German-American and English-American components, while the rest of the Anglo-American majority—the Irish and Scottish ethnic groups—would become distinct parts of the mosaic. Then there could be no dominant ethnic group within the community of groups.

Such an outcome of the mosaic could produce a major shift in political and economic power according to the 1990 Census figures. The ten largest ethnic groups include German-Americans at 23.3 percent of the total population; Irish-Americans at 15.6 percent; English-Americans at 13.1 percent; African-Americans at 9.6 percent; Hispanic-Americans at 9.0 percent, and American Indians at 3.5 percent. Consequently, the departure of the Irish-Americans, many of whom are Catholic, from the heavily Protestant combination of German-Americans and English-Americans would reduce the 52 percent German-Irish-English majority to a 36.4 percent minority. Moreover, the 22.1 percent combination of African-Americans, Hispanic-Americans, and American Indians would numerically outstrip both the English-Americans and the Irish-Americans while almost matching the German-Americans.

Hence, the defenders of the melting pot cling to their separation of race from ethnicity, since its abandonment would fatally undermine the entire melting-pot culture. To this end, the language of the mass media reinforces this distortion of reality in subtle ways. For instance, the term ethnic is invoked to mean White, and the term racial to mean Black. Ethnic conflict means conflict that does *not* involve Blacks, whereas racial conflict means conflict involving Blacks.

However, the social divisions created by the melting pot have not been restricted to the immigrant and native-Black levels of society which have been pitted against each other by the top, WASP level. On the contrary, the sharpest crises in our national history, such as the Civil War, the class struggles of the 1930s, and the civil rights battles of the 1960s, arose because of splits created within the ethnically homogeneous Anglo-Saxon society by the social consequences of the melting-pot system. Since the WASP elite has always ruled the United States, and still does, its view of the melting pot is critical to an understanding of the roles played by ethnicity and race in melting-pot society.

THE NOVEMBER 9, 1989, issue of the *New York Review of Books* published an informative personal memoir by the venerable journalist Joseph W. Alsop, a member of the WASP elite known as the WASP ascendancy.

Mr. Alsop recalls the superior attitude even the best of the WASP ascendancy exhibited toward the White ethnic groups (minorities) in the melting pot when he notes in passing that "Eleanor Roosevelt in those days was not only mildly anti-Semitic, which she later honorably overcame; she was also quite obstinately anti-Catholic, which remained until the end of her days." Assimilation into WASP society was restricted to Northwest-European Protestants "who were on their way up in the world": Scots and Dutch, as well as French, Swedish, and Protestant (but not Catholic) Irish. If the outsiders rose high enough, "they had to be really pretty awful not to be promptly absorbed into the WASP ascendancy."

Then Alsop presents an illuminating view of the melting pot in the 1920s:

> In America when I was young we did not have just
> one excluded minority suffering from discrimination

like the black minority today, and no efforts were going forward to end the exclusion of any American minority. Instead we had an enormous array of more or less excluded minorities. The best-off of these was probably the Jewish American minority, who suffered from social anti-Semitism, were subject to an admissions quota from universities like Harvard, but otherwise did very well indeed. Then there were all the so-called ethnic minorities belonging to the Catholic church and to other exotic churches that flourish in Eastern Europe. Of them it is enough to say that finding an Italian or a Polish or a White Russian name in a position of high government responsibility, or even in any serious university, would have been quite astonishing when I was a young man.

Here the "enormous array of more or less excluded minorities," does not include *any* non-White minorities, since the racial minorities were not even in the melting pot and thus were not part of *American* society. By contrast, the reference to the exclusion of *American* minorities suggests that the White ethnic minorities were included in *American* society despite their exclusion from WASP society.

Alsop's 1920s hierarchy of White ethnic groups inside the melting pot underscores the anti-Catholic and pro-Western biases of the melting-pot culture. Americanized Jews come first, followed by ethnic "Catholics" and then by even more ethnic "Eastern Europeans" with their "exotic churches." Any semblance of opportunity equal to that of the WASPS was denied to all melting-pot groups: "Careers were not simply open to talent; careers were open to talent with the right kind of origins and the right kind of names."

The link between the traditional melting pot and today's version is provided by Alsop's remark that in the 1920s "we did not have just one excluded minority suffering from discrimination *like the black minority today.*" According to him, the traditional melting pot excluded White ethnic minorities from WASP society and discriminated against them, but it included them in American society *as groups* and gave them *unlimited* opportunity for *individual* advancement. By contrast, the non-White racial minorities were barred from *group* inclusion in the melting pot and thus suffered from *restricted* individual opportunity. All these racial groups *except the "black minority"* have now been admitted to the melting pot as groups [EMPHASIS MINE].

The Alsop memoir concludes with an expression of relief that exclusion and discrimination are no longer the norm for minorities ("thank God . . . all of this seems to me to be over now"), combined with an eloquent call for inclusion of the Black minority into a new, multicultural American society that evokes the mosaic idea:

> The last great task facing the United States is to extend equal shares to the black minority. . . .
> . . . So we must somewhere along the line find a new American culture and a new American view of history before we produce new wise men more representative of the mixed America that gives me so much pride.

Mr. Alsop implies that instead of repairing the melting pot, we should eliminate it so we can repair our society.

Most American historians, however, defend today's biased melting pot described by Alsop even while acknowledging the traditional melting pot's failures and injustices, their principal argument being that the single melting-pot culture is the only way to escape the divisiveness of a multiethnic society. But I think the opposite is true: today's melting pot *creates* divisiveness in a country that is as multiracial as it is multiethnic by promoting the dominance of stratified ethnic groups inside the melting pot over the excluded Black minorities.

THE MELTING POT was defended in the July 8, 1991, issue of *Time* magazine by historian Arthur Schlesinger, Jr.'s article, "The Cult of Ethnicity, Good and Bad." Asserting that "we have always been a multiethnic country," Mr. Schlesinger confirmed the traditional melting pot's subordination of race to ethnicity by admitting that it barred all non-Whites and banned them from American society:

The new American nationality was inescapably English in language, ideas and institutions. The pot did not melt everybody, not even all the white immigrants; deeply bred racism put black Americans, yellow Americans, red Americans and brown Americans well outside the pale.

However, he failed to explain how *today's* melting pot has dealt with the exclusion of non-Whites, asserting merely that "American culture at last began to give shamefully overdue recognition to the achievements of groups subordinated and spurned during the high noon of Anglo [WASP] dominance." The crucial fact that the Black minority remains excluded from the melting pot was ignored.

Instead, Mr. Schlesinger blamed the victims of the traditional melting pot's ethnic stratification and racial exclusion for forming what he calls a "cult of ethnicity [which has] erupted both among non-Anglo whites and among nonwhite minorities":

It gives rise, for example, to the conception of the U.S. as a nation composed not of individuals making their own choices but of inviolable ethnic and racial groups. It rejects the historic American goals of assimilation and integration. And, in an excess of zeal, well-intentioned people seek to transform our system of education from a means of creating "one people" into a means of promoting, celebrating and perpetuating separate ethnic origins and identities. The balance is shifting from *unum* [one] to *pluribus* [many]. That is the issue that lies behind the hullabaloo over "multiculturalism". . . .

. . . The situation in our universities, I am confident, will soon right itself. But the impact of separatist pressures on our public schools is more troubling. If a Kleagle of the Ku Klux Klan wanted to use the schools to disable and handicap black Americans, he could hardly come up with anything more effective than the "Afrocentric" curriculum. And if separatist tendencies go unchecked, the result can only be the fragmentation, resegregation and tribalization of American life.

Mr. Schlesinger's criticism lumps the small Black-separatist minority in the Afrocentric movement with the majority that seeks equal ethnic recognition. The Black victims of cultural exclusion from the White-dominated melting pot are accused of threatening the "fragmentation, resegregation and tribalization of American life" despite the failure of American society to allow their attainment of "the historic American goals of assimilation and integration." As I see it, the WASP "cult of ethnicity," rather than Afrocentrism, established the "inviolable ethnic and racial groups" whose conflicts have fragmented American society, and it is the melting pot that admitted non-Whites in a manner that exacerbated both ethnic and racial tensions.

Because the traditional melting pot institutionalized the superiority of ethnic status over racial status, the White ethnic minorities resisted the claim of *ethnic* parity advanced by the non-White ethnic minorities who shed their previous racial-minority classification as they were gradually accepted into the melting pot. For instance, new European immigrants were accepted by White ethnic neighborhoods, whereas non-White ethnic minorities who had lived in the U.S. for generations were generally not welcomed. As a result, the ethnic tensions inside the new melting pot took on a multiracial character, while the ethnicity-race conflict continued with heightened intensity and greater complexity between the racially diverse ethnic minorities inside the pot and the excluded native-Black racial minority outside it.

However, *both* the White and the non-White ethnic minorities rejected Schlesinger's idea of *individual* integration into American society; instead they continued to demand integration *as ethnic groups* and left assimilation to individuals. On the other hand, the excluded Black minority demanded integration either *as a single racial group* (as Blacks) or *as a single ethnic group* (as African-Americans) but rejected integration as individuals or as diverse ethnic minorities (Jamaican-Americans, Nigerian-Americans, native African-Americans, immigrant Blacks).

Mr. Schlesinger closed by describing a new melting pot that offers

American-born *members* of White and non-White minority groups (but not the *groups* as groups), integration into American society and ultimate assimilation into WASP society as a reward for abandoning their ethnic identification:

> Most American-born members of minority groups, white or nonwhite, see themselves primarily as Americans rather than primarily as members of one or another ethnic group. A notable indicator today is the rate of intermarriage across ethnic lines, across religious lines, even (increasingly) across racial lines. "We Americans," said Theodore Roosevelt, "are children of the crucible."

The "American-born members of minority groups, white or nonwhite," are well able to speak for themselves, but Mr. Schlesinger spoke ably for that part of the WASP elite which established today's melting pot. He covered up the exclusion of Blacks as a group from the melting pot by accurately including them as individual *members* of their group on a par with the *members* of all other groups. What he neglected to add was that the Black minority *group* is the only one not automatically included in today's melting pot in its entirety, even though its individual *members* can enter the melting pot if they meet its subtly discriminatory *individual-entry* requirement consisting of either middle-class or immigrant family values.

If this clarification is taken into account, Mr. Schlesinger appears to be proposing the merger of the top, WASP level with the middle, ethnic level consisting of all White and non-White minorities except the Black minority. This was implied by his recognition that frequent intermarriage is occurring across ethnic, religious, and "even" racial lines, and by his use of the statement by Theodore Roosevelt, a leader of the WASP ascendancy, that "*we* Americans are children of the crucible." Of course, Mr. Schlesinger omitted the fact that Roosevelt was identifying himself as a member of a melting pot in which there were no non-Whites at all.

The idea of merging WASP society with today's melting-pot society that excludes the Black minority can be seen to stem from the anxiety of the WASP elite about the numerical minority status of their ethnic group. This minority will become even smaller as the U.S. population becomes more non-White in the immediate future. If today's melting pot were to include all Blacks as a single ethnic group and all White and non-White ethnic groups were to have equal status, the ethnicity-race conflict would disappear, and WASP society would no longer enjoy automatic dominance.

To avoid this threat to its power, the WASP elite has perpetuated the ethnicity-race conflict by incorporating all immigrant non-White minorities, including immigrant African-Americans, in the melting pot while continuing to exclude the large native-Black minority.

THE PRESENCE OF NON-WHITE MINORITIES in the melting pot is not yet firmly established, since many members of White ethnic minorities oppose the acceptance of non-White minorities as ethnic equals. A piece by syndicated columnist Patrick Buchanan, an Irish Catholic, in the *Washington Times* of August 19, 1991, decried the "mortal threat" which, in his view, open immigration and multiculturalism pose to "American civilization." Buchanan was calling for the termination of non-White immigration when he cited the figure of 90 percent maintained by the traditional melting pot as a suitable White majority in the United States: "In 1950 we were a nation of 150 million, 90 percent of European descent. . . . But in 1991 we are a nation of 250 million, less than 77 percent of European stock."

Although there are deep divisions within White ethnic groups over the inclusion of racial groups in the ethnic melting pot, Mr. Buchanan's views are important because they reflect the Republican party leadership's decision to pit ethnicity against race for political gain. The essence of Buchanan's political outlook was revealed when he warned the August 1992 Republican National Convention that America was engaged in "a cultural war as critical to the kind of nation we shall be as the Cold War itself," adding that "this war is for the soul of America." And his chilling example of a battle in his "war" was White troopers, "M-16s at the ready," dispersing a Black "mob" during the May 1992 Los Angeles riot: "And as those boys took back the streets of Los Angeles block by block, my friends, we must take back our cities and take back our culture and take back our country."

Those remarks prompted the *Boston Globe* of August 19, 1992, to comment editorially that "in Buchanan's vision of urban America, black people figure as rioters to be faced down or shot." New York's Governor Mario Cuomo, who has consistently identified himself as an ethnic from the melting pot, compared the Republican convention's emphasis on family values and its calls for cultural uniformity to Hitler's emphasis on cultural purity:

> What do you mean by culture? That's a word they used in Nazi Germany. What are you saying? . . .
> . . . Why do they attack New York all the time . . . ?
> I'll tell you why. Because when you see New York City, you see all those different colors, all that ethnicity, all those poor people. What they're telling you is that that is them—that's the others, that's not us. It's us and them, and it's frightening.

With these remarks, aimed especially at Patrick Buchanan, Governor Cuomo dramatized the profound split among ethnic Whites over whether to defend today's melting pot against the unrestricted entry of native Blacks or to move gradually toward the mosaic. Since a majority of ethnic Whites still favor preservation of the melting pot, Cuomo was swimming against the tide when he defined "us" as including not only "all that ethnicity" and "all those different colors" but also "all those poor people." In short, he was talking about the mosaic.

At the same time Governor Cuomo's proven record of political skill leads me to believe that he has detected considerably greater support for the mosaic among ethnic Whites than is publicly apparent. Still, most leaders of White ethnic groups face an intractable problem whenever they contemplate supporting the mosaic—they must reject the familiar and comfortable melting pot entirely in order to be free of the divisive ethnicity-versus-race conflict that is the foundation of melting-pot theory and practice. To their credit, many of them have stretched melting-pot ideology far enough to include all non-White groups who are not Black, and "even" Blacks who are immigrant-descended or native-Black middle-class, but their own constituencies have rebelled at the idea of including native Blacks *as a group*.

Consequently, melting-pot ideology has conveniently classified the majority of native Blacks—the low-skilled working class and the poor—as a Black underclass and excluded it from the melting pot as a *racial* underclass. Instead of admitting this group into the melting pot along with new Black immigrants, most ethnic Whites advocate "ethnicizing" the members of this bottom level in order to equip them with "adequate values" for entry.

An August 29, 1991, article in the *New York Times* lamented the "overt" Black rejection of "the integrationist goals implicit in the melting pot" and quoted an array of weighty sources who compared the melting pot to the family, called for strengthening "ethnic identity," and complained that "too many ethnic problems are hushed up." The emphasis on integration and on a stronger ethnicity reflects the demand of the ethnic-White leadership that the Black underclass *assimilate* into the melting pot by becoming similar to White ethnics. This attitude imitates the insistence of the WASP elite that White ethnics assimilate into WASP society. Therefore, the article fails to acknowledge that the members of the Black underclass *are already ethnic in their own way* but are excluded from the melting pot on purely racial grounds. This racially based withholding of ethnic status can be seen as the reason why ethnic problems are "hushed up," and it explains why African-Americans have rejected melting-pot "integration": they refuse to settle for anything less than integration as a group on a par with the integration of all other ethnic groups. But ethnic Whites refuse to accept any semblance of parity with the Black underclass, and therefore their leaders resort to the use of ethnic arguments to mask racial discrimination.

An interesting example of this aspect of the clash between ethnicity and race appeared in the Winter 1991 issue of *Reform Judaism* in which Rabbi Alexander M. Schindler, president of the Union of Hebrew Congregations, deplored "the current climate of racial and ethnic assertiveness disuniting our . . . society," thus acknowledging the distinct racial and ethnic levels of American society. He went on to quote Arthur Schlesinger, Jr.'s warning about "the splintering of a once homogeneous America" with approval, and to urge preservation of an essentially traditional melting pot that would "interweave" the many "ethnic threads" into a single "tapestry." No mention was made of any *racial* "threads."

It is in this context that Rabbi Schindler launched a strong criticism primarily of multiculturalism as expressed by *Black* demands for the same ethnic status that ethnic Whites have used to acquire a share of political and economic *power:*

> We face the threat of a multiculturalism run amok, of the understandable quest for recognition perverted by the less admirable quest for power. . . .
>
> . . . In the inner city, the Martin Luther Kings and Bayard Rustins have been succeeded by the Sharptons and Maddoxes; builders of bridges are being replaced by those who construct barricades and bunkers.

Note that Rabbi Schindler used the hostile phrase "multiculturalism run amok" as a metaphor to describe the demand of the African-American minority for group cultural status. Here the "recognition" to which Schindler referred approvingly represents the present melting-pot status quo, whereas the "power" of which he disapproved represents the African-American demand for *equal* rights.

"The inner city" is a euphemism for urban areas to which most of the Black underclass is confined. Neither Martin Luther King nor Bayard Rustin were ever dominant leaders of a Black underclass which traditionally has been led by more militant and nationalist leaders such as Malcolm X and Stokeley Carmichael. Rev. Al Sharpton and attorney Alton Maddox are the successors of those leaders, just as Rev. Jesse Jackson and Democratic party chairman Ron Brown are the successors of Martin Luther King and Bayard Rustin. The times and the issues have changed, and, therefore, Rabbi Schindler's understandable and well-meaning nostalgia for the 1960s is harmful. The longer the melting pot continues to exclude the Black underclass, the more powerful the challenge by "the Sharptons and Maddoxes" will become. Ultimately, if the melting pot does not yield, new political and cultural leaders having the stature and moral authority of Rev. King, the mature Malcolm X of 1964–1965, and Paul Robeson are likely to emerge. Their goal would be to unite all classes of African-Americans in a sustained mass struggle against the melting-pot system— a struggle that would rival the civil rights movement in scope and determination.

The opposing sides in such a conflict would differ markedly from the contending forces in the civil rights revolution and would be more evenly divided. Supporters of the mosaic would be arrayed against defenders of the melting pot in a struggle that would be similar to the Civil War in the sense that the entire American governmental and institutional system would be in dispute. The trigger for such a turn of events would be a joint decision by the Black working class and middle class to mount a direct challenge to the melting pot.

Although this possibility at present appears to be remote because of the ideological and programmatic disarray of African-American leadership, one need only recall the rapidity with which the powerful movements of the 1960s followed the dormant 1950s. So one can appreciate the dilemmas faced by liberal White-ethnic leaders and Black leaders alike, but at the same time they must all be prodded gently but firmly to face the melting-pot's ethnicity-race contradiction head-on.

A MORE EXPLICIT DELINEATION of today's ethnic melting pot can be found in *Ethnic America* by Black economist and historian Dr. Thomas Sowell:

> Groups that arrived in America financially destitute have rapidly risen to affluence when their cultures stressed the values and behavior required in an industrial and commercial economy. Even when color and racial prejudices confronted them—as in the case of the Chinese and Japanese—this proved to be an impediment but was ultimately unable to stop them. Nor was their human capital even a matter of bringing specific skills with them. . . .
>
> . . . While not racially distinct from American Negroes, West Indians have had a different cultural background and have remained socially distinct from the other blacks around them. . . .
>
> . . . Unlike the southern rural migrants, 80 percent of the West Indian immigrants were from cities. The contrast between the West Indians and American Ne-

groes was not so much in their occupational backgrounds as in their behavior patterns. West Indians were
much more frugal, hard-working, and entrepreneurial.
Their children worked harder and outperformed native
black children in school. . . .

Dr. Sowell's argument served as the foundation for today's melting
pot because it unapologetically attempted to justify the exclusion of the
majority of native Blacks. Note that Dr. Sowell alternates between the pre-
civil rights "American Negroes" and "native black," with lower case
spelling, thus minimizing *ethnicity* compared to race. In the case of the
former, he could have written "Negro Americans" which has greater ethnic
weight.

According to Sowell, *all* immigrant ethnic groups of all races arrived
in America with cultural values superior to those of native Blacks, and,
therefore, they were able to succeed "even when color and racial prejudices
confronted them." His crowning example of the perceived superiority of
West-Indian culture over native-Black culture was designed to "prove" that
native Blacks lack the family values exhibited by the immigrants who are
admitted to the melting pot.

Dr. Sowell's argument suffers from serious flaws—his comparison of
mostly working-class and middle-class Black immigrants from stable
families to members of the native-Black underclass from unstable families;
the failure to note the significant preference for lower-qualified Black
immigrants over higher-qualified native Blacks in the competition for
unskilled jobs, and the lack of any reference to the significant support often
received by immigrant Blacks from their native country, among others.
But these faults are less important than the fact that both the WASP elite and
the ethnic-White leadership have adopted the Sowell view in order to deny
native Blacks the ethnic status required for group entry into the melting
pot.

The extension by these two elites of the ethnicity-race clash by
pitting immigrant-descended Americans of all races against the Black
underclass has undermined our entire society and provoked a powerful
and potentially dangerous surge of racial estrangement which is spreading

throughout all classes of African-Americans. The demand for the equal ethnic status represented by the term African-American is merging with a resentment against racial exclusion and the growing feeling among members of the Black underclass that they are in a "race war" for survival.

THE GRIM SOCIAL LANDSCAPE of the 1990s has caused the ethnicity-race confrontation between the middle and bottom layers of our society to be overtaken by a struggle within the WASP elite over the future of today's melting pot: should it intensify the ethnicity-race division by forging a melting-pot coalition against native Blacks, or should it end the exclusion of the Black underclass and move toward the mosaic? It is here that we shall find the key to ending the ethnicity-versus-race conflict that continues to rot our nation. And it is from here that the nascent mosaic alternative emerged to stem the Reagan-Bush effort to revive the cult of the old WASP ascendancy.

The debate over the future of today's melting pot has been transformed into a debate over whether to replace the melting pot with a mosaic. The lead article in the July 8, 1991, issue of *Time* magazine may have exaggerated somewhat when it claimed that "gone, or going fast, is the concept of the melting pot." However, it revealed the crux of the debate within WASP ranks when it added that "gone too is the emphasis . . . that rights reside in the individual rather than with social or ethnic classes and that all who come to these shores can be assimilated." In other words, the melting pot can't assimilate many non-White immigrants, not to speak of the Black underclass, and only *group* rights, rather than just individual rights, can guarantee African-Americans equal opportunity.

This means that the full inclusion of African-Americans into American society requires not only the abolition of the melting pot but also the abandonment of two pillars of the American Constitution and Declaration of Independence—the primacy of individualism over communitarianism and the priority of individual *liberties* over group *rights*. The mosaic alternative speaks to the latter issue because its implementation—the elimination of the ethnicity-race conflict—requires the *enforcement* of both racial and economic group rights simultaneously.

The melting pot's middle-class-values entry requirement is clearly discriminatory, since such values are the ones which the melting pot is supposed to *teach* immigrants. So for *economically disadvantaged native Blacks only,* the goals of the melting pot have been converted into the entry requirements. What is behind this circular contradiction, however, is more than merely race and poverty; the essence of the problem lies in the cherished melting-pot myth that America is a middle-class nation and therefore serves as the ideal example of liberal democracy.

Today's melting pot artificially divides America into two classes: a middle class that includes everyone above the median annual household income of about $30,000, and an underclass consisting of everyone below an annual household income of about $15,000. The wealthy become ultra-successful individual members of the middle class and are never mentioned as a separate class. Households with an annual income between $15,000 and $30,000 disappear either into the underclass as the working poor or into the middle class as working people. The appearance given is that of a population which is about 70 percent middle-class and about 30 percent underclass. The words working *class* are all but forbidden.

Since a middle-class *life style* requires an annual household income of roughly $50,000 and the wealthy *class* consists of the top 2 percent of the population with annual household incomes above $200,000, the actual class distribution of the American people is radically different from that claimed by the melting-pot myth: 2 percent rich who own half the national wealth; 37 percent middle class; 47 percent working class; 14 percent underclass.

So melting-pot ideology has imposed a middle-class culture on a working-class nation while abandoning a predominantly White underclass of 35 million (roughly 25 million Whites; 7.5 million Blacks; 2.5 million other non-Whites) to a miserable poverty in the midst of plenty. And all this is not only tolerated but supported in order to preserve the melting-pot culture. It's time for the melting pot to go and for the underclass to join the rest of our society.

But no set of values can by themselves empower the underclass to make the transition to the middle class. The most important empowerment is job training plus a decent job, since the primary experience for eventually running a business is regular employment. Comprehensive economic and social policies that can integrate the underclass into American society are prerequisites for shedding the burden of the ethnicity-race conflict and uniting our people, but the will to institute such policies depends on resolving that conflict. Therefore, the only way out of this vicious circle lies in moving beyond ethnicity and race.

Professor William Julius Wilson, the eminent Black sociologist, advocated this approach as far back as 1978 in his path-breaking book *The Declining Significance of Race:* "The challenge of economic dislocation in modern industrial society calls for public policy programs . . . that go beyond the limits of ethnic and racial discrimination by directly confronting the pervasive and destructive features of class subordination." He neglected to add the precondition that to transcend the "limits" of ethnic and racial bias one must first break out of the melting pot by overcoming the separation of ethnicity from race.

Seventeen years before the publication of Professor Wilson's book, President John F. Kennedy struck a similar theme in his inaugural address when he said: "If a free society cannot help the many who are poor, it cannot save the few who are rich." Similarly, it could be stated that individual liberties are worth little if human rights, including economic rights, are not guaranteed to every citizen *and every group of citizens* by the federal government. This idea sparked the movement from which the multiculturalist mosaic has emerged to challenge the melting pot in the 1990s.

2

MULTICULTURALISM AND THE BUSH SUPREME COURT

ecisions of the u.s. Supreme Court on such diverse issues as abortion, criminal justice, and freedom of speech exert a powerful influence on our cultural life, but they merely reflect the more fundamental, though less obvious, cultural role played by the Court in regulating the interrelationships between government, society, and the individual. This is true because cultural freedom requires freedom of the individual from repression not only by the federal government but also by society. The degree to which the federal government may intervene to defend the individual from society is the defining issue separating conservative and liberal Supreme Court justices.

Conservatives claim that the civil liberties guaranteed by the original Constitution protect the society of individuals from government, while liberals believe that the civil rights incorporated in the Bill of Rights amendments to the Constitution require government to protect the individual from society. Most individuals who are at risk from society belong to minority groups, so their effective protection indirectly violates the liberal principle of not recognizing group rights, thereby dividing the liberal constituency. It is within this framework that President George Bush attempted to harness the Supreme Court to his purpose of reshaping American culture to fit his individualist conservative image.

Conservative Republican presidents Richard Nixon, Ronald Reagan, and George Bush all achieved powerful presidencies, but they could not wrest the balance of power from Congress without the support of the Court. President Bush's successful nominations of conservative judges David H. Souter and Clarence Thomas to the Supreme Court in 1990 and 1991, respectively, established a decisive six to three conservative majority on the nation's highest court by expanding the group of four conservative judges appointed by President Reagan: Chief Justice William H. Rehnquist, Sandra Day O'Connor (the first White, female justice), Antonin Scalia, and Anthony M. Kennedy. The selection of Souter and Thomas was part of a carefully designed Bush plan to tilt the governmental balance of power in favor of his presidency by making the Supreme Court even more conservative.

President Bush's ultimate goal was to refashion the melting-pot culture into a racially and sexually inclusive version of the old one. All men and women, regardless of race, who adhered to the traditional melting-pot values (i.e., the "family values" of 1992 political jargon) were to be welcomed into American society as full-fledged *individuals.* All persons, regardless of their talent and ability, who did not accept the implicit rules and standards of the melting pot were to be denied the status of individuals endowed with a full complement of federally protected individual liberties. Any multiculturalism that was not explicitly approved by the new race-neutral American culture was to be delegitimized, and civil rights, which include group rights, were to be undermined.

Each of President Bush's two Supreme Court nominees served the dual purpose of popularizing the new Court majority in the eyes of middle-class America and providing Bush with a loyal ideologically committed supporter. In Justice Souter's case, the Bush ideological agenda was masked by the very ordinariness which formed the core of the nominee's popular appeal, while Judge Thomas's right-wing conservative views were obscured by the Bush administration's shameless exploitation of Thomas's color. The American public, faced with a superficial, biased, and often mendacious presentation of events, was given little chance of understanding the complex political and cultural issues being contested.

Nevertheless, the national debate over sexual harassment which was generated by the Thomas confirmation hearings altered our nation's cultural consciousness for the better. This happened because the issues and protagonists were joined in a manner which publicly illuminated not only the liberal-conservative conflict but also the contrast between the melting-pot culture and the mosaic culture—that is, between the White male value system and the value system which incorporates the values of minorities. As a result, the struggle which began when the Bush administration played its race card ended with the issue of values—i.e., of *culture*—transcending the familiar racial and sexual perceptions of most Americans.

JUSTICE DAVID SOUTER's confirmation process in 1990 was virtually free of controversy. Souter, an unpretentious and pleasantly quiet-spoken product of the relatively poor, overwhelmingly White, conservative state of New Hampshire, had almost no judicial record or identifiable judicial philosophy except a consistent tough-on-crime posture, and he successfully resisted all attempts at ascertaining his judicial philosophy or personal attitudes on major social issues. His disarmingly modest personal style deterred even the most liberal Democratic senators from serious opposition to his confirmation, despite the fact that his main patron was the extremely conservative John Sununu, a former governor of New Hampshire and President Bush's chief of staff.

In his first nine months on the Supreme Court bench, Justice Souter predictably demonstrated that he was a law-and-order conservative but gave no significant clues as to his judicial stance on race, religion, abortion, and Constitutional law. However, on May 23, 1991, he cast the deciding vote in the five to four Supreme Court decision to uphold a federal ruling barring abortion advice at federally funded clinics. His vote marked a basic shift in the balance of the Court toward President Bush's personal brand of conservatism on social and cultural issues. Yet the significance of Justice Souter's vote was overshadowed by the far-reaching dissent of nominally conservative Justice Sandra Day O'Connor.

In joining the three dissenting liberal Justices Thurgood Marshall, Harry A. Blackmun, and John Paul Stevens, she did far more than deny the Reagan-Bush conservatives a more comfortable six to three majority: her dissenting opinion struck at the heart of President Bush's relentless efforts to acquire increased presidential powers. First, she defended a broad interpretation of the First Amendment against a narrow interpretation favored by the Bush conservatives; second, her opinion was based firmly on the principle of judicial restraint—the idea that the Court must not reach constitutional questions in advance of the necessity of deciding them; third, she implied a respect for congressional intent by admonishing the five Justices who signed the majority opinion that: "we should not tell Congress what it cannot do before it has chosen to do it."

This realignment among the conservative justices meant that on those issues most crucial to Bush the best outcome that could probably be hoped for was a tenuous five to four pro-administration decision. This would not be good enough in the election year of 1992. Worse still, a mere five to four majority on the fundamental issue of eliminating the enforcement of civil rights legislation might invite disaster in the face of a united opposition by all minorities, including White women. This latter danger was magnified a month later, when on June 20, 1991, the Supreme Court, by a decisive six to three majority, ruled that the 1965 Voting Rights Act applies to all elections for judges. This ruling, which was directed against racially discriminatory voting practices or district boundaries, supported the principle that group rights still require federal protection. On this critical issue, Justice Souter joined Justice O'Connor in preserving one of the pillars of multiculturalism.

IT WAS IN SUCH A CONTEXT that Associate Justice Thurgood Marshall, the only African-American ever to sit on the Supreme Court and a sharp critic of the Court's conservative trend during the Reagan-Bush years, announced his retirement on June 27, 1991. In the last of the twenty-five dissenting opinions which he wrote in his final term, Marshall advised his colleagues not to "squander" the legitimacy of the Court "as a protector of the powerless."

President Bush praised Justice Marshall's "extraordinary and distinguished service to his country," adding that Marshall's career "is an inspiring example for all Americans." Apparently, Bush felt constrained to speak well of Justice Marshall despite the fact that Marshall had been less than charitable toward the Reagan and Bush presidencies. He had expressed his contempt for Reagan with the comment: "I wouldn't do the job of dog-catcher for Ronald Reagan." And he had dismissed President Bush: "It's said that if you can't say anything good about a dead person, don't say it. Well, I consider him dead."

President Bush, by breaking with the right wing of the Republican party and appointing another liberal African-American judge to replace Justice Marshall on the Supreme Court, could have changed course toward "a kinder, gentler nation" and made progress toward neutralizing the issue of race in u.s. politics. Instead, Bush chose Judge Clarence Thomas who from the outset was a willing tool in an effort to employ the race issue in the service of suppressing both the liberal Democratic tradition and the mosaic culture championed by the supporters of multiculturalism.

Clarence Thomas, a forty-three-year-old Black Republican who was serving as a United States appeals court judge for the District of Columbia at the time of his nomination by Bush, is the second Black person ever to be given an opportunity to serve on the u.s. Supreme Court. As a publicly avowed right-wing conservative who has risen through Republican ranks and as a judge with an undistinguished record of judicial, legal, or scholarly accomplishment, Thomas stands in stark contrast to his predecessor Thurgood Marshall, a legendary civil rights lawyer with twenty-four years of outstanding service on the Supreme Court as an apostle of liberalism. And although he is Black, Judge Thomas has consistently gone out of his way to place himself apart from and in opposition to African-American culture and majority opinion. Specifically, he opposes affirmative action and all other "race-conscious legal devices" while espousing the ideology of radical individualism and the melting-pot culture.

These credentials were precisely the ones that made Judge Thomas the perfect nominee to confound the Bush administration's liberal opponents: the supporters of affirmative action could hardly oppose the president's "racially preferred" affirmative-action nominee on the ground that he was merely "qualified" rather than the best qualified. There was no opening for opposition on general philosophical grounds either—how could liberals effectively attack a one-hundred-percent-American Black of humble southern origin who fervently espouses the credo of radical individualism? As far as specific issues were concerned—for instance, affirmative action, abortion, individual liberties, constitutional law— Thomas was instructed to follow the principle already established during the confirmation hearings of Judge David Souter: "It's improper for me to discuss what I would do in deciding specific cases, so I can't answer that question." Past controversial statements were to be covered by saying that they might not necessarily apply in the lofty environment of the Supreme Court.

It was a brilliantly conceived strategy that gave President Bush a virtually unbeatable hand to play: White liberals who attacked Thomas could be accused of a racist double standard because they had not similarly attacked the White nominee, Souter. Dissenting Blacks would have to attack "a brother," knowing that any alternative White nominee would probably be just as conservative as Thomas. White women who feared that Thomas would vote to outlaw abortion would have to attack a Black male with the attendant risk of canceling the growing collaboration between the women's movement and the Black movement. And Black women attacking Thomas because of his opposition to both affirmative action and choice regarding abortion would be subject to attacks by other Blacks for trying to "impede the advancement of a Black man."

On the other hand, conservatives could be counted on to accept the Black nominee because of his impeccable conservative credentials, while the general White public would accept him because of his comforting melting-pot, radical-individualist values (he would be perceived by Whites as "an American Black, not one of those African Blacks"). Opposition to Thomas would splinter the Democratic constituencies and unite the Republican ones. At the same time, Judge Thomas would symbolize the opening of the melting pot to Blacks who accept politically correct conservative ideology, thus making the Republican party more attractive to conservative Black voters. The race card could thus be exploited among Blacks and Whites alike.

President Bush kept determinedly to this script at the press conference where he introduced his nominee to the public:

> Judge Thomas's life is a model for all Americans, and he's earned the right to sit on this nation's highest court. . . . I kept my word to the American people and to the Senate by picking the best man for the job on the merits. And the fact he's minority, so much the better. But that is not the factor, and I would strongly resent any charge that might be forthcoming on quotas when it relates to appointing the best man to the court. That's the kind of thing I stand for.

The skeptical press corps knew very well that Judge Thomas, with only one year on the United States Court of Appeals for the District of Columbia, was one of the least qualified nominees, male or female, White or Black, whom Bush could have chosen. Even according to the standard for minority affirmative action—the best qualified within the particular minority category—Thomas was far down the list. Among the most highly qualified Black judges are two Black women—Amalya L. Kearse of the Second Circuit in New York and Judith W. Rogers, chief judge of the District of Columbia Court of Appeals on which Thomas served. Then there is New York Federal District Judge Robert Carter who followed Thurgood Marshall as head of the NAACP Legal Defense Fund.

President Bush had nominated a Black judge who could serve his political and ideological purposes solely because he was Black, not because of his abilities. However, the reporters who were present stopped short of pointing out that a White person with such meager qualifications could never have been nominated for a seat on the Supreme Court. This failure of the mass media to expose the contradictions inherent in the Thomas nomination helped to produce deep divisions among White liberals and among Blacks over whether to oppose Judge Thomas's confirmation.

White liberals were divided by the combination of Judge Thomas's strong advocacy of individual liberties with his vehement opposition to group rights, since this coupling presented the choice of reinforcing individual liberties at the cost of undermining group rights, or of safeguarding group rights along with individual liberties. Most of the liberals who oppose group rights either supported Thomas or were neutral, whereas most of those who support group rights were strongly against him. Consequently, supporters of civil liberties were to some extent arrayed against supporters of civil rights.

Blacks were split also. The Black civil rights leadership, with some exceptions, generally opposed Judge Thomas because of his hostility to the civil rights laws guaranteeing the group rights of minorities. Thomas's support came from Black conservatives who share his ideology; from those Black liberals for whom individual assimilation is a central priority, and from those Black nationalists for whom the fact that Thomas is Black outweighs all other considerations.

A minority of White liberals threw in the towel almost immediately. Dean Guido Calabresi of Yale Law School proclaimed that he "despised the current Supreme Court," but he supported the Thomas nomination because: "I know him, and I know he is a decent human being who cares profoundly for his fellows." Nat Hentoff, liberal columnist for New York's *Village Voice,* wrote in defense of Thomas that there was "an encouraging sign" of how he might vote on some matters of civil liberties, since Thomas had said that he was raised "to survive under the totalitarianism of segregation."

However, a majority of the White liberal leadership organized a powerful nationwide campaign to prevent Judge Thomas's confirmation.

A majority of African-American leaders opposed the Thomas nomination despite strong support for Judge Thomas among their constituents. Some Black political, civic, religious, and social organizations expressed their opposition by large margins (for example, the entire congressional Black Caucus with the exception of its lone Republican member, and fifty out of the fifty-one directors of the NAACP). So did the entire thirty-five-member Executive Council of the AFL-CIO, largely in response to the desires of the Black trade-union leadership representing millions of Black union members. Almost no major Black organizations and few Black celebrities supported the nomination. Justice Thurgood Marshall's acerbic comment on the selection of his successor was to compare him to a snake: "beware of a black snake as well as a white snake—they both bite."

The reason for Black leaders' determined resistance to the Thomas nomination can be found in Clarence Thomas's own words, which deny not only the existence of an African-American culture but even the legitimacy of Black group interests. Excerpts from his speeches and writings, published in the *New York Times* of July 2, 1991, and passages from an Op-Ed piece in *The Los Angeles Times,* November 15, 1985, are particularly revealing:

> The tragedy of the civil rights movement is that as blacks achieved the full exercise of their rights as citizens, government expanded, and blacks became an *interest group* in a *coalition supporting expanded government.*
>
> . . . The argument that the views of black leadership are consonant with those of black Americans misses the point, since most blacks are not represented by black politicians, nor are most blacks members of organizations that claim to represent them. . . . The real issue here, however, is not who represents black America. . . . Rather, the real issue is why, unlike other individuals in this country, black individuals are not entitled to have and express points of view *that differ from the collective hodgepodge of ideas that we supposedly share because we are members of the same race.*
>
> . . . We certainly cannot claim to have progressed much in this country as long as it is insisted that our intellects are controlled *entirely* by our pigmentation, with its countless variations, even though our individual experiences are *entirely* different [EMPHASIS MINE].

Here Judge Thomas has reduced African-Americans to a misguided "interest group" that "supposedly" shares a "collective hodgepodge of ideas" which should be cast off so that African-Americans can become "black individuals." Then he claims that Blacks who express a culture different from the melting-pot culture are "insisting that our intellects are controlled entirely by our pigmentation." These statements reveal Judge Thomas's failure to grasp a central point: most Black *individuals* refuse to separate their intellect from their *culture* in order to satisfy the demands of racially biased American *society*.

As far as Thomas's claim that the personal experiences of Black people are "entirely" different is concerned, it strains credulity beyond the breaking point in view of his statements about being raised to survive "in spite of the dark oppressive cloud of governmentally sanctioned bigotry" ("Why Black Americans Should Look to Conservative Policies").

THE BLACK LEADERSHIP'S OPPOSITION to Judge Clarence Thomas's nomination was based squarely on the issues raised by Thomas's conservative ideology. Their position was that the Thomas nomination threatened vital economic, social, and political *group interests* of Black Americans, despite the fact that Thomas is Black. Group interest was placed above simplistic *color* solidarity. At the same time, many African-American leaders publicly criticized President Bush's selection of Judge Thomas as an exploitation of the race issue for political gain.

For its part the Bush administration launched a powerful propaganda campaign depicting Clarence Thomas as an all-American melting-pot hero and a cultural role model for Black Americans. The small but vocal Black conservative establishment was pressed into frenzied support activity in the mass media and within the African-American community, whereas the massive and growing opposition to the nomination commanded little media coverage.

Despite this, a public-opinion poll published on the eve of Judge Thomas's Senate confirmation hearings showed results that were hardly encouraging to Thomas supporters: two-thirds of both Whites and Blacks had no opinion, and this recalled the similar response of the public just prior to Judge Robert H. Bork's confirmation hearings in 1987 after which the Senate rejected his nomination by President Reagan. Whites who had an opinion favored Judge Thomas's confirmation by 26 percent to 10 percent because of his conservative ideology, with those opposed to confirmation citing the same reason—his conservatism. Blacks who had an opinion favored confirmation by 23 percent to 15 percent (a somewhat smaller ratio than for Whites) because of Thomas's race and his boyhood poverty, with those opposed citing his opposition to affirmative action. These statistics revealed that Bush's "race card" had worked in unintended ways.

Whites split along conservative-liberal lines, with race playing no significant part; moreover, most Whites believed Bush's fantasy that he had nominated the best qualified person, so the issue of a "Black nominee" did not arise for them. Blacks split over the issue of race, as intended, but in the "wrong" manner. The 15 percent who opposed Thomas were the Black elite—precisely those whom Bush was trying to recruit into today's melting pot and for whom Thomas was to serve as a role model. They quite logically rejected him because of his opposition to the affirmative action programs which had benefited them and him alike. By contrast, the 23 percent of Blacks who supported Thomas were mostly low-income Blacks who backed Thomas from blind racial solidarity (any Black judge is better than a White one).

Conservative Black columnist Tony Brown put the best face on this paradox in a July 23, 1991, column titled, "Clarence Thomas: Black Masses Say Yes, Black Elite Say No."

Since the members of the Black elite are overwhelmingly liberal, the liberal-conservative conflict within the African-American community was quickly resolved in favor of the liberals; Black conservatives were reduced to making a racial argument which appealed primarily to Black-nationalist constituencies who backed Thomas but whose political clout was minimal.

Because both the Black and the liberal constituencies remained sorely divided, despite an anti-Thomas consensus within both leaderships, the victory of Black liberals over Black conservatives produced an unexpected result. The sharpened divisions among Blacks and among liberals reduced the Republicans' ability to exploit the race issue in electoral politics. The spectacle of a multiracial Democratic liberal coalition fighting a multiracial Republican conservative coalition to prevent confirmation of a conservative *Black* Supreme Court nominee undermined more than two decades of Republican success in implying to White voters that liberals (Democrats) are pro-Black, while conservatives (Republicans) are pro-White. It also negated some major stereotypical notions long held by White Americans about Blacks.

But the Bush administration played the race card once more by warning the Senate Democrats that if Judge Thomas was not permitted to avoid questions concerning his opinions on basic issues, as was the case during Judge Souter's confirmation hearing, they would be accused of a White-liberal racist double standard. This threat confined the confirmation debate to legalistic language that was impossible for the general public to decipher. Thomas's evasiveness was a liability and was exploited by the Democratic majority on the Senate Judiciary Committee which conducted the hearing, but it had little effect on the public.

Nevertheless, Judge Thomas's subtly nuanced statements in reply to tough questioning on controversial issues of constitutional law exposed the ideological profile of a right-wing conservative when they were combined with his previous writings. This profile stiffened the opposition to his confirmation: the Senate Judiciary Committee, by a seven to seven tie vote, refused to recommend Judge Thomas's confirmation by the full Senate and set the stage for a dramatic Senate debate on the fundamental principles that were at stake in the controversy over the Thomas nomination.

Three fundamental constitutional issues were raised by Judge Thomas's testimony before the Senate Judiciary Committee in September of 1991: 1. the legitimacy of invoking a higher, natural law based on religious belief when interpreting the u.s. Constitution; 2. the relationship between the Constitution, society, and the individual; and 3. the political balance between the presidency and Congress. Judge Thomas's positions on all three issues were revealed to be much clearer than the media would have us believe. It was on the issue of natural law that Thomas was questioned most closely by the senators, since in his previous writings (*Center Magazine*, November-December 1987) he had argued that:

> Natural rights and higher law arguments are the best defense of liberty and of limited government. . . .
> . . . The rule of law in America means nothing outside constitutional government and constitutionalism, and

these are simply unintelligible without a higher law. Men
cannot rule others by their consent unless their common
humanity is understood in light of transcendent standards provided by the Declaration's [the Declaration of
Independence] "Laws of Nature and of Nature's God."

This statement implies that natural law is God's law and is the only
sound basis for interpreting the Constitution. The Declaration of Independence, and not the Constitution itself, is then cited as the legal justification
for this approach.

Democratic Senator Joseph Biden, the chairman of the Judiciary
Committee, questioned Thomas relentlessly on this issue, but Thomas
conceded only that he would not "adjudicate" (that is, *decide*) cases on the
basis of natural law; he was careful not to deny that he might use natural law
for the more important purpose of *interpreting the Constitution*. Later, under
questioning by Democratic Senator Howard Metzenbaum of Ohio,
Thomas modified his position by stating that natural law is nothing more
than *the* (not just *a*) background to the Constitution, adding that: "It is not
a method of interpreting or a method of adjudicating in the constitutional
law area." This was still short of eliminating natural law as *a basis* for
interpreting the Constitution.

The second controversy which erupted during the Senate's hearings
on the Thomas nomination concerned Thomas's interpretation of the
Constitution in relation to government, society, and the individual. In
1987 he had written the following comments published in the *Wall Street
Journal* on February 20 and October 12:

Much of the current thinking on civil rights has been
crippled by the confusion between a "colorblind society"
and a "colorblind Constitution." The Constitution, by
protecting the rights of individuals, is colorblind. But a
society cannot be colorblind, any more than men and
women can escape their bodies. It would destroy limited
government and liberal democracy to confuse the *private,
societal realm (including the body and skin color) and the public,
political realm (including rights and laws)*. . . .

> . . . *I firmly insist that the Constitution be interpreted in*
> *colorblind fashion* [EMPHASIS MINE].

This issue of a color-blind (and therefore group-blind) Constitution and its interpretation in matters affecting the relationship between society and the individual bears directly on the right of individual privacy included in the liberty clause of the Fourteenth Amendment, which guaranteed the citizenship of slaves freed after the Civil War. Judge Thomas's view is that the color-blind interpretation of the Constitution *must* be applied to a *society* which he acknowledges is not and "cannot be" color-blind. Moreover, he defines the societal realm as the private (i.e., individual) realm. By this he implies that society is made up of melting-pot individuals who, under the radical-individualism theory of liberal democracy, must be protected from intrusive federal civil rights regulations. Such a policy would make it difficult to protect minority-group individuals *from* society, so civil rights advocates opposed Judge Thomas's confirmation vehemently.

The third major controversy which developed during the Thomas hearings concerned the relationship between Congress and the presidency, since Judge Thomas's recent writings and lectures had revealed a pronounced bias in favor of the presidency and an unconcealed hostility toward Congress. After Colonel Oliver North's claims of virtually unrestrained presidential power in his testimony before the joint congressional committee investigating the Iran-Contra affair, Thomas praised North for "exposing congressional irresponsibility." Later he commented that, "There is little deliberation and even less wisdom in the manner in which the legislative branch conducts its business." And in 1988 he invoked natural rights in supporting Supreme Court Justice Antonin Scalia's lone dissent against the Court's ruling which upheld the statute establishing federal counsels who are independent of the executive branch.

Thomas's testimony before the Senate Judiciary Committee did nothing to alter that impression. Even Republican Senator Arlen Specter from Pennsylvania, an ardent Thomas backer, was not satisfied with Thomas's replies to questions about whether Thomas would respect congressional intent. Democratic Senator Ted Kennedy of Massachusetts summed up the position of seven out of the eight Democratic senators on the Judiciary Committee when Thomas had finished his testimony:

In effect, President Reagan and President Bush have carried out a triple play against the role of Congress. First, in the guise of executing the laws, they have used their executive branch power to rewrite and constrict statutes they dislike. Second, they persuade the Justices they have named to the Supreme Court to disregard plain legislative history about congressional intent and sustain narrow executive branch readings as minimally plausible in interpretations of the law. Third, they dare Congress to try and pass a new law to restore the correct interpretation in the face of a veto by the President.

My concern is that Judge Thomas, based on his record, is likely to become a willing disciple of these search and destroy missions of the Court.

The Bush administration, having failed to get a recommendation for confirmation from the Senate Judiciary Committee and facing an all-out, partisan debate in the full Senate, worried about the final confirmation vote in spite of public claims of an overwhelming Senate majority leaning in favor of confirming Judge Thomas. The media campaign in support of confirmation was intensified, and the race issue continued to be emphasized by the administration and by Republican senators.

For example, Senator Arlen Specter said of Thomas:

I think he brings a very, very important measure of diversity to the Court. I think it's very important that an African-American be on the Court now, within the chambers of those nine Justices; that they hear the views of African-Americans in this country.

The cynicism of these remarks by Senator Specter, especially his use of the appellation "African-Americans," is stunning when one considers that Thomas's views are opposite to those of most Blacks, and that a racially diverse Court is being advocated to support an allegedly color-blind Constitution and government.

Most liberal Democratic senators were rendered ineffectual by this skillful use of the race issue, and their fears were magnified by the strident but unsubstantiated threats issued by both conservative Blacks and the Bush administration to the effect that there would be a backlash by Black voters against liberal White senators who dared to vote against the confirmation of Judge Thomas. There were some notable exceptions, however. Senator Howard Metzenbaum of Ohio said:

> President Bush made a cynical choice in selecting Clarence Thomas, believing that no White liberal could vote against a black man. I said then that this white liberal would have no problem voting against a black man if I believe that man would erode and erase the hard-won individual rights and liberties the Court has protected. [Note Senator Metzenbaum's separate mention of rights and liberties, implying a distinction.]

The last phase of the Thomas confirmation drama was played out against the background of a series of unexpected and uncontrollable events that altered the political playing field in a manner that was devastating to the Bush administration. On October 6, 1991, two days before the full Senate was scheduled to vote on his confirmation to serve on the U.S. Supreme Court, Judge Thomas was publicly accused of sexually harassing Anita F. Hill, a Black tenured professor at the University of Oklahoma Law Center, during 1981 and 1982 when she served as his personal assistant at the Equal Employment Opportunities Commission (EEOC).

Although a month earlier the FBI, after interviewing Prof. Hill, had given the Senate Judiciary Committee her affidavit detailing the alleged sexual harassment by Judge Thomas, neither the Democrats nor the Republicans on the all-White, all-male committee had deemed the Hill affidavit to warrant further investigation and had buried it. Now women's groups across the nation seethed with indignation, and women voters deluged both Republican and Democratic senators with demands that open hearings of the Senate Judiciary Committee be held on Anita Hill's charges before the Senate vote was taken on the Thomas nomination. The issues of sexual harassment in the workplace took over the public stage from the fading racial issue, especially since Professor Hill was both Black and relatively conservative.

Despite the effectiveness of President Bush's race card in frightening part of the White liberal leadership, significant sections of White liberal constituencies had been able to organize powerful pressure on the Democratic senators, most of whom are heavily dependent on liberal votes. And since virtually the entire Black political establishment mobilized to assist in this effort, the attacks by Black conservatives against White liberals carried little or no weight. Now a powerful army of activist White women joined the opposition against the confirmation of Judge Thomas.

Moreover, an important consequence of Judge Thomas's testimony was overlooked by the media: his "White" erudition and effectiveness, combined with the distinct African-American cultural style in his subtleties of speech and behavior, had an unforeseen impact on the White public. In these "Black" externals, he was not a carbon copy of a White conservative, so he contradicted White stereotypes of Blacks. Ironically, the public role played by the very person whom Bush selected to destroy the legal foundation of multiculturalism had the effect of popularizing diversity. Judge Thomas played the role of an authoritative Black male with assurance, and, therefore, the general public was more inclined to examine the issues on their merits, free of the long-held racial and sexual stereotypes which derive from melting-pot values.

In this uncertain political environment, a delay of the Senate confirmation vote until after Anita Hill's charges had been heard in open hearings was approved unanimously by the full Senate. Tough negotiations and adept maneuvering by the Democratic leadership had forced President Bush to cave in when the Republican leadership warned him that the vote would go against Thomas if it were held on schedule.

The *New York Times* of October 10 reported that the White House "was hunkered down to make a heavy assault on Professor Hill," and noted that "no one in the Republican camp seems to take the anger among women in Washington this week as a warning." As the Republicans launched a no-holds-barred defense of Judge Thomas and a character-assassination campaign against Ms. Hill, Senator Alan Simpson of Wyoming, a Republican member of the Judiciary Committee, warned ominously that: "Anita Hill . . . will be injured and destroyed and hounded and harassed—real harassment, different from the sexual kind."

According to the deal made between the Senate Democratic and Republican leaderships, Judge Thomas would appear before the Judiciary Committee with a prepared statement first and would not be questioned, then Professor Hill would be questioned under oath, and when she completed her testimony Judge Thomas would have the option of submitting himself to questioning under oath. Finally, the committee would hear supporting witnesses for both sides.

The entire nation was glued to television sets as this hearing proceeded; and what it witnessed was high drama.

Judge Thomas angrily, categorically, and convincingly denied all of Anita Hill's allegations and then denounced the confirmation process and, by implication, the Judiciary Committee itself, saying that:

> I have not done what she has alleged. And I still don't know what I could possibly have done to cause her to make these allegations. . . .
>
> This is not American. This is Kafkaesque. It has got to stop. . . .
>
> I am not going to allow myself to be further humiliated in order to be confirmed. . . .
>
> I will not allow this committee or anyone else to probe into my private life. . . .
>
> Yesterday, I called my mother. She was confined to her bed, unable to work, and unable to stop crying. Enough is enough. . . .
>
> I will not provide the rope for my own lynching, or for further humiliation.

With that, he departed.

It was an impressive performance, and President Bush immediately declared that "this decent and honorable man has been smeared." But according to Bob Herbert, a Black columnist for the *New York Daily News,* the president was a bit hasty:

> The next act belonged to Hill and it was incredible, shocking, astounding. And it was bad news for Thomas.

> Maintaining the poise, dignity and credibility that she had shown at a press conference on Monday, Anita Hill told a story that rocked the Caucus Room. . . .
>
> For hours, the Thomas supporters on the Judiciary Committee tried to shake her story. . . .
>
> Hill remained steadfast and credible. . . .
>
> . . . Hill's story remained intact. In fact, she had come across as so credible that not one of the Senators was willing to accuse her of lying. . . .
>
> For Thomas, the worst news was the growing sense that his nomination was doomed. Every Senator was aware that the entire nation was watching, including millions of outraged women.

An hour after Anita Hill had completed her testimony, Judge Thomas reaffirmed his categorical denial of all of Professor Hill's charges. Then he systematically took control of the hearing on the strength of his dramatic use of the race issue. This political weapon, which had yielded limited results in the hands of the Bush administration, would devastate the Judiciary Committee Democrats when it was wielded by Clarence Thomas playing the role of enraged Black victim. But first, with the aid of the well-organized group of seven Republican members of the committee, he carefully set the stage.

He surprised his audience when he stated that he had not watched Hill's testimony, remarking angrily that he had "heard enough lies." Then he altered the entire framework of the discussion between himself and the Judiciary Committee by unleashing a controlled rage against the committee for allowing the confidential report of Hill's original allegations to leak to the press, and for holding public hearings on them. Simultaneously, the Republican senators mounted a sustained and vicious attack on the credibility and integrity of Professor Hill, in her absence, making it difficult for the Democrats to press Judge Thomas effectively. The headline in the *New York Times* the next day read: "ACCUSER (HILL) COMES UNDER ATTACK AS SENATORS QUESTION THOMAS."

Perhaps the cheapest shot was taken by Senator Arlen Specter, who had led the hostile questioning of Professor Hill, when he declared weightily that Hill had committed perjury and then read excerpts from her testimony outside of their original context.

In his original questioning of Hill, Specter had asked her repeatedly about a story in the October 9 *USA Today* which claimed Hill had been told by Senate staffers that her affidavit would lead to pressure on Thomas to withdraw. Hill said that the reporter who wrote the story had spoken to her over the telephone, and her recollection of the conversation was poor; however, she did remember that the conversation was unpleasant and adversarial. The verbatim record of the testimony then reads:

> *Specter:* Did anyone ever tell you that by providing the statement . . . there would be a move to press Judge Thomas to withdraw his nomination?
>
> *Hill:* I don't recall any story [i.e., newspaper story] about . . . using this [i.e., her statement] to press anyone.
>
> *Specter:* Well, do you recall anything at all about anything related to that? [Specter is no longer talking about the news story.]
>
> *Hill:* I think I was told that my statement would be shown to Judge Thomas, and I agreed to that. [Hill is now referring to a conversation with a Judiciary Committee staff member.]
>
> *Specter:* But was there any suggestion, however slight, that the statement with these serious charges would result in a withdrawal so that *it wouldn't have to be necessary for your identity to be known, or for you to come forward under circumstances like these?*
>
> *Hill:* . . . Not that I recall. I don't recall anything being said about him being pressed to resign [i.e., in the context of Hill remaining anonymous and not publicly coming forward.] [EMPHASIS MINE.]

Professor Hill thus testified that no one had discussed with her the possibility that her *anonymous charges* might cause Judge Thomas to withdraw, and said that she had authorized the Judiciary Committee to show her statement to Thomas himself. Senator Specter's spurious charges of perjury against Professor Hill rested on the fact that Hill testified that a committee staff member had mentioned the possibility of Thomas's withdrawal *after* he had been shown Hill's allegation and after the FBI investigation that produced those allegations had taken place.

If we now refer back to Senator Specter's last question to Hill, which linked Thomas's withdrawal to Hill's *anonymity,* we can see the trap Specter was setting. When he dramatically leveled his charge of perjury against Professor Hill, he quoted the first question and answer in the excerpt above and then skipped directly to Hill's answer to his later question, without including the question itself. This prompted a crisp response from Chairman Biden who read the full text of the excerpt into the record.

But these Republican tactics placed the Democrats ever more on the defensive; as the *New York Times* later put it: "Republicans Gain In Battle By Getting Nasty Quickly." It was in this atmosphere that Judge Thomas electrified the national audience as he skillfully appealed to both White guilt and Black sympathy:

> We still have underlying racial attitudes about black men and their views of sex. And once you pin that on me, I can't get it off. . . .
>
> . . . These are charges that play into racist, bigoted stereotypes, and these are the kind of charges that are impossible to wash off. . . .
>
> . . . And if you want to track through this country in the 19th and 20th centuries the lynchings of black men, you will see that there is invariably, or in many instances, a relationship with sex, and an accusation that that person cannot shake off. . . .
>
> . . . I have been harmed. My family has been harmed. . . . I wasn't harmed by the Klan. I wasn't harmed by the Knights of Camelia. I wasn't harmed by the Aryan Race. . . . I was harmed by this process . . . which accommodated these attacks on me.
>
> . . . I would have preferred an assassin's bullet to this kind of living hell . . . .

> ... From my standpoint as a black American, as far as
> I'm concerned, it is a high-tech lynching for uppity
> blacks who in any way deign to think for themselves, to
> do for themselves, to have different ideas. It is a message
> that unless you kow tow to an old order, this is what will
> happen to you. You will be lynched, destroyed, carica-
> tured by a committee of the u.s. Senate rather than hung
> from a tree.

Directed at a panel of fourteen White male senators, these remarks
tended to shift the focus from sexual harassment to race, and clouded the
issue of Thomas's credibility regarding Hill's charges with an appeal for
sympathy toward a persecuted Black man. And it was credibility that
would decide the Senate confirmation vote. Since Professor Hill's credibility had survived the hearing and could not be demolished after her
departure, Judge Thomas could salvage his confirmation only by establishing his own credibility under adversarial questioning. Otherwise a vote by
a Democrat to confirm him would invite voter retaliation by a combination
of White women, White liberal males, and a majority of Blacks.

This was no easy task, since Thomas's credibility was vulnerable in
three areas: 1. his alleged interest in pornographic movies; 2. his admission
that he had driven Hill home a number of times and been in her apartment
on at least one occasion; and 3. his denial that he had ever asked her out
socially, even for lunch. He also faced the overall difficulty of having
denied *everything* Hill said. This had created an almost universal impression
that either Hill or Thomas could be believed, but not both. Since at this
point it was unlikely that he had any chance of proving Hill a liar, his
performance had to be spectacular enough to convince both the public and
the press (but not the senators) to believe him while also believing Hill.

It is this dilemma that caused Thomas to use inappropriate racial
imagery instead of reiterating his denial of Hill's charges. After all, what
possible connection could there be between a lynch mob after a Black man
accused of raping a White woman, and a coalition of liberal White women,
a moderate Black woman, liberal White men, and liberal Blacks trying to

prevent a conservative Black man backed by a constituency of conservative White men from dismantling civil rights legislation? The primary significance of Thomas's words was not in their content but in their sincerity and passion. And, fortunately for him, that is exactly how the public received them.

Why did this tactic, which did not fool the public even though it won widespread sympathy, neutralize the Democratic senators on the Judiciary Committee? Contrary to the conventional wisdom which held that the Democrats were afraid Black voters would vote against them if they rejected Thomas's nomination, and that the Democratic leadership was incompetent, their dilemma was just as uncomfortable as that of the Republicans. They were not primarily concerned about the Black vote, but rather about the conservative White male vote and the White female vote.

If they were perceived as letting Thomas go scot free, the White female vote would damage them, perhaps fatally, in light of Hill's credibility. On the other hand, overly zealous attacks on Thomas would be seen by conservative White males as unfair to a fellow melting-pot male who had the opportunity of a lifetime and had paid his melting-pot dues. Besides, Thomas's juxtaposition of sex and race subtly reminded them that the alleged harassment was "only" of a Black woman, not of "a flower of White womanhood." Of course, this was not an insurmountable problem for several northern liberal Democrats, and they tried to go after Thomas. But it was *the* problem for the conservative and moderate southern Democrats, including Chairman Biden, who constituted the crucial swing votes in the confirmation battle.

The outcome most helpful to the re-election prospects of Democratic senators was for there to be a "credibility tie" between Thomas and Hill. Then the entire Senate would be off the hook, and each senator would be free to vote on the basis of sheer opportunism if he or she so chose, claiming to believe both of them but casting the safe vote after the appropriate amount of hand-wringing. This is exactly what happened, despite the obvious fact that it was not possible for the two completely opposite accounts of Hill and Thomas to be true. The problem for the Democrats on the committee was to allow Thomas to win a draw, and the race issue introduced so forcefully by Thomas provided them with the cover for doing so. The rest was theater.

JUDGE THOMAS'S COMMAND PERFORMANCE won him his credibility draw, and the subsequent parade of witnesses supporting the two sides merely confirmed the stand-off. The Senate confirmation vote was too close to call until the vote was tallied, and the national perceptions of the issues of sex and race were fundamentally altered by the public's exposure to the Thomas confirmation hearings. The primary result was that sexual harassment and the issue of women's rights displaced the race issue despite Thomas's confirmation. The Senate vote on Judge Thomas reflects this, because the bare fifty-two to forty-eight majority for Thomas revealed a significant erosion from the sixty-two to thirty-eight estimated majority Thomas enjoyed before Professor Hill's charges became public.

The key Senate votes that provided Judge Thomas's victory margin came from seven southern Democrats who feared the White male conservative vote in their relatively conservative states: Nunn and Fowler of Georgia; Hollings of South Carolina; Robb of Virginia; Shelby of Alabama; Breaux and Johnston of Louisiana. The idea that in such states the Black vote might defect from these Democrats was misguided, since all of their prospective opponents on the Republican ticket were certain to make openly racist appeals to White voters, thereby alienating Black voters far more than a Democratic vote against Thomas could have.

The impact of the Thomas confirmation battle went beyond educating the American public on the subject of sexual harassment—for the first time, it exposed a vast White television audience to a representative cross-section of the Black elite, it improved White America's perception of Black America, and it bolstered the self-image of African-Americans. Consequently, the effectiveness of the race issue in electoral politics was reduced. For example in the Louisiana gubernatorial election that took place soon after Judge Thomas's confirmation the 55 percent White vote for the racist candidate David Duke was significantly lower than the predicted 64 percent, whereas the overwhelming Black turnout of 80 percent, of whom 96 percent voted for the Democratic candidate, was decisive in defeating Duke by a landslide.

The Republican party found itself on the defensive on the issues of both race and women's rights as the 1992 electoral contest began, despite President Bush's victory in the confirmation battle. Bush won the Supreme Court only to lose the presidency.

One of the most interesting assessments of Clarence Thomas's second round of confirmation hearings appeared in an October 20, 1991, *New York Times* Op-Ed piece by Harvard sociology professor Orlando Patterson, nominally a Black liberal, in which President Bush's version of the melting pot, complete with its White male values, was translated into a package for sale to African-Americans.

Professor Patterson's opening paragraph offered an unrivalled evaluation of this round as: "one of the finest moments in the modern history of America's democratic culture, a riveting, civic drama that fully engaged the electorate in an exposure and examination of its most basic fears and contradictions concerning class, race, sex and gender."

But then Patterson used class, race, sex, and gender to defend Thomas by demeaning White and Black women alike. After suggesting that White feminists cannot explain the "startling realization" that Judge Thomas "might well have said what Prof. Anita Hill alleges and yet be the extraordinarily sensitive man his persuasive female defenders claimed," Patterson criticized the feminist movement for protesting sexual harassment which he claimed "working-class" southern White women and "especially" Black women are willing to tolerate:

> Implicit in these hearings was an overdue questioning of the legalistic, neo-Puritan and elitist model of gender relations promoted by the dominant school of American feminists.
>
> . . . He [Thomas] may well have said what he was alleged to have said, but he did so as a man not unreasonably attracted to an aloof woman who is aesthetically and socially very similar to himself, who had made no secret of her own deep admiration for him.
>
> With his mainstream cultural guard down, Judge Thomas on several misjudged occasions may have done

something completely out of the cultural frame of his white, upper-middle-class work world, but immediately recognizable to Professor Hill and most women of Southern working-class backgrounds, white or black, especially the latter.

This attempt to justify the sexual harassment that Clarence Thomas was accused of inflicting upon Anita Hill fails for two main reasons.

First, the description of Judge Thomas's "work world" as *White* and upper-middle-class is a distortion. Actually, his staff at the EEOC included many upper-middle-class *Blacks* whose presence contradicts Patterson's speculation that Thomas may have lowered his "mainstream guard" which he needed in the "cultural frame" of his job.

Second, Professor Patterson's description of southern Black cultural traditions as accepting sexual harassment is inaccurate. Southern Black women do not view sexual disrespect, not to say sexual harassment, as a tolerable way for Black men to relate to them. The viciously racist loose-morals stereotype of working-class Black women was created to legitimize the sexual harassment of Black women of all classes by *White* men. As for southern Black culture, working-class or otherwise, sexual harassment is held in contempt, if only because southern Black men used to risk their lives to defend Black women from White men.

Patterson only compounded his error when he went on to say:

> I am convinced that Professor Hill perfectly understood the psycho-cultural context in which Judge Thomas allegedly regaled her with his Rabelaisian humor (possibly as a way of affirming their common origins), which is precisely why she never filed a complaint against him.
>
> Raising the issue 10 years later was unfair and disingenuous: unfair because, while she may have been offended by his coarseness, there is no evidence that she suffered any emotional or career damage, and the punishment she belatedly sought was in no way commensurate with the offense, and disingenuous because she has lifted a verbal style that carries only minor sanction in

one *subcultural* context and thrown it in the overheated
cultural arena of mainstream, neo-Puritan America where
it incurs professional extinction [EMPHASIS MINE].

Rabelaisian humor was surely not a way to "affirm their common
origins." Professor Hill failed to file a complaint because she did not want
to risk her own career or to damage Judge Thomas's, and sexual
harassment *made public* does not carry "only minor sanction" in the Black
community. But what is most significant in this passage is the demeaning
reference to a "subcultural context" which supposedly defines African-
American culture relative to the "mainstream cultural arena." Moreover, the
case of Professor Anita Hill and Judge Clarence Thomas is a classic; the
Black man accused of harassing the Black woman was the ultimate
authority in the workplace as head of the EEOC, so Professor Hill faced the
forbiddingly high risk of making a *public* complaint.

Professor Patterson ended his piece by signaling that the Bush
administration welcomed the Black middle class into the melting pot, and
by accusing White liberals of stereotyping Blacks as a "monolithic group":

What has emerged is not only the indifference of the
white public to the racial aspect of the proceedings but
the degree to which white men and women identified
their own interests and deepest anxieties with the two
African-American antagonists. . . .

African-Americans must now realize that these hearings were perhaps the single most important cultural
development for them since the great struggles of the
civil rights years.

. . . What all African-Americans won from their pain,
"perfected by this deed," this ritual of inclusion, is the
public cultural affirmation of what had already been
politically achieved: unambiguous inclusion; unquestioned belonging. The culture of slavery is dead.

. . . Superficial liberal stereotypes of blacks as victims
or bootstrap heroes are seen for what they are: a new
form of racism that finds it hard to imagine African

Americans not as a monolithic group but . . . [as] a diverse
aggregate of . . . individuals. . . .

Patterson was telling "African Americans" [note the strongly ethnic
term, without the hyphen] that America's melting pot is open to them as
never before. The "culture of slavery"—that is, the culture of Black
exclusion—"is dead." He offered the Black middle class the "public cultural
affirmation" of "unambiguous inclusion" and "unquestioned belonging."
However, he failed to mention the middle-class entry requirement that still
excludes the majority of native Blacks from the melting pot, implying class
distinction only indirectly in his contradictory antiliberal rhetoric.

Through his unrealistic claim that Black group solidarity is a liberal
stereotype, Patterson indirectly invited the Black middle class to abandon
the victimized and excluded Black underclass by recognizing "class
differences." Then he accused liberals of creating the *conservative* Black-
bootstrap-hero stereotype Bush used to tout Thomas, and ignored the
victimization of the majority of native Blacks while actually criticizing the
"superficial liberal stereotype of blacks as victims."

WHAT PROFESSOR PATTERSON REVEALED in his *New York Times* Op-Ed
article was the Republican blueprint for the 1992 presidential campaign—
no more crude race card with its clearly recognizable appeal to the racism
of White males, but a continued attack on feminism, on those perceived to
lack prescribed family values, and on group rights. The melting pot was to
clear the way toward a color-blind, but not sex-blind, society of equal
individuals. The minorities who refused to enter this new national
brotherhood and sisterhood were to be cast as retrograde elements bent on
subverting our core American values at the behest of those ever-treacher-
ous liberals who have replaced the Communists as the new subversives.

This contradictory and racially charged antiliberal line has been
woven into Republican party ideology and is certain to poison American
electoral politics for a long time, but the prospect that Clarence Thomas is
likely to adopt a similar approach as a Supreme Court Justice is even more
alarming.

The present u.s. Supreme Court will affect all aspects of our cultural, political, economic, and social life far beyond the 1992 and 1996 presidential elections, and Justice Clarence Thomas's vote will be a decisive factor in its rulings. Therefore, virulent political combat surrounded every aspect of his nomination to the Supreme Court bench. In an important sense the confirmation of Judge Thomas shaped the 1992 election campaigns of both the Republican and Democratic parties.

From here on, a Republican president can overcome a Democratic Congress with the aid of the new Supreme Court. But a Democratic president will require overwhelming Democratic margins in both houses of Congress to overcome the resistance of the Supreme Court. The political battle triggered by Judge Clarence Thomas's nomination has established a framework for the political wars of the current decade.

3

PAUL ROBESON
AND THE
UNIVERSALITY OF
BLACK CULTURE

*In my music, my plays, my films, I want to carry always
this central idea—to be African.*
—PAUL ROBESON, 1934

aul Robeson (1898–1976), one of the twentieth century's
greatest concert singers and actors, represents the antithesis of Judge Clarence Thomas in Black life. Robeson
was willing to risk all in resisting melting-pot ideology
and challenging the cultural foundations of American
racism. In contrast with Thomas's subservience to White authority, he
continued the tradition of the independent Black leader who champions
the interests of his own people.

Paul Robeson's personification of the African-American cultural
tradition derived from the same source that provided Rev. Martin
Luther King, Jr.'s moral and philosophical base—the religious culture of

the Black South with its core values of American slaves. This culture, forged in the crucible of the slave-ship hell and slavery's chains, constructed an intricate and sophisticated communications web that united the myriad African ethnic groups scattered over a vast territory and was not understood by most Whites. Its center consisted of the traditions common to all the African ethnic groups—traditions which nourished the preservation of each group's culture and were enhanced in return by those cultures.

In this sense, the slave culture had a natural universal side which transcended the ethnic and religious differences among the large, diverse, and constantly changing Black population of the u.s. during the nineteenth century. This universalist tendency was reinforced by both the inclusion of the Black freedmen's culture and the necessary absorption of modified aspects of American culture. And since the Bible was the only book slaves were legally permitted to read, the religious expression of the slaves' culture became interwoven with the Judeo-Christian tradition.

The African-American church subsequently emerged as the cultural focus of Black life in America by combining both the Afrocentric and universalist sides of the slaves' culture, thus supporting those Blacks who integrated into American society, as well as the Black majority left behind in the segregated non-White society outside the melting pot. However, American culture always refused to acknowledge the Afrocentric side of Black culture and insisted on restricting it to its universal side. Those Blacks who are admitted to American society are required to abandon their Afrocentrism by pretending that they are children of the melting pot.

Although they were separated by a generation, both Reverend King and Paul Robeson refused to abandon *either* their Afrocentrism *or* their universalism, despite the conflicting pressures and blandishments of American culture and Black separatism.

Three years before Reverend King was born, Paul Robeson made his spectacular arrival on the American cultural scene during the Harlem Renaissance of the 1920s. Together with his pioneering accompanist-arranger, Lawrence Brown, my father went on to become one of the world's greatest concert artists of the twentieth century. His deep roots in African-American slave culture enabled him to embrace the universal essence of the ancient European cultures through his identification with the universality of the Black cultural tradition.

Those roots came from my grandfather, Rev. William Drew Robeson, a runaway plantation slave from North Carolina who was pastor of the Witherspoon Street Presbyterian Church in Princeton, New Jersey, in the 1890s; built the St. Luke African Methodist Episcopal Zion Church in Westfield, New Jersey, in the decade prior to World War I; and then was pastor of the St. Thomas A.M.E. Zion Church in Somerville, New Jersey, from 1910 until his death in 1918. He taught Paul the nonviolent assertion of full human dignity in the face of anti-Black discrimination and hatred. My father referred lovingly to this legacy in his 1958 autobiography *Here I Stand*:

> The glory of my boyhood years was my father. . . .
> . . . I marvel that there was no hint of servility in my father's make-up. . . . From him we learned, and never doubted it, that the Negro was in every way the equal of the white man. . . .
> . . . I heard my people singing! . . . from choir loft and Sunday morning pews—and my soul was filled with their harmonies. . . . I heard these songs in the very sermons of my father. . . . The great, soaring gospels we love are merely sermons that are sung.

THE REVIEWS OF PAUL ROBESON'S first concert season of 1925–1926 referred explicitly and even reverently to the cultural significance of his artistry.

On April 20, 1925, the music critic of the *New York Times* wrote: "His Negro Spirituals . . . hold in them a world of religious experience; it is their cry from the depths, this universal humanism, that touches the heart. . . . Sung by one man, they voiced the sorrow and hopes of a people."

And in an article in *The New Republic*, titled "The Man with His Home in That Rock: Paul Robeson," Elizabeth Shepley Sergeant wrote:

> Paul Robeson . . . is a symbol . . . of the increasing

important place of the American Negro on the American stage.... It is earnestly to be hoped that the men like Paul Robeson with his evangelical tradition and Lawrence Brown with his Florida verve . . . are establishing a "classic" Spiritual tradition that will long live in American music. . . .

Let us give thanks that we were not born too late to hear this Negro Chaliapin render the Spirituals reverently, with wildness and awe, like a trusting child of God.

However, not all of Paul's songs included in the programs of his earliest concerts were spirituals. Throughout his concert career, one of Paul's favorite composed songs was "Water Boy," a Black secular song written by the well-known White composer Avery Robinson. Some years ago, I found an interesting reference to that song in my father's 1929 diary: "Of course, technique might help me grow . . . but that might not make me a *greater* artist. 'Water Boy' is my best record—[made] when I was untrained." Seventeen years later, his intuitive affinity for the song was confirmed.

In 1946 my father received a letter, accompanied by an African battle axe, from a member of an anthropological expedition to a remote village in southern Angola. Several records were played on a portable gramophone for the assembled villagers, and one of the songs was my father's rendition of "Water Boy." As the song ended, the village chief rose, went to his hut, and brought back a ceremonial battle axe which he laid before the gramophone as a gift to "the great chief across the water."

One might wonder how Paul Robeson could speak to the heart of an African chief through a song written by a White composer, but Paul was not surprised. By then his search for his African cultural heritage had led him to research the origins of "Water Boy." Black singer Robeson discovered that White composer Robinson had heard the song sung by a Black Alabama chain gang in a particular county of Alabama where the culture of rural Blacks is derived from the culture of the southern Angolans.

In the years between the Harlem Renaissance and 1946, my father traveled far and wide in a determined quest for artistic and personal growth. Like many gifted African-American artists and intellectuals of the 1920s, Paul chose to escape the stifling cultural atmosphere created by the melting pot. Because he sensed the essential shallowness of American culture, he decided to establish his artistic career in the richer cultural soil of England and the European continent. He also understood that the White cultural establishment in America would never willingly allow him to transcend its crude Black stereotypes.

In 1927 Paul Robeson moved his family headquarters to London, England, where he became a dominant figure in the popular culture for the next decade. It was in London that he "discovered Africa." In his handwritten notes from the period 1934–1936 I found the following entry:

> Africa—there is the future of the Black man. From there will come his real contribution to the culture of the world.... I am now working at Swahili, one of the Bantu tongues, and have consulted many sources on comparative Bantu sounds. I found them most subtle.... In these African languages is the content of the Negro spirit—the same spirit that one finds in music and sculpture.... As one of African descent, I feel this strange necessity to (spiritually at least) find my roots.

During this same period, Paul's travels across Europe on concert tours brought him into contact with many cultures in which he found reflections of his own culture. In 1936 he wrote the following in a page of notes inserted into a Russian edition of poetry written by the great Russian poet Alexander Pushkin, whose great-grandfather, on his mother's side, was an African from Abyssinia:

> It is interesting that Pushkin, the shaper of the Russian language, like Chaucer and Shakespeare rolled into one, was of African descent. So the Russian language as spoken today passed through the temperament of a man of African blood.... Pushkin means more to me than any other poet.

By then, Paul Robeson had enriched his repertoire with songs created from the folk idiom by many famous European composers, including Bach, Moussorgsky, and Mozart. A year later, he had an extraordinary experience which linked Mozart to the culture of African antiquity. Paul found himself on location in Cairo, Egypt, during the making of the film *Jericho*. Henry Wilcoxon, his costar in the film, took him on a visit to the Great Pyramid of Gizeh.

Their guide led them to the Pharaoh's chamber at the geometric center of the pyramid where they all noticed an unusual echo. Wilcoxon urged Paul to sing a chord, and when Paul complied, the echo sounded like it had come from a huge organ. As the reverberations finally died out, Paul, without hesitation, stepped to the exact center of the chamber and sang the aria "O' Isis and Osiris" from Mozart's opera *The Magic Flute*. The entire chamber vibrated sympathetically like an enormous natural high-fidelity speaker, producing an unforgettable sound of unbearably majestic beauty. An African-American singer had made a connection with ancient Africa through one of Europe's greatest composers, whose music was inspired by the legend of the African prince and princess who colonized ancient Egypt.

PAUL ROBESON'S LINKAGE of African culture to ancient Western culture drew a significant comment from the famed British historian, Arnold Toynbee, in his book *A Study of History:*

> A distinguished Negro American singer . . . came to realize that the primitive culture of his African ancestors . . . was spiritually akin to all the non-Western higher cultures, and to the pristine higher culture of the Western world itself, in virtue of its having preserved a spiritual integrity which a late Modern Western secularized culture had deliberately abandoned. . . .
>
> . . . Paul Robeson was putting his finger on the difference between an integrated and a disintegrated culture.

Mr. Toynbee is talking about the "pristine higher" culture of

Shakespeare and his predecessors, which was far superior to modern Western culture; moreover, unlike most White Americans, he recognizes that Paul Robeson symbolizes the Negro who happens to be an American, rather than the American who happens to be a Negro. Toynbee then goes on to quote Robeson:

> I discovered that . . . African languages—thought to be primitive because monosyllabic—had exactly the same basic structure as Chinese. I found that Chinese poems which cannot be rendered in English would translate perfectly into African. I found that the African way of thinking in symbols was also the way of the great Chinese thinkers. . . . I found that I, who lacked feeling for the English language later than Shakespeare, met Pushkin, Dostoyevsky, Tolstoy, Lao-tsze, and Confucius on common ground.

My father's comment that he "lacked feeling for the English language later than Shakespeare" registers his affinity for Shakespeare's multiculturalism. This universality derives from the ancient Anglo-Saxon culture of Chaucer, and it is Paul's understanding of this culture that informed his definitive interpretation of the title role in Shakespeare's *Othello*. A leading British Shakespearean critic, John Dover Wilson, called the Robeson performance on Broadway in 1943–1944 the most notable one in the present century.

Paul studied *Othello* in four foreign languages: French for its soft, almost caressing quality when Othello speaks about his love for Desdemona; German for a special kind of harshness when reference is made to military matters; Russian because of its extraordinary range of imagery and its capacity for the expression of subtle shadings of emotion; and Yiddish for its light and sardonic humor and its bittersweet sadness. He also studied the pre-Elizabethan English in which Chaucer wrote, learned the role in Shakespeare's Elizabethan English, and studied the ancient Venetian and Moorish cultures.

The result was described in a 1971 radio interview by Margaret Webster, the director of the record-breaking Broadway production of Paul

Robeson's *Othello* with Jose Ferrer as Iago and Uta Hagen as Desdemona:

> Paul brought qualities with him which I never have seen
> equaled before or since. The moment he stepped on that
> stage, he was not only a black man but a great black
> man—a man of stature. Somehow or other, he put the
> play in focus.

Although Ms. Webster recognized the centrality of a great personality to the role of Othello, the tell-tale words "somehow or other" reveal that she could not understand *how* Paul "put the play in focus." The reason for this becomes clear from an interview she gave to *New York Times* critic Elliot Norton prior to the Broadway opening of *Othello* (August 16, 1942). According to Norton,

> Miss Webster's idea of "Othello" . . . centers in the belief
> that both the text and the sense of the play require a
> Negro in the title part. . . . Everything points to his
> believing himself a member of a race which is not fully
> equal; it is this which makes him easy prey for Iago. Miss
> Webster points out that he is not sure of himself.

Paul Robeson's approach to the role was markedly different from this:

> Othello has killed Desdemona. From savage passion?
> No. Othello came from a culture as great as that of
> ancient Venice. He came from an Africa of equal stature,
> and he felt he was betrayed—his honor was betrayed,
> and his human dignity was betrayed.

My father believed that Othello's vulnerability to Iago stemmed from his feeling of *superiority* over the Venetians. So he paid little attention to what were, to him, their petty intrigues. Such a concept is based on a deep belief in multiculturalism, while Margaret Webster's view comes from the familiar commitment to a dominant Western civilization in which anyone from a non-Western culture *must* feel inferior.

The response of the critics to the Broadway opening confirmed the fidelity of Paul Robeson's Othello to Shakespeare's intent. Louis Kronenberger of *PM* (October 20, 1943) wrote: "Robeson's Othello has so great a natural assurance as never to feel doubt; in a sense, he is lost once so utterly unfamiliar a thing as doubt enters his mind. . . . Where shall we find an Othello to equal him?"

Howard Barnes of the *New York Herald Tribune* (October 31, 1943) wrote:

> The magnificent Margaret Webster production is the first I have seen in which a Negro played a role obviously designed for him, and . . . it takes on more meaning and grandeur than I could have believed possible. . . . There are those who have found Robeson's performance less than satisfactory, objecting to his deliberate delivery of lines in the early scenes, and his gestures of hapless anger as he is caught up in a web of jealousy. For my money, it is exactly these accents . . . which illuminate the tragedy for the first time on a stage.

Margaret Marshall of *The Nation* (October 30, 1943) was among the small minority who openly objected to the multiculturalism represented by a Black Othello:

> Paul Robeson . . . performs passably well, but he creates no illusion. . . . He is not the Moor as Shakespeare conceived him. Both Mr. Robeson and Miss Webster have tried to prove that Othello is a Negro; they have attempted also to prove that "Othello" is a play about race. Both theories are false and foolish. . . . In Shakespeare's conception the essential quality of the Moor is his foreignness. He is the exotic character—so exotic as to bewitch, for all his denials, the innocent English—or Venetian—Desdemona.

During the play's pre-Broadway run, Leo Gaffney of the *Boston Daily Herald* had demonstrated his racial bias more crudely: "His [Robeson's] Moor is too black, too burly, too obvious."

Rudolph Elie, Jr., the *Variety* critic, was prophetic in his review of Robeson's performance during the 1942 summer tryout of *Othello* when he concluded that,

> the play silences for all time the folderol centering around the furious controversy that Othello was not intended as a Negro and should consequently not be played by one. Fact of the matter is that Robeson's performance is of such a stature that no white man should ever dare to presume to play it again.

However, Mr. Elie, like Miss Webster, missed the main point—it was Paul Robeson's ability to tap the multiculturalism of pre-Renaissance Western culture, rather than *just* his color, that made his performance possible. Salvini, a leading actor of Italian ancestry who was in touch with the ancient European culture, was an Othello far superior to the Othellos of many leading White *and* Black actors imprisoned within modern Western culture.

Paul Robeson's Othello made a powerful impression on an America in which the minstrel show was still a pervasive ritual, and some of the most persistent stereotypes of the Black male were permanently undermined at a time when my father was only one generation removed from slavery. I can recall an evening in 1944 when a White man with a southern drawl who was about my father's age respectfully asked my father for an autograph. His name was Robeson, he said, adding that we got *our* name from *his* father. Dad's face clouded over for a moment, but then he smiled, signed his autograph, and handed it to the man, saying: "Let's just say my father worked for your father." After all, it was the son of the slave owner who had asked the son of the slave for an autograph!

THE RESPONSE OF AMERICAN popular culture to this challenge to its Black stereotypes was to tout Paul Robeson as an *American* national hero, a living monument to that cornerstone of *American* civilization—the opportunity of an individual of humble origins, even a Black individual, to reach the pinnacle of success. The clearest example of this can be found in the association of Paul Robeson with a staple of the popular culture: the musical *Show Boat* and its theme song "Ol' Man River."

Jerome Kern, one of the greatest composers of American musical theater, composed the music for *Show Boat* in 1926, and the famous lyricist, Oscar Hammerstein II, wrote the lyrics. The theme song "Ol' Man River" was dedicated to Paul Robeson; his rendition of it captivated audiences around the world and became his artistic signature. Edna Ferber, author of the book *Show Boat*, described a 1932 performance at New York's Casino Theater in a letter to the renowned writer and critic Alexander Woollcott:

> I . . . looked at the audience and the stage at the very moment when Paul Robeson came on to sing "Ol' Man River." In all my years of going to the theater . . . , I never have seen an ovation like that given to any figure of the stage, the concert hall, or the opera. . . . That audience stood up and howled. They applauded and shouted and stamped. Since then I have seen it exceeded but once, and that was when Robeson, a few minutes later, finished singing "Ol' Man River." The show stopped. He sang it again. The show stopped. They called him back again and again. Other actors came out and made motions and their lips moved, but the bravos of the audience drowned all other sounds.

Listening to my father sing "Ol' Man River" became a landmark experience in American culture, so the lyrics acquired a significant symbolism. The original lyrics are still sung today, except for the first two lines which my father had already modified by 1932. Oscar Hammerstein II had written:

> Niggers all work on the Mississippi,
> Niggers all work while the white folks play,

and Paul Robeson changed these lines to:

> Colored folks work on the Mississippi,
> Colored folks work while the white folks play,

The rest of the lyrics conform to the nondefiant lament allowed by the popular culture of the 1920s, as illustrated by the following excerpt:

> Pullin' dem boats from the dawn till sunset,
> Gettin' no rest till the judgement day,
> . . . .
> Tote that barge and lift that bale,
> Ya gits a little drunk and ya lands in jail.
> I gits weary and sick of tryin'
> I'm tired of livin' and scared of dyin',
> And Ol' Man River, he just keeps rollin' along.

But after his triumph in the Broadway *Othello,* Paul rewrote the lyrics of "Ol' Man River" to challenge the Black stereotypes of the popular culture overtly—his rendition of the song became the symbolic equivalent of the raised Black fist:

> There's an old man called the Mississippi,
> That's the old man I don't like to be.
> What does he care if the world's got troubles;
> What does he care if the land aint free.
> . . . .
> Tote that barge and lift that bale;
> You show a little grit and you lands in jail.
> But I keeps laffin' instead of cryin',
> I must keep fightin' until I'm dyin',
> And Ol' Man River, he just keeps rollin' along.

Paul Robeson's decision to challenge American racism head-on was based on his refusal to accept the terms under which non-Whites were integrated into American society. Although he had been accepted as the equal of Whites because of his extraordinary achievements, Paul rejected the framework of the society as he found it and demanded fundamental social, political, economic, and cultural change. He insisted that not just outstanding Black individuals, but the entire African-American people be accepted as full citizens into all aspects of national life.

MY FATHER'S REJECTION of the stereotypical images mandated for Blacks by American culture coincided with his active participation in the civil rights movement of the late 1940s. In March of 1947, at a concert in Salt Lake City, Utah, he startled the audience after his final song by holding up his hand to still their ovation; then he announced that they had heard his last formal concert for two years, and that he would be singing songs of struggle and resistance to civil rights and labor audiences. "From now on," he said, "I shall sing . . . only at gatherings where I can sing what I please."

Paul explained to the press that he had always refused to sing before segregated audiences in the South; instead, he sang at Black universities where White people could attend and sit among their Black neighbors. He added that he would continue to sing on college campuses and for trade union organizations after he left the concert stage.

Paul Robeson was true to his word, and his artistic appearances on behalf of civil rights and labor causes led him to become a spokesman for the growing national civil rights movement. On September 11, 1947, at a Madison Square Garden rally sponsored by the Progressive Citizens of America, Paul evoked a tradition which countered the melting pot:

> Let us—a unified power of labor, liberals, Negroes, the Jewish people, descendants of foreign born, all oppressed groups . . . protect our true American tradition. Let us turn this country toward the course of history—a world of all the people, . . . a world where men of every race and creed may walk the earth in true dignity.

A year later, Paul spoke in a similar vein about his tour through the deep South on behalf of the Progressive party presidential campaign of former vice president Henry Wallace. On that trip Paul and many others had risked their lives while leading the first voter registration drive among southern Blacks since Reconstruction, and his words bear a striking similarity to those spoken by the civil rights campaigners of the 1960s:

> I've just come from a very long tour up and down the breadth of America. . . . I was most moved by what happened in the deep South. They told us . . . we couldn't

come into Memphis, Tennessee. . . . We went into
Memphis. People said, "you're not going to have a
meeting." We said, "we *are* going to have a meeting."
And we got one of the biggest Negro auditoriums; a
Negro minister gave us one of the finest places in
Memphis. . . .

. . . We went on to New Orleans; to Mobile, Alabama;
to Charleston, South Carolina; to Savannah, Georgia.
. . . Here again, one felt that the Negroes of Savannah
understood what Wallace meant when he came into the
South. That here for the first time it was not a question of
. . . a few civil rights—it was a question of striking at the
liberation, the complete liberation of the Negro people
in our time.

Here Paul Robeson speaks of the "complete liberation" of African-
Americans, not merely about "a few civil rights." Over forty years ago, he
rejected the limited absorption of all Black individuals into the melting pot
which is still being offered today; what Robeson was insisting on was the
inclusion of African-Americans into American society as a distinct people.
I believe it was this, and not primarily his left-wing radicalism, that caused
him to be persecuted so ferociously by the u.s. government. A decade later,
having survived the secret war waged against him by the Federal Bureau
of Investigation and the Central Intelligence Agency, Paul illuminated the
path of the nascent civil rights movement of the late 1950s and early 1960s
in his autobiography *Here I Stand,* published in 1958:

As I see it, . . . freedom can be ours, here and now: the
long-sought goal of full citizenship under the Constitution is now within our reach. We have the power to
achieve that goal—what we ourselves do will be decisive. . . .

. . . We ask for nothing that is not ours by right, and
herein lies the great moral power of our demand. It is the
admitted *rightness* of our claim which has earned for us the
moral support of the majority of white Americans. . . .

. . . *Wherever and whenever we, the Negro people, claim our*

lawful rights with all of the earnestness, dignity and determination
that we can demonstrate, the moral support of the American
people will become an active force on our side.

But Paul also looked beyond the civil rights struggle to the struggles that would come after it. Noting that African-Americans had been relegated to the lowest rungs of society since before the founding of the American republic, he pointed out that

> the equal *place* to which we aspire cannot be reached
> without the equal *rights* we demand, and so the winning
> of those rights is not a maximum fulfillment but a
> minimum necessity. . . . Even with the removal of all
> barriers, we still have a long climb in order to catch up
> with the general standard of living.

Then Paul proposed an approach toward the exercise of power by Black Americans in pursuit of their vital interests.

In a chapter entitled "The Power of Negro Action," my father combined his support of massive nonviolent resistance with a call for a fully independent Black leadership:

> Nothing is more important than to establish the fact
> that we will no longer suffer the use of mobs against
> us. Let the Negro people of but a single city respond
> in an all-out manner at the first sign of a mob—in
> mass demonstrations, by going on strike, by organizing
> boycotts—and the lesson will be taught in one bold
> stroke to people everywhere. . . .
> . . . Effective Negro leadership must rely upon and be
> responsive to no other control than the will of their
> people. . . . Good advice is good no matter what the
> source, and help is needed and appreciated from wher-
> ever it comes, but Negro action cannot be decisive if the
> advisers and helpers hold the guiding reins. For no
> matter how well-meaning other groups may be, the fact
> is our interests are secondary at best with them.

Yet Paul Robeson saw no contradiction between this expression of independent African-American power and universal human brotherhood. "Even as I grew to feel more Negro in spirit, or African as I put it then," he wrote, "I also came to feel a sense of oneness with the white working people whom I came to know and love." He asserted the "oneness of humankind" and pointed to the universality of ethnic cultural traditions. "I base nothing on distinctions of race," Paul had written in the 1930s. "Color distinctions cannot be avoided; neither can cultural differences. . . . [But] I am more profoundly impressed by likenesses in cultural forms which seem to me to transcend the boundaries of nationality."

PAUL ROBESON WAS ONE of the main cultural links between the last generation of Black slaves and the generation of independent Black leaders who spearheaded the civil rights revolution of the 1960s. The creative manner in which he developed his cultural philosophy and used his artistic talents led a panel of Black historians to include Robeson among the ten most important Black men in American history. In an article published in the August 1972 issue of *Ebony,* they wrote that when his scholarship became better known, Paul would "win recognition as the finest ideologist of black nationalism since Sidney of the early 1840s . . . , [and] as one of the century's most perceptive commentators on the cultures of the East, the West and Africa."

The late James Baldwin alluded to Paul Robeson's historic cultural stature and his symbolic meaning to Baldwin's generation in the following eloquent passage of an open letter written in 1977 on behalf of a group of Black notables who were protesting against a Broadway play titled *Paul Robeson* which, they felt, trivialized Robeson's life and misrepresented his character:

> Robeson is not yet a historical figure, has not yet entered the limbo of the public domain. He lives, overwhelmingly, in the hearts and minds of the people whom he touched, the people for whom he was an example, the people who gained from him the power to perceive and the courage to resist. It is not a sentimental question. He lived in our times, we lived in his. . . .

Thus, it is not a matter of setting a historical record straight, or a matter of historical interpretation. It is a matter of bearing witness to that force which moved among us.

. . . The man the play presents is not Paul Robeson. That is all we are saying. . . . We *must* say this so that our children's children's children will know better than we did how to honor and protect him when they meet him in their own lives.

4

BLACK AND WHITE HISTORY

ust as the U.S. popular culture in the aftermath of World War II rejected Paul Robeson's assertion of full human dignity and true personhood, this culture has always rejected the idea that the Black male slave was a full human being. The superiority of the *White* male—the concept which I see as central to melting-pot ideology and which justifies the exclusion of non-Whites from the melting pot—is measured against the assumed inferiority of the *Black* male.

The modern institutionalization of this perceived inferiority has been built on the melting-pot interpretation of slavery's impact on African-Americans, and, therefore, the history of slavery has been filtered into U.S. popular culture almost exclusively through White male perceptions. White historians, conservatives and liberals alike, have, with few exceptions, distorted the history of American slavery in a manner tending to legitimize the view that Blacks are culturally inferior to Whites.

Conservatives have generally approached the subject directly and simply: they have taken the position that slavery was essentially justified because African-Americans were considered to be genetically inferior to European-Americans. According to the conservative view, history proves that the White race is superior to the Black race.

Liberals find this concept unacceptable, yet firmly support the melting-pot ideology of White male superiority. They have solved this dilemma by claiming that the cruelties of slavery produced Black inferiority by eradicating Black culture and dehumanizing the Black male. Their argument is that slavery, rather than genetics, made the Black man inferior to the White man.

This argument is supported by two unsubstantiated and artificially connected assumptions: 1. Any normal White man subjected to the extremely harsh conditions endured by the Black male slave would have been dehumanized; and 2. *therefore,* Blacks would have had to be superhuman to retain their humanity under slavery, since Whites could not have done so.

The first proposition, which is dubious according to available historical data about White slaves and White indentured servants, is purely speculative in the sense that the only accurate comparison would be an American fantasy in which a Black society owned White slaves.

The second proposition is fundamentally different from the first, which at least relies on White speculation about White dehumanization. The very idea that slavery dehumanized Blacks *because* of its assumed capacity for dehumanizing Whites is based on guesses by free Whites about the internal psychological and emotional reactions of enslaved Blacks. The fact that such guesses are highly unreliable is confirmed by the consistent inability of antebellum southern Whites to tell the difference between a future slave rebel, like Nat Turner, and an Uncle Tom, even after prolonged and close personal contact.

Furthermore, mountains of historical evidence are available as proof that Black slaves did indeed retain their humanity under slavery by adapting their highly developed culture to harsh new conditions. White ignorance of Black culture served as a foil for the refined ability of the slaves to conceal their true attitudes from Whites, and the result was an almost universal White fantasy of generally contented slaves which could be penetrated only by slave rebellions, the Civil War, and Reconstruction.

Since melting-pot ideology cannot survive without the myth of Black male inferiority, liberal historians perpetuate this image by trivializing African-American slave culture and slave resistance.

ONE OF THE MOST REVEALING examples of this well-meaning but flawed historical analysis can be found in historian Martin B. Duberman's book of essays, *The Uncompleted Past.* In the chapter "William Styron's *Nat Turner* and *Ten Black Writers Respond*," Professor Duberman comments on the three principal historians of slavery in the u.s.: Ulrich Phillips, whose justification of slavery in *American Negro Slavery* remained definitive until the 1960s; Kenneth Stampp, whose 1956 work, *The Peculiar Institution*, exposed the cruel injustice of slavery and argued that the slaves remained fully human; and Stanley Elkins, whose 1959 book *Slavery* claimed that the harshness of slave life dehumanized the slaves, making them childlike. Duberman criticized Phillips and Stampp, but tended to agree with Elkins.

Although Professor Duberman's commentary on Phillips's apology for slavery as an institution rejected both the idea that slavery was "mild" or "paternal" and the notion that "the Negro's childish temperament" was in any sense a genetic trait, Duberman left open the possibility that the childishness of the slaves might be a *culturally derived* racial trait—that is, a trait acquired through learning. Duberman wrote:

> [Phillips] believed slavery was a civilizing force: it re-
> moved Africans from their benighted homeland and
> introduced them to the blessings of Christianity and
> Progress. But the civilizing process could go only so far,
> for the Negro's childish temperament, however "ami-
> able" and "ingratiating," made some form of subordinate
> status and guardianship inescapable. Phillips's character-
> ization established the stereotype of Black Sambo, the
> shuffling, genial, happy darky. He saw Sambo's traits as
> genetic, not cultural—that is, given by nature, not
> acquired through learning.

Professor Duberman went on to reject the view that the Black Sambo image could be *genetic,* but he did not entirely reject Phillips's picture of the

Black slave. Rather, he allowed for the possibility that "Sambo's traits" might be cultural.

In my view, the idea that the culture of slavery's institutions imposed Sambo traits on the personalities of the slaves is mistaken. The slaves possessed a powerful culture that antedated their enslavement and survived slavery to manifest itself in today's native-Black culture. Moreover, the culture of the slaves produced the Sambo *behavior* as a defense *against* the culture of slavery.

Professor Duberman appears to ignore this possibility in criticizing Kenneth Stampp's *The Peculiar Institution,* in which Stampp documented the psychological strength and resilience of the slaves despite the cruelties of slavery. After characterizing Stampps's portrait of the slave as a full human being as "bizarre," and accusing Stampp of a "reluctance to pursue the pernicious consequences of slavery," Duberman wrote:

> He [Stampp] resisted the conclusion which seemed to follow from his own evidence: that a cruel and coercive system of labor must have had a destructive psychological effect on its laborers. . . .
>
> . . . Stampp tends to see the slave, in full manliness and vigor, engaging in day-to-day resistance to oppression; his typical slave is closer to Toussaint L'Ouverture than to Black Sambo. [Toussaint L'Ouverture was a legendary Black political and military figure who led Haiti's enslaved Black masses in a rebellion which freed Haiti from the yoke of Napoleon's France.]

Professor Duberman apparently misunderstood Stampp's portrayal of slave resistance, in which Stampp described the coercive aspect of the slave system from the points of view of both master and slave:

> Here, then, was the way to produce the perfect slave: accustom him to rigid discipline, demand from him unconditional submission, impress upon him his innate inferiority, develop in him a paralyzing fear of White men, train him to adopt the master's code of good

behavior, and instill in him a sense of complete dependence. This, at least, was the goal. But the goal was
seldom reached. Every master knew that the average
slave was only an imperfect copy of the model. He knew
that some bondsmen yielded only to superior power—
and yielded reluctantly. This complicated his problem of
control [PAGE 148].

. . . The great majority of disarmed and outnumbered
slaves, knowing the futility of rebellion, refused to join in
any of the numerous plots. Most slaves had to express
their desire for freedom in less dramatic ways. . . .

The survival of slavery, then, cannot be explained as
due to the contentment of slaves or their failure to
comprehend the advantages of freedom. They longed
for freedom and resisted bondage as much as any people
could have done in their circumstances, but their longing
and resistance were not enough even to render the
institution unprofitable to most masters. The masters had
power and . . . developed an elaborate technique of slave
control [PAGE 140].

Thus Stampp argues that the Black slave was *neither* Black Sambo nor
Toussaint L'Ouverture, but rather a spectrum of human personalities
between those extremes. Yet Professor Duberman continued his argument
for the dehumanized slave image by attributing to Stampp an "unwilling-
ness to lend credence to the view that Negroes were—or are—'different'":

By insisting that "Negroes are, after all, only white men
with black skins," Stampp is forced to minimize the
special experience of slavery and to describe its effects in
a way that threatens to replace Phillips's slanders and
stereotypes with new unrealities. . . . Such a portrait, in a
bizarre reversal of Stampp's actual intentions, ends by
denying the Negro his common humanity, for he cannot
be "like everyone else" if, unlike everyone else, he does

not react to endless indignity and brutalization with some despair and self-hate.

However, Stampp's comment about "white men in black skins" was made in the broader context of Stampp's distinction between cultural differences and human traits, and this context makes clear an intent that appears to have been misinterpreted by Duberman:

> I have assumed that the slaves were merely ordinary human beings, that innately Negroes *are,* after all, only white men with black skins, nothing more, nothing less. I did not, of course, assume that there have been, or are today, no cultural differences between white and black Americans. Nor do I regard it as flattery to call Negroes white men with black skins. It would serve my purpose as well to call Caucasians black men with white skins. I have simply found no convincing evidence that there are any significant differences between the innate emotional traits and intellectual capacities of Negroes and whites. This gives quite a new and different meaning to the bondage of black men; it gives their story a relevance to men of all races which it never seemed to have before.

The core of Professor Stampp's argument is that there are no significant differences in human traits between people of different races or ethnic groups, despite wide differences in cultures. "Innate emotional traits and intellectual capacities" are universal, whereas cultures differ from group to group. This implies that a culture—even one as harsh as slavery—cannot alter human traits significantly.

On the other hand, Professor Duberman apparently holds that cultural differences reflect differences in human traits "acquired through learning." This implies that human traits can be altered by a cultural environment such as slavery or the melting pot.

Professor Stampp's view implies that the absence of any significant differences in human traits precludes any type of hierarchy based on race, ethnicity, class, or gender. I call this view *progressive,* since it differs fundamentally from the *liberal* view which justifies a cultural hierarchy on the basis of culturally perceived differences in human traits. Thus, Stampp, the progressive, aptly ended his book with a quotation from a former slave: "'Tisn't he who has stood and looked on, that can tell you what slavery is, 'tis he who has endured. . . . I was black, but I had the feelings of a man as well as any man."

Professor Duberman's denial of the distinction between cultural and human traits appears to be based on his belief in the melting-pot *culture* which is supposed to melt the human traits of people from various cultures into new, American human traits. Such an outlook tends to attribute cultural deviations from the melting-pot norms to deviations of *human traits* from the prescribed American traits.

The Duberman essay, though written in the 1960s in the wake of the civil rights movement, is encumbered by the same melting-pot ideology that failed to challenge slavery and compulsory racial segregation. In this limited sense, Professor Duberman reflects some of the attitudes of liberal historians toward slavery a century earlier, in the mid-1800s, when the abolitionist movement was growing and slave rebellions and conspiracies in 1800 (Gabriel Prosser's conspiracy), 1822 (Denmark Vesey's conspiracy), and 1831 (Nat Turner's rebellion) had traumatized not just the South but the entire nation.

ONE OF THE MOST PERCEPTIVE nineteenth-century commentators on American liberal democracy is the liberal French historian Alexis de Tocqueville. In two penetrating essays, "Race Relations in America" and "Blacks in America," de Tocqueville laid out the classic liberal interpretation of melting-pot ideology as it applies to slavery and Black-White relations. It is instructive that, despite his uncompromising rejection of any ideology which accepts a racial hierarchy based on *genetic* differences, Tocqueville is also unequivocal in his rejection of equal status for Blacks as a people. Only isolated Black *individuals,* he writes, can ever aspire to such a position:

> I do not imagine that the white and black races will ever
> live in any country upon an equal footing. But I believe

the difficulty to be still greater in the United States than elsewhere. An isolated individual may surmount the prejudices of religion, of his country, or of his race, and if this individual is a king, he may effect surprising changes in society; but a whole people cannot rise, as it were, above itself. . . .

. . . The mulattoes are the true means of transition between the white and the Negro; so that wherever mulattoes abound, the intermixture of the two races is not impossible.

The 1960s concept of integration, as advanced by liberals, was a modification of Tocqueville's view: the sole difference lay in a radical increase in the number of individual Blacks who were admitted into American society. Moreover, today's liberals continue to point to assimilation as the only permanent solution to the race problem, even as they call for the admission of Blacks into the melting pot.

The essays by Tocqueville also foreshadowed the modern Black Sambo theories which are based on acquired behavior, rather than on genetics. He insisted that:

The Negro enters upon slavery as soon as he is born; nay, he may have been purchased in the womb, and have begun his slavery before he began his existence. Equally devoid of wants and enjoyment, and useless to himself, he learns, with his first notions of existence, that he is the property of another who has an interest in preserving his life, and that the care of it does not devolve upon himself. Even the power of thought appears to him a useless gift of Providence, and he quietly enjoys the privileges of his debasement.

This picture of the dehumanized slave was central to the liberal position on the critical issue of whether to abolish slavery. Tocqueville stated that position bluntly:

If it be impossible to anticipate a period at which the

> Americans of the South will mingle their blood with that of the Negroes, can they allow their slaves to become free without compromising their own security? And if they are obliged to keep that race in bondage in order to save their own families, may they not be excused for availing themselves of the means best adapted to that end?

In the America of the mid-nineteenth century, only the abolitionists supported immediate and unconditional freedom for the slaves. Conservatives, liberals, and even progressives were opposed to full-scale emancipation. Moreover, many northern liberals were apologists for the slave-owner class and held the view that freedom for the slaves would compromise the "security" of White southerners. This attitude was recognized by Tocqueville's version of the Black Sambo image of *free* Blacks:

> If he becomes free, independence is often felt by him to be a heavier burden than slavery; for having learned, in the course of his life, to submit to everything except reason, he is too much unacquainted with her dictates to obey them. A thousand new desires beset him, and he is destitute of the knowledge and energy necessary to resist them: these are master [i.e., temptations] which it is necessary to contend with, and he has learnt only to submit and obey. In short, he sinks to such a depth of wretchedness, that while servitude brutalizes, liberty destroys him.
>
> . . . The Negro makes a thousand fruitless efforts to ingratiate himself with men who repulse him; he conforms to the tastes of his oppressors, adopts their opinions, and hopes by imitating them to form a part of their community. Having been told from infancy that his race is naturally inferior to that of whites, he assents to the proposition, and is ashamed of his own nature.

This self-fulfilling characterization was then used by Tocqueville to argue *against* freedom for the slaves:

I am obliged to confess that I do not regard the abolition of slavery as a means of warding off the struggle of the two races in the United States. The Negroes may long remain slaves without complaining; but if they are once raised to the level of free men, they will soon revolt at being deprived of all their civil rights; and as they cannot become the equals of the whites, they will speedily declare themselves as enemies. In the North everything contributed to facilitate the emancipation of the slaves; and slavery was abolished without placing the free Negroes in a position which could become formidable, since their number was too small for them ever to claim the exercise of their rights. But such is not the case in the South.

Even this foreign observer could perceive that the mere *claim* to the exercise of equal Black rights was unacceptable to *northern* Whites. There could be no clearer statement of the melting-pot principle that rights must not be exercised by a group—especially by *Blacks* as a group. The same principle is reflected in liberal ideology by the notions that Black-White *equality* conflicts with White *liberty* (i.e., privilege), and that Black-White cultural differences represent acquired differences in human traits. Consequently, liberals oppose *group rights* for Blacks on the ground that rights should be restricted to *individuals* who meet melting-pot cultural standards.

Progressives reject this position on the ground that cultural differences *do not* represent significant differences in human traits, and that, therefore, Blacks and Whites are equal in human terms *as groups,* not merely as individuals. Therefore, progressives advocate *group rights* to guarantee equal treatment of Blacks and of other minority groups who are culturally different from the majority group.

Against this background, it is fitting that the man who played the central role in the abolition of American slavery was not a liberal but a progressive.

ABRAHAM LINCOLN, both in the Lincoln-Douglas debates and as president during the Civil War, addressed the issue of slavery in a unique way that has been misunderstood and thus distorted by historians holding a variety of political views. He differed with conservatives, liberals, and abolitionists alike, yet he acted in a way that destroyed slavery and allowed the freed slaves to exercise their newly acquired rights.

Lincoln differed with both conservatives and liberals on three fundamental issues: 1. slavery as an institution; 2. the attitude of the founding fathers and the Constitution toward slavery; and 3. the elimination of slavery. He differed with the abolitionists on only one of these issues—his slower timing and milder prescription for the elimination of slavery. But he rejected "all this quibbling" about the inferiority of "this man and the other man, this race and that race," and urged Americans to "unite as one people throughout this land, until we shall once more stand up declaring that all men are created equal."

Abraham Lincoln's debate with Senator Stephen A. Douglas in 1858, when Lincoln unsuccessfully challenged Douglas for his seat in the u.s. Senate, offers a clear view of Lincoln's moral positions on slavery. In my opinion, the following three excerpts are, in retrospect, among those most representative of Lincoln's true convictions.

The first excerpt is of special interest because in it Lincoln addresses the morality of slavery, in the context of preventing its expansion:

> The real issue in this controversy—the one pressing on every mind—is the sentiment on the part of one class that looks upon the institution of slavery *as a wrong,* and of another class that *does not* look upon it as a wrong. The sentiment that contemplates the institution of slavery in this country as a wrong is the sentiment of the Republican party. . . .
>
> They [Republicans] insist that it should, as far as may be, *be treated* as a wrong; and one of the methods of treating it as a wrong is to *make provision that it shall grow no larger.*

Lincoln's uncompromising condemnation of slavery as a "wrong" was the basis for his interpretation of the founding fathers' attitude toward that "peculiar institution." This is evident in the second excerpt, where Lincoln claimed that the Constitution expresses a negative attitude toward slavery:

> It is not true that our fathers, as Judge Douglas assumes, made this government part slave and part free. Understand the sense in which he puts it. He assumes that slavery is a rightful thing within itself—was introduced by the framers of the Constitution. The exact truth is that they found the institution existing among us, and they left it as they found it. But in making the government they left this institution with many clear marks of disapprobation upon it. They found slavery among them, and they left it among them because of the difficulty—the absolute impossibility—of its immediate removal. . . . I have proposed nothing more than a return to the policy of the fathers.

Lincoln's reference to the "absolute impossibility" of the *immediate removal* of slavery requires elaboration. He is referring to the practical dilemma, rather than the moral one, which faced the men who adopted the Constitution.

At that time, according to the 1790 census, the recorded U.S. population of about 3,930,000 included roughly 3,000,000 Whites; 50,000 free Blacks, and 880,000 Black slaves. (American Indians were not counted.) Blacks thus constituted about 25 percent of the total population, and freeing them all at once would irreversibly and radically have altered the *class* balance of power between those who owned property and those who did not. Furthermore, the sudden elimination of slave labor and the entry of hundreds of thousands of free workers into the labor market would have shattered the economy in the absence of a fundamental change in the economic system.

As for evidence supporting Lincoln's claim that the Constitution disapproved of slavery, one can point to the word "person" in reference to the slaves throughout the text, the right of the federal government to terminate the slave trade after the year 1808, and the inclusion of free Blacks among "the people of the United States" having full citizenship rights. In any case, what is important here is not so much the strength of the evidence, but Lincoln's firmness in his assertion that the Constitution intended the abolition of slavery at some future time.

The third excerpt focuses once again on slavery as a moral issue:

> The real issue . . . is the eternal struggle between two principles—right and wrong—throughout the world. They are the two principles that have stood face to face from the beginning of time and will ever continue to struggle. One is the common right of humanity, and the other is the divine right of kings. . . . No matter in what shape it comes, whether from the mouth of a king who seeks to bestride the people of his own nation and live by the fruit of their labor, or from one race of men as an apology for enslaving another race, it is the same tyrannical principle.

Here Lincoln's comparison of slavery to the "divine right of kings" and his inclusion of the slaves in the "common right of humanity" place him closer to the abolitionists than to the liberals. Yet his failure to embrace immediate abolition, regardless of the consequences, caused his clash with the abolitionists, as evidenced in Lincoln's August 1862 letter to Horace Greeley:

> I would save the Union. I would save it the shortest way under the Constitution. . . . If there be those who would not save the Union unless they could at the same time *save* Slavery, I do not agree with them. If there be those who would not save the Union unless they could at the same time *destroy* Slavery, I do not agree with them. My paramount object in this struggle *is* to save the Union, and is *not* either to save or destroy Slavery.

President Lincoln was being consistent with his position advocating the *peaceful* elimination of slavery within the framework of a Union held together by whatever force was required. When he concluded, a little more than three months later, that the Union could not be saved without freeing the slaves, he did so in a manner guaranteeing all freed *persons* full citizenship rights and the *protection* of those rights.

Lincoln's Emancipation Proclamation of January 1, 1863, constituted his decisive action which irreversibly eliminated slavery. He wrote:

> All persons held as slaves within any state or designated part of a state, the people whereof shall then be in rebellion against the United States, shall be then, thenceforward, and forever, free; and the Executive Government of the United States, including the military and naval authority thereof, will recognize and maintain the freedom of such persons, and will do no act or acts to repress such persons, or any of them, in any efforts they may make for their actual freedom. . . .
>
> And I hereby enjoin the people so declared to be free to abstain from all violence, *unless in necessary self-defense*; and I recommend to them that, in all cases when allowed, they labor faithfully for reasonable wages.
>
> And I further declare and make known that such persons, of suitable condition, will be received into the armed service of the United States to garrison forts, positions, stations, and other places, and to man vessels of all sorts in said service [EMPHASIS MINE].

There are four striking aspects to the proclamation other than the complete and unconditional freedom granted to the slaves, who at that time constituted one-eighth of the total population.

First, the entire power of the executive government, including, specifically, its military power, is invoked to protect the freedom of the slaves after they have reached free soil.

Second, since the Civil War was still very much in the balance at the time of the proclamation, the statement that the Union military forces would not interfere with any efforts of the slaves to free themselves recognized the *right* of slaves to fight for their freedom.

Third, President Lincoln's "enjoining" of the slaves to abstain from "all violence, *unless in necessary self-defense*" should be read in the context of the previous point—the right of the slaves to free themselves. With these two statements, Lincoln was telling the slaves not to engage in violence against southern Whites *except in pursuit of their escape to the North,* while guaranteeing the right of self-defense to all Black people as a *general principle.*

Fourth, the explicit admission of the former slaves into all phases of military service accomplished two major objectives—one immediate, and one of a longer-term nature. The first objective was to deny the South its slave work force and to recruit the slaves into the Union armed forces—about 250,000 Blacks, most of them former slaves, served in the Union military, and an even greater number supported the Union military effort in other ways. The second objective was to establish a permanent and major Black presence in the Union armed forces in order to deter race warfare in the South *or* in the North when Blacks began to *exercise* their new rights.

THIS BROADER CONTEXT provides the background for my return to the discussion with which I began this chapter—liberal historian Martin B. Duberman's essay on liberal writer William Styron's novel *The Confessions of Nat Turner.* Mr. Styron's fictional story and Professor Duberman's defense of it combine to present a classic example of today's sophisticated distillation of Alexis de Tocqueville's far cruder nineteenth-century liberal attitude toward slavery.

Mr. Styron's novel imagines the personality of Nat Turner, a major Black historical figure who led the most significant slave rebellion in American history, to fit liberal ideological preconceptions about the outward manifestations, emotional reactions, and inner thoughts of Black slaves during the first half of the nineteenth century. On that point, Professor Duberman attempted no defense of Mr. Styron—in fact, his criticism of Styron for making Nat Turner neither "vivid" nor "believable" could serve as an indictment of the entire novel: "Nat never comes alive as an individual. He speaks his lines well, but we sense a ventriloquist near at hand."

Professor Duberman does not elaborate his criticism beyond that single sentence, perhaps because at that point in his essay he had already lavished praise on the very "lines" which Nat delivers "well."

Mr. Styron's Nat Turner is constantly speaking in a manner which reinforces and embellishes the crude Black Sambo image cultivated by conservative historians. For example,

> It seemed that my black shit-eating people were surely like flies, God's mindless outcasts, lacking even that will to destroy by their own hand their unending anguish [PAGE 27].

And Nat expresses contempt for the field slaves:

> As a child I am contemptuous and aloof, filled with disdain for the black riffraff which dwells beyond the close perimeter of the big house—the faceless and mindless toilers who at daybreak vanish into the depths of the mill or into the fields beyond the woods, returning like shadows at sundown to occupy their cabins like so many chickens gone to weary roost [PAGE 136].

Later, Nat demeans the "childlike spirit" of a slave with "intelligence":

> It was not easy at first—leading this simple, unformed, and childlike spirit to an understanding of the way and an acceptance of the light—but I can recall several things working in my favor. There was his intelligence for one thing, as I have said: unlike so many of the other black boys, half drowned from birth in a kind of murky mindlessness in which there appeared not the faintest reflection of a world beyond the cabin and the field and the encompassing woods, Willis was like some eager, fluttering young bird who might soar away if only one were able to uncage him. Perhaps growing up near the big house had something to do with this, only briefly had he known the drudgery of the fields [PAGE 202].

Having saturated his characterization of Nat Turner with contempt for Black slaves, Mr. Styron, like Alexis de Tocqueville, perpetuated the myth that they could not handle even the prospect of freedom, still less survive as free men. Styron's eighteen-year-old Nat is terrified at the news he will be set free at age twenty-five:

> *A free man.* Never in a nigger boy's head was there such wild sudden confusion. For as surely as the fact of bondage itself, the prospect of freedom may generate ideas that are immediately obsessed and half crazy, so I think I am being quite exact in saying that my first reaction to this awesome magnanimity was one of ingratitude, panic, and self-concern. . . .
>
> . . . The idea of leaving it [the plantation] filled me with a homesickness so keen that it was like a bereavement. To part from a man like Marse Samuels, whom I regarded with as much devotion as it was possible to contain, was loss enough; it seemed almost insupportable to say goodbye to a sunny and generous household. . . .
>
> . . . "But I don't want to go to any Richmond!" I heard myself howling at Marse Samuel, galloping after him now. "I don't want to work for any Mr. Pemberton! *Naw* sir!" I cried. "Unh *unh*, I want to stay right here!" (Thinking now of my mother's words long ago, and still another fear: "*Druther be a low cornfield nigger or dead than a free nigger.*") [PAGES 193–194.]

Professor Duberman's commentary on Mr. Styron's book was critical of those who "insist that *all* slaves craved freedom," since in his view, "Only when slavery is viewed as an essentially benign institution . . . can it follow that it left no deep personality scars on its victims." Duberman did not venture to say what the nature of those scars might have been. Nor did he allow for the possibility that the scars were different than the fictionalized ones described by Styron. But he did express the opinion that Styron's failure to achieve a believable characterization of Nat Turner was due to Styron's decision to "put aside . . . his own truth in order to serve those twenty-odd scraps of paper we call Nat Turner's 'confessions.'"

This was a curious judgment, since the "twenty-odd scraps of paper" constitute, despite having been recorded by a White representative of the

Virginia authorities, the only historical record of what the real Nat Turner actually said. Moreover, Mr. Styron used only about one fifth of the "confessions" and significantly altered important statements even in that small portion. He also ignored much of the eyewitness commentary by Thomas Gray, the man who took Nat Turner's confession.

For instance, the real Nat Turner revealed that his mother and grandmother were central to his religious training, and that his parents taught him to read and write. Yet in Styron's novel, Turner's grandmother dies soon after she gives birth to Nat's mother, and the young White women in the master's household teach him to read and write.

Similarly, Styron's image of Turner as a somewhat cowardly, indecisive leader is not substantiated by Thomas Gray's recollection of his interrogation of Turner:

> He is a complete fanatic, or plays his part most admirably. On other subjects he possesses an uncommon share of intelligence, with a mind capable of attaining anything; but warped and perverted by the influence of early impressions.
>
> . . . The calm, deliberate composure with which he spoke of his late deeds and intentions, the expression on his fiend-like face when excited by enthusiasm, still bearing the stains of the blood of helpless innocence about him; clothed in rags and covered with chains; yet daring to raise his manacled hands to heaven, with a spirit soaring above the attributes of man; I looked on him and my blood curdled in my veins.

In the face of such major misrepresentations of historical truth by Mr. Styron, Professor Duberman speaks of "Styron's occasional distortion of detail" and asserts that Styron's presentation of Turner "is true in broad outline to the limited historical evidence we have." The underlying reason for Duberman's attitude may reside in a subsequent passage of his essay, which expresses today's liberal version of radical individualism:

> Faith in the importance of Black History, moreover,

seems to me based on the double assumption—*so uncommon in our culture*—that the individual can best find fulfillment in the group, and that the group best gains an understanding of its future purpose by examining its own past history. To me, the opposite of these propositions seems truer: that the individual is most likely to find fulfillment by exploring his "specialness"—how he differs from all others—and that a group is most likely to formulate and pursue goals adequate to the needs of the present if it avoids intense involvement with or adulation of the past [EMPHASIS MINE].

Here the key words, "so uncommon in our culture," expose Duberman's commitment to the melting-pot culture ("our culture"), as well as his alienation from Black culture ("so uncommon").

There are other essays in Professor Duberman's book, *The Uncompleted Past,* that reflect this liberal cultural position. In his essay on the autobiography of W.E.B. Du Bois, Duberman reflects the liberal tendency to define Blacks in terms of their response to Whites:

Du Bois made mystic references throughout his life to the Negro's inherited qualities of sensuousness, rhythm, humor, and pathos, and spoke of the Negro's duty to maintain his racial integrity so that he might fulfill his special mission to humanity. In his fury at white racism, in his determination to give his people the psychological weapons needed to defend themselves against white slander, Du Bois, like Rap Brown after him, sometimes resorted to the very terminology he ordinarily denounced, to that insistence on innate racial differences which in other moods he railed against so bitterly, so justifiably. Which perhaps only proves what the majority in this country has for so long denied: that Afro-Americans are, above all, Americans. Brought up in a racist culture, they, too, will sometimes exhibit symptoms of racism.

Here Professor Duberman blurs the distinction between human traits and cultural differences. Thus, Du Bois called for racial integrity in the service of asserting the universality of Black, as well as White, human traits, while Duberman assumed that racial integrity denies human universality. Similarly, Rap Brown called for Black power for the practical purpose of resisting racially oppressive White power, while Duberman mistakenly concluded that Black rebellion against White oppression requires an ideology which is the mirror image of White racism. Finally, Duberman's statement that "Afro-Americans are, above all, Americans" implies a minimal cultural difference between Blacks and Whites that contradicts his own assumption of differences in human traits.

No aspect of american society is more wary of a powerful Black male image than u.s. presidential politics. And no individual in recent memory has been more threatening to the national political hierarchy than Rev. Jesse Jackson with his 1984 and 1988 runs for the Democratic presidential nomination. The result of those campaigns has been the empowerment of Black voters to the point where they have become the decisive political force within the Democratic party and a serious threat to the domination of the party by its White liberal elite.

It is, therefore, not surprising that this elite sought out a Black liberal as a surrogate who would attempt to influence public opinion against Rev. Jackson. The classic modern example of such a Black liberal surrogate was the late Roy Wilkins, long-time head of the National Association for the Advancement of Colored People (NAACP), who served the interests of the liberal wing of the Democratic party for over three decades, beginning in 1949. During that time, he was not averse to assisting the u.s. government in its efforts to undermine independent Black leaders—specifically, Paul Robeson and Martin Luther King, Jr.

The 1986 book by Adolph L. Reed, Jr., *The Jesse Jackson Phenomenon: The Crisis of Purpose in Afro-American Politics,* is a more recent example of a Black liberal's assault on an independent Black political figure in the interest of White liberals.

The anti-Jackson bias of this monograph is obvious from its opening evaluation of Rev. Jesse Jackson's 1984 presidential campaign as "a ritualistic event—a media-conveyed politics of symbolism, essentially tangential to the crucial debate over reorganization of American capitalism's governing consensus." However, the superficiality of Mr. Reed's approach is underscored by his failure to discuss, or even to define, "the critical debate."

Instead of analyzing "the Jackson phenomenon" within the context of American society, Mr. Reed confines Jackson within the narrow limits of the competition between two factions of the Black elite: the "traditional protest elite," and the "newer cohort of elected officials." Yet in view of Reed's astute description of the "client relationship that binds Black elites primarily to external sources of patronage," one marvels at his refusal to recognize the central feature of the Jackson campaign—its powerful challenge to this very client relationship.

The primary target of Mr. Reed's attack is the link between African-American culture and independent Black politics—a link which, in his view, threatens liberal democracy. One of his main assaults is aimed at the political role of the Black church, the institution which is the chief support of African-American culture and serves as a center of Black politics; however, his arguments are consistently weak.

First, Mr. Reed's position that the Black church is not a significant political force (he speaks contemptuously of the "myth of a politically active Black church") has been refuted by the massive support given by Black churches nationwide to Rev. Jesse Jackson's 1984 and 1988 presidential campaigns.

Second, Reed's notion that there is, in his words, "a fundamental tension between the church and politics in the Black community—both historically and in the present," is refuted by the frequent election of Black clergymen to political office and by the fact that the major slave revolts were rooted in the religious traditions of the Black slaves.

Finally, Mr. Reed offers an inappropriate application of "the critique of religion developed by Karl Marx in the 1840s" to the relationship between politics and the church among African-Americans in the twentieth century and under slavery. The margin by which Mr. Reed's attempted correlation misses the mark can be judged by the fact that Marx's concern was the church's interference with the political solidarity of a class-wide homogeneous group across cultural differences, while the African-American case involves the church's indispensability to the political solidarity of a culturally homogeneous group across class differences.

What Mr. Reed defends is liberalism, and his main argument is that mass-movement politics based on independent Black political power is somehow "undemocratic." He claims the "superiority of procedural mechanisms—such as elections—for establishing leadership in a normally functioning liberal polity," and urges cultivation of a spirit of "civic liberalism" in Black politics.

However, Reed's Black champions of democracy are conservatives who oppose the vital interests of the great majority of Blacks. According to him, "by pressing an unpopular [conservative] position . . . , the 'new conservatism' may assist the cause of democracy [i.e., liberalism] among Afro-Americans."

Here Mr. Reed is openly representing White liberals in opposing independent Black politics, and in doing so he finds common cause with those Black conservatives who serve the interests of White conservatives rather than Black interests.

It is, therefore, fitting that *The New Republic* of June 2, 1986, carried a highly laudatory review of Mr. Reed's book by Professor C. Vann Woodward, a distinguished White liberal historian. Having accepted Reed's analysis and conclusions at face value, Professor Woodward admonished the Democrats: "If they cannot handle the Jackson troubles better than they did last time, given what they know of the perpetrator, the fault will be largely their own." This reflection of the fear and animosity Rev. Jesse Jackson inspires in the liberal establishment is a tribute to the potential power of independent Black politics.

THE INDEPENDENCE OF BLACK POLITICAL LEADERSHIP is closely bound up with the struggle for multiculturalism and the challenge to liberal melting-pot ideology. A culturally based Black political movement of any kind is a threat to the entire melting-pot system and is, therefore, anathema to liberals, including many of those who were all-out supporters of the civil rights movement. Thus, liberal historians, Black as well as White, are hostile to multiculturalism and loyal to Mr. Reed's "liberal polity."

Against such a background, it is especially refreshing to hear the clear voice of a *radical* Black male, even after the passage of almost a century and a half. The following portion of Frederick Douglass's Fourth of July address in 1852 to the citizens of Rochester, New York, is a reminder that even then there existed a radical alternative to the liberal tradition. It proved to be an alternative which informed President Abraham Lincoln's historic actions against slavery a decade later, and it still rings true today:

> It is not light that is needed, but fire; it is not the gentle shower, but thunder. We need the storm, the whirlwind, and the earthquake. The feeling of the nation must be quickened; the conscience of the nation must be roused; . . . the hypocrisy of the nation must be exposed; and its crimes against God and man must be denounced.
>
> What to the American slave is your Fourth of July? I answer, a day that reveals to him more than all other days of the year, the gross injustice and cruelty to which he is the constant victim. To him your celebration is a sham; your boasted liberty an unholy license; your national greatness, swelling vanity; . . . your denunciation of tyrants, brass-fronted impudence; . . . your prayers and hymns, your sermons and thanksgivings, with all your religious parade and solemnity, are to him mere bombast, fraud, deception, impiety, . . . a thin veil to cover up crimes which would disgrace a nation of savages.

5

LIBERAL EDUCATION'S MELTING POT

ecause the melting pot's radical individualism and subordination of race to ethnicity are central to White America's liberal democracy, melting-pot ideology dominates the liberal education provided by White universities. Therefore, campus culture treats everyone except native Blacks as melting-pot *individuals* having a cultural (i.e., ethnic) status; native Blacks are treated as *members* of a racial minority group that is outside the melting pot, and are denied cultural status. Cultural legitimacy is confined to the core values of melting-pot culture.

By contrast, Black universities provide a native-Black cultural environment in which the melting-pot culture is adapted to African-American needs, and Black students are treated as *Black individuals* having an African-American cultural status. The multicultural education offered on these campuses encourages the exploration of a wide range of cultural values while providing a thorough understanding of both the racial and ethnic aspects of native-Black culture.

As I see it, the inability of melting-pot liberalism to accommodate racial diversity along with ethnic diversity is the primary cause of racial conflict on predominantly White campuses. "Cultural diversity," liberal education's euphemism for *curriculum* diversity, is a substitute for *multiculturalism:* Blacks will be provided with recognition in the curriculum but must not manifest a culture different from that of Whites. The Black response has been to demand a cultural diversity that accepts the imposed, *exclusively racial,* status of the Black minority as equal to the *ethnic* status of the White majority.

The struggle over the curriculum is essentially a political conflict over *whose* diversity shall prevail—the multiethnic diversity imposed by the White majority, or the multiracial diversity demanded by the Black minority; the diversity of ethnic groups which excludes the Black minority, or the diversity of *equal* racial groups.

Diversity that includes native Blacks can be achieved only if minority affirmative action in student admissions and faculty hiring openly includes affirmative action for native Blacks as a *separate* category rather than as part of the *composite* minorities category. This is the case because native Blacks are the only minority still excluded from the melting pot, and, therefore, the practice of combining them with other non-White ethnic groups and White women in a single minorities category covers up the *racial* exclusion of the Black minority. This exclusion can be remedied only by *group* racial preference; *individual* racial preference is not sufficient to offset discrimination against a *group.*

Liberal education's attempt to preserve the monocultural melting pot in the face of the multiculturalist movement hinges on restricting native Blacks to entry as middle-class individuals instead of as a group, since their entry as a *racial* group would destroy the exclusively *ethnic* basis of the melting pot. However, the liberal-conservative coalition that has risen to defend the melting pot cannot openly embrace the overtly racist cause of barring only the native-Black group from the melting pot.

And so the phrase political correctness has emerged as liberal education's most potent weapon in its battle against multiculturalism. The crusade of a nationwide coalition of prominent liberals and conservatives against political correctness targets a small, predominantly White, leftist political grouping within a massive, predominantly Black, multiculturalist constituency for the purpose of discrediting the demands of the unintegrated Black minority on campus. The real conflict between White monoculturalism and Black multiculturalism is misrepresented as a struggle between the melting-pot correctness of liberal democracy and the political correctness of communist totalitarianism.

This strategy was highlighted in the spring of 1991 by Dean Donald Kagan, of Yale College, who declared on national television that the political-correctness "tyranny of the Left" on campus exceeded the excesses of the infamous "Red Scare" of the 1950s. Recalling that he was a student in those days, Kagan asserted that there is less academic freedom in the 1990s than McCarthyism permitted then.

Although in the 1950s thousands of faculty members and students were fired, expelled, dragged before investigating committees, spied upon by the Federal Bureau of Investigation, forced to sign loyalty oaths, or compelled to inform on colleagues, not a single case of such treatment at the hands of political-correctness advocates is on record. Yet no high-ranking member of the Yale University administration challenged Dean Kagan's overstatement.

One reason for this lack of rebuttal may have been that the political-correctness scare was welcomed by many liberal administrators as a respectable excuse for suppressing the struggles of the Black minority for cultural inclusion. In any case, evidence of anti-Black sentiment within the campaign against political correctness soon emerged on many campuses in the form of successful free-speech movements to rescind behavior codes outlawing the racial harassment of Black students.

IN THIS CONTEXT, *Illiberal Education: The Politics of Race and Sex on Campus* by Dinesh D'Souza, a research fellow at the American Enterprise Institute, earned lavish praise from both conservatives and liberals, ranging from former judge Robert H. Bork on the right to Morton Halperin of the American Civil Liberties Union (ACLU) on the left. In D'Souza, an immigrant native of India, they found an ideal apologist for the resistance of both White and non-White immigrant ethnic groups to equal melting-pot status for native Blacks. He made attacks on the Black minority respectable by placing virtually exclusive responsibility for the multiculturalist movement on Black cultural assertiveness.

As a middle-class member of a culture in which English is the official language and Western traditions permeate the educational system, Mr. D'Souza shares the majority attitudes of the dominant Anglo-Saxon ethnic group while also empathizing with the immigrant traditions of both White and non-White ethnic minorities. But he is remote from native-Black culture. A personal anecdote reveals how different his outlook is from that of native Blacks when he describes how, as an exchange high-school student in Arizona, he asked a White girl to the Homecoming dance and she replied that she would have to ask her parents:

> The next day I asked, "What did they say?" She looked at me, "Who?" "Your parents," I said. "Say about what?" At first I was simply astounded, but then I realized, with a sinking feeling, that I had approached *the wrong girl*. It was only later that I realized what my problem was: I thought all white women looked alike. . . .
> . . . My own experience helped me realize that no matter what our skin color or background, it is not easy to transcend our cultural particularity [PAGE 22].

This mindset is the mirror image of the attitude expressed by the American White majority to whom all Blacks are racial-minority others who look alike. Mr. D'Souza's majority thinking makes it difficult for him to understand that a Black-minority high school boy in Arizona would be most unlikely to forget which White-majority girl he had asked to a dance, and that Blacks are compelled by their inferior status to make clear distinctions among Whites. Moreover, D'Souza conceals the main problem in American Black-White relations by his assertion of an inability of Blacks and Whites *alike* to "transcend" their "cultural particularity." Actually, both Whites and Blacks are compelled by the melting pot to overcome their cultural provincialism; the conflict between them arises because Blacks are the only ones excluded from the melting pot as "them."

Consequently, most Blacks either demand inclusion in the melting pot as members of their racial group or refuse to identify with melting-pot culture. One could imagine that Mr. D'Souza's lack of a racial-minority perspective leads him to misinterpret the Black demand for racial *inclusion* as a demand for special treatment, and to misconstrue the Black resistance to some aspects of melting-pot culture as a rejection of liberal education's high academic standards.

Throughout his book D'Souza blames the Black minority for the escalating racial strife on majority-White campuses, evoking the image of a "victim's revolution" in which the victims are primarily Black and the revolution is abetted by timid administrators and left-leaning faculties. "Diversity, tolerance, multiculturalism, pluralism" are the principles of the revolution, and its goal, he says, is to "transform liberal education in the name of minority victims." But in his 304 pages, including notes, Mr. D'Souza never does specify this transformation; nor does he explain how administrations that are almost exclusively White and faculties that are barely 4 percent Black are acceding to a revolution of Black victims among hostile majority-White student bodies.

Instead, he advocates suppression of the Black minority's cultural identification and elimination of affirmative action in the name of preserving liberal education as the basis for liberal democracy:

> Liberal education is consistent with democracy; indeed, it enables democratic rule to reach its pinnacle.
> . . . Democracy is not based on the premise of equal endowments, but of equal rights. It does not guarantee success, but it does *aspire* to equal opportunity. This opportunity is extended not to groups, as such, but to individuals, because democracy respects the moral integrity of the human person, whose rights may not be casually subordinated to collective interests. Democracy requires representation, but in no sense does it mandate proportional representation based on race [EMPHASIS MINE; PAGE 250].

What is significant here is that D'Souza augments his repetition of melting-pot dogma on the primacy of individual rights over group rights with three propositions that undercut the affirmative-action policies which protect Blacks from discrimination and have been supported by decisions of the U.S. Supreme Court: 1. Democracy need only "aspire to" equal opportunity instead of guaranteeing it; 2. equal opportunity is specifically *denied* to groups; and 3. political representation by *race* is not "required," but no such waiver of "required" representation is applied to ethnicity or gender.

His attribution of responsibility for the escalation of racial harassment of Black students to Blacks is central to D'Souza's argument that "pluralism" and "diversity" on campus are merely euphemisms for Black separatism and special treatment. Despite the fact that 25 percent of Black students complain of racial harassment on majority-White campuses, D'Souza minimizes what he admits is the "proliferation" of racist insults to Blacks by accusing "all sides" of "a good deal of excess" and by claiming that "racial confrontations on campus are mere symptoms of . . . an academic revolution" whose "distinctive insignia" are Black-related.

In this framework his linkage of "most" racial incidents to "preferential treatment" and "double standards" benefiting Blacks provides the rationale for the so-called "new racism" of White university students who "know exactly what is going on," i.e., that "minorities" means Blacks who are "privately" suspected to be culturally inferior to Whites:

> The old racism was based on prejudice, whereas the new racism is based on conclusions. . . .
>
> . . . The new bigotry is not derived from ignorance, but from experience. It is harbored not by ignoramuses, but by students who have direct and first-hand experience with minorities in the close proximity of university settings. The "new racists" do not believe they have anything to learn about minorities; quite the contrary, they believe they are the only ones who are willing to face the truth about them. . . .
>
> . . . Both university leaders and minority activists sense the durability of the new racism, and its resistance to correction by means of liberal reeducation. . . .

> . . . Many administrators are privately ambivalent about combating these private suspicions about minorities, because they share them. Most of them, too, are among the new racists on the American campus. . . .
>
> . . . The new racism cannot be fought with the more vehement application of preferential treatment, teach-ins, reeducation seminars, and censorship; indeed, these tactics, which are tailored to address the old racism, only add to the new problem. In fact, to a considerable extent they are the problem [PAGES 240–242].

Thus, having blamed the "new racism" on Blacks, Mr. D'Souza would combat it by terminating "preferential treatment" (i.e., affirmative action for *Blacks*) and by rescinding campus "codes" which "censor" the racial harassment of Blacks by Whites. Of course, he does not add that these combined policies would mean a return to the "old racism," especially since many administrators "are among the new racists."

D'SOUZA AVOIDS THE ISSUE of Black exclusion by challenging the need for *either* cultural *or* racial diversity on the ground that a "first-rate" liberal education requires only "diversity of mind," rather than diversity of *cultures* or *people.* So the monoculturalism of the melting pot is extolled as superior to a multiculturalism that is caricatured in the chapter "Travels with Rigoberta." Shakespeare's *Othello* is compared with Alice Walker's *The Color Purple*; Chinese, Indian, and Middle Eastern societies are included among the non-Western societies that have "created works of literature and art of the highest order," but African society is excluded; the African influence on the cultures of Egypt, Greece, and Rome is denied; the contributions of Afro-Europeans and Afro-Americans to the cultures of modern Europe and America are omitted, and we are presented with the claim that "curiosity about other cultures appears to be a distinctively Western trait."

The title of the chapter reflects an effort to trivialize non-Western cultures by ridiculing the oral tradition of Rigoberta Menchu, a Guatemalan Indian woman whose autobiography has become part of the new

Stanford University curriculum. It is D'Souza's misfortune that only a year after he dismissed Ms. Menchu's work because it "detailed the mundane," the thirty-three-year-old Ms. Menchu was awarded the 1992 Nobel Peace Prize "as a vivid symbol of peace and reconciliation across ethnic, cultural and social dividing lines." Similarly, D'Souza made no reference to the current leading Black writer in the Western Hemisphere, Afro-Caribbean poet and playwright Derek Walcott, who was subsequently awarded the 1992 Nobel Prize for literature.

Mr. D'Souza returns to this argument for melting-pot monoculturalism in his concluding chapter by invoking the universality of Shakespeare's *Othello* to defend a Western-oriented curriculum which addresses "the basic issues of equality and human difference." According to D'Souza, *Othello* tackles these issues in the context of "*ethnic* and *sexual* difference"; I see Shakespeare's central themes as *cultural* and *racial* differences. D'Souza interprets *Othello* as the story of "a cosmopolitan [i.e., melting-pot] *society's* struggle to accommodate an alien while maintaining its cultural identity," but I see Shakespeare as portraying an Othello whose tragedy is *his* struggle to maintain a distinct cultural identity by refusing to accommodate an alien Venetian melting pot.

As I read *Othello,* it is a multicultural story based on a clash between two different and equal cultures—the Moorish culture of Africa and the Venetian culture of Europe. It is the antithesis of a melting-pot story because Othello's tragedy was his unmeltable nature. D'Souza, unable ideologically to accept the idea of another culture *equal* to European culture, displaces Shakespeare's central cultural theme with "the specter of a dark-skinned man sexually assaulting a white woman." *Sexual* difference with a racial subtext is used to displace *cultural* difference.

Othello is also a play about *race* as much as it is a play about *culture.* The Moor is not only from a different and powerful culture; he is *Black* with a "sooty bosom," and a Black man who comes from an African culture equal to Venetian culture is unacceptable to melting-pot ideology. Therefore, in America Othello was cast as an exotic Arab in order to convert the *racial* theme of the play into an *ethnic* theme. So the role was played exclusively by White actors in brownface until 1943 when Paul Robeson played the role as Shakespeare wrote it. Mr. D'Souza insists that *Othello* is a play about *ethnic* difference rather than about *racial* difference, confirming once again that the melting pot pits ethnicity against race and cannot accommodate racial diversity.

Finally, Mr. D'Souza says that "Othello . . . depended on Desdemona's love to legitimate his full citizenship," whereas I think that Shakespeare has Othello depending on his consummate military skills as a general, rather than on Desdemona's love, to "legitimate" a status which is far above that of "full citizenship." Othello speaks as an equal to the Duke of Venice before his Court, and the Duke treats Othello as an equal. Moreover, far from depending on Desdemona's love to secure his social position, he has married her in secret and considers his behavior to be no one's business but his own:

> That I have ta'en away this old man's daughter,
> It is most true; true, I have married her:
> The very head and front of my offending
> Hath this extent, no more.

MR. D'SOUZA'S REJECTION of racial diversity is especially evident in his chapter on Black colleges, "In Search of Black Pharaohs," and focuses on Howard University in Washington, D.C., a city in which the majority of the population is Black. The cultural environment and educational accomplishments of Black universities are ignored in favor of reportage on campus protests, on student alienation from the administration, and on a curriculum which D'Souza considers to be too Afrocentric. The chapter attempts to substantiate D'Souza's view that young Blacks "feel socially deligitimized . . . by the sense that they have no past from which to draw self-respect and dignity," and, as a result, it omits any reference to the native-Black cultural traditions rooted in slavery which Black universities so successfully draw upon.

The unique contributions of native Blacks to American society and the universality of native-Black culture are central to the curriculum on majority-Black campuses, while the common cultural background shared by the faculties and the student bodies, facilitates student motivation and success. Although only about one-third of Black college students attend majority-Black universities, at least half of Black college graduates are produced by these institutions. Fully half of America's Black business leaders and elected officials, as well as a majority of Blacks holding doctoral degrees, are graduates of Black colleges. Yet the average endowment per student at majority-Black private colleges is only 53 percent of the endowment at small majority-White private colleges, and over 40 percent of the students at majority-Black colleges come from families with incomes below the poverty level.

Not only does Mr. D'Souza ignore these facts, but he attempts to cancel out the central role which historically Black universities have played in adapting native-Black culture for the achievement of success in an essentially alien and hostile melting-pot environment. For example, D'Souza does refer to Rev. Martin Luther King, Jr. as "a homegrown American who formulated his rhetoric in classic American terms, invoking Jefferson and Lincoln," and does quote Rev. King's philosophy of massive nonviolent civil disobedience aimed at awakening moral shame and achieving ultimate redemption and reconciliation. However, he fails to add that King, a product of a southern Black college, led a Black mass movement against the South's violent, diehard, White racism and compelled the White majority to confront the moral inferiority of its ethnocentric, individualist culture.

D'Souza insists that young Blacks who are "in a search for cultural identity" should not look for that identity either in the native-Black tradition or in the African tradition. Instead, they must accept their identity within "Western civilization" which "is a towering human accomplishment" that has no satisfactory equal.

Consequently, he negates the value of majority-Black colleges by quoting approvingly from Barnard scholar Jacqueline Fleming's study of Black colleges which pictures these institutions as "anachronisms in contemporary society, relics of segregation which have outlived their usefulness." From this he concludes that political protest at Howard is caused merely by the need of the students at Black colleges "to establish their relevance" and to demonstrate Black solidarity across class lines. Only later, in a chapter on what he sees as subversion of academic standards at Duke University, does D'Souza cite evidence, from the same Jacqueline

Fleming study, confirming that, "although students at black colleges start out less well prepared than their black counterparts at mainstream institutions, they show more progress and development during their four years."

Thus, Mr. D'Souza's idea of diversity excludes racial diversity in any form, including the continued existence of Black universities. However, he does acknowledge class diversity and supports "policies of preferential treatment" for students from low-income families who cannot afford college. Yet he overlooks the fact that *Black* colleges have been pursuing this policy on a large scale for years.

AFFIRMATIVE ACTION IS CENTRAL to equal opportunity in higher education and is directly linked to the kind of multiculturalism which is being sought. Mr. D'Souza's kind of multiculturalism boils down to cultural dominance of the majority culture over minority cultures. While in his chapter on the "victim's revolution," D'Souza states that "America is rapidly becoming a multiracial, multicultural society," his next paragraph reveals that this is to occur only when "America loses her predominantly white stamp" due to the extrapolation of current immigration and birth-rate patterns over many decades. Meanwhile, he is quite clear about how the present White majority should preserve Western cultural traditions: "it is in the nature of democratic societies that the majority ultimately prevails in a test of force."

This kind of multiculturalism leads to the melting-pot diversity that excludes the Black minority group, so Mr. D'Souza opposes racial affirmative action as a matter of principle. However, he turns reality upside-down: "Racial division is the natural consequence of principles that exalt group equality above individual justice . . . ; a program that began as a campaign to *eliminate* race as a factor in decision making has come to *enforce* race as a factor in decision making."

There are three fundamental flaws in this reasoning.

1. "Racial division" in the form of *enforced* segregation was the *cause* of racial affirmative-action legislation, rather than its "consequence."

2. Racial affirmative action was designed to end the *group* exclusion of Blacks by enforcing racial preference for a relatively small number of Black *individuals*. Thus, Blacks were protected only partially and indirectly

against group injustice so that White liberal democracy could *avoid* granting group rights to Blacks.

3. Racial affirmative action substitutes *individual* rights for *group* rights—the reverse of D'Souza's claim that it sacrifices "individual justice" for "group equality." This is why today's melting pot discriminates with impunity against Blacks as a group, but does not dare to discriminate openly against individual Blacks.

Mr. D'Souza's apparent conclusion is that since racial affirmative action amounts to *individual* racial preference for the purpose of preventing *group* racial discrimination, this logic can be applied in reverse: the elimination of *individual* racial preference can be invoked to re-impose *group* discrimination on the Black minority in the name of opposing quotas.

The Bush-Quayle administration launched just such an antiquota attack against affirmative action on majority-White university campuses in 1990–1992. Its success was revealed by an article in the *New York Times* of September 30, 1992, dealing with racial-minority (i.e., Black) admission policies. A Department of Education investigation of racial preference in minority admissions to the law school at the University of California at Berkeley was so intimidating that the school voluntarily changed its rules applying to Black applicants. From now on, Blacks who were previously allowed to compete only against one another will have to compete against the general pool of minority applicants. This amounts to the *total abolition* of specifically Black affirmative action and its replacement with *strict meritocracy* within the minority category. The result will be a sharp reduction in the number of native Blacks admitted.

Because native Blacks are the only minority still excluded from the melting pot, they score lower than other minorities, on the average, on college entrance examinations. So a strictly meritocratic admissions policy would virtually eliminate Blacks from universities to which entry is highly competitive. Therefore, affirmative action is designed primarily to permit Blacks to be admitted ahead of others having higher test scores, provided that the Black applicants meet the *minimum* admissions requirements. The conservative attempt to eliminate racial preference is actually an effort to terminate affirmative action entirely by labeling it as a quota system for Blacks.

In view of this, it is important to note that this conservative definition of the term quota contradicts the U.S. Supreme Court's definition, as expressed in the 1986 majority opinion by Justice Sandra Day O'Connor. She clearly defined quota as a preference applied to persons who are *unqualified*: "A fixed number or percentage of persons of a particular race, color, religion, sex or national origin which must be attained, or which cannot be exceeded, regardless of whether such persons meet the necessary qualifications to perform the job." Consequently, racial preference for Blacks who are *minimally qualified* is not a quota according to the Supreme Court.

Here lies the real reason behind the fuss about quotas—the determination of all White and non-White ethnic groups in the melting pot to preserve the competitive advantages their middle classes derive from the exclusion of the Black minority. The controversy over admissions to Georgetown University Law School which erupted in the Spring of 1991 provides an interesting example of this ethnic backlash against racial preference. In his April 24, 1991, syndicated column in the *New York Post,* Patrick Buchanan denounced the Georgetown Law School's affirmative action program for accepting highly qualified Black applicants because White applicants with even higher qualifications had been turned down. Decrying this policy as "discrimination in reverse," Buchanan wrote:

> Kids of Irish, Italian, Polish and Greek ancestry are getting the shaft when they apply to Georgetown because they are white. Their applications are being round-filed, though their scores and grades are higher than those of black kids being admitted. . . . There is never going to be peace at the G.U. Law Center until black students can look white students in the eye, and say, "I got here the same way you did, buddy, through achievement!" That is what blacks can say to their peers in athletics, the arts and the armed forces.

Mr. Buchanan conveniently forgot the melting-pot preference that these White ethnic groups have enjoyed and continue to enjoy at the expense of the excluded Black minority. Moreover, his reference to Black achievement in sports as compared to the academy is hypocritical in the extreme, since universities with major sports programs and a shamefully low percentage of Black students invariably give racial preference, as well as questionable financial benefits, to Black athletes lacking even the minimum academic qualifications in order to exploit their athletic ability.

Buchanan also failed to explain his omission of Jews and Asians from his exclusively White list of ethnic groups who were "shafted" by Black preferential treatment, the reason being that Jews and Asians are already represented on college campuses in numbers exceeding their population percentage. Since they have benefited so spectacularly from the melting pot, they choose not to complain as long as the melting pot remains intact, even though they are often underrepresented according to academic achievement.

Nevertheless, I suspect that not a few of them harbor feelings similar to those of ethnic Whites, that are reflected by Dinesh D'Souza near the end of his book:

> Racial harassment is getting so bad that for the first time, the *Wall Street Journal* reports, many black students are avoiding troubled institutions and applying to safe— often historically black—universities. Because universities have exhausted the patience of the most sympathetic advocates of the victim's revolution, the backlash against preferential treatment and sensitivity education will continue to get worse. Nobody will say so, but the truth is that a large number of students and faculty have simply *had it* with minority double standards and intimidation. Until they change their policies, universities are likely to see a dramatic increase in racial tension and racial incidents, with a corresponding upsurge of violence. The worst is yet to come [PAGE 228].

So, according to Mr. D'Souza, it turns out that the victim's revolution is really affirmative action which has imposed racial diversity on melting-pot campuses and transformed liberal education into quasi-multicultural education. As I see it, the real rebellion is a counter-revolution spearheaded by ethnic Whites against the majority of university administrators and faculty members. Their goal is to roll back affirmative action, to minimize racial diversity on campus by repairing the damaged melting pot, and to restore monocultural liberal education.

They have powerful allies off campus: when D'Souza writes that *the universities* "have exhausted the patience of even the most sympathetic advocates of the victim's revolution," he is referring to the liberals who have joined conservatives in a nationwide political coalition against affirmative action. These defenders of the melting pot are so determined to force universities to abandon their affirmative-action policies that they are apparently willing to condone an "upsurge of violence" to accomplish that end.

AFFIRMATIVE ACTION AS A POLICY to achieve racial diversity on majority-White campuses by admitting virtually all Blacks who meet the admission qualifications has been spectacularly successful. As a result, the Black middle class has become competitive with White and non-White ethnic middle classes in American society and has acted out the success story of the immigrant tradition. Having finally gained entry to the melting pot with the aid of the civil rights revolution and affirmative action, the Black middle class has predictably registered economic and educational advances comparable to those of previous ethnic middle classes immediately following their entry.

However, much like Jews and Asians, Blacks in the melting pot have chosen to retain their culture while functioning successfully in the majority, White world. In response to this choice by the Black middle class, today's melting pot is attempting to inflict a double penalty upon the entire Black minority.

First, non-middle-class native Blacks continue to be excluded from the melting pot, and, therefore, a majority of African-Americans is disadvantaged relative to all other ethnic groups.

Second, the melting-pot campaign against affirmative action is designed to coerce the Black middle class into abandoning its culture and its leadership of African-American political solidarity by threatening to cripple its ability to compete with the rest of America's middle class.

The attempt to reverse affirmative action is being opposed with considerable success by Blacks in alliance with some liberals and most progressives, but the exclusion of non-middle-class native Blacks from the melting pot is not generally acknowledged by either middle-class Blacks or liberal Whites. The neglect of this central class issue stems from the fact that real quotas for the underqualified and the unqualified are mandatory, not only for non-middle-class Blacks, but for all non-middle-class Americans if they are to have a decent life in today's u.s. society.

What blocks even the discussion of such a policy is the fierce resistance to affirmative action and quotas for native Blacks which emanates from the White and non-White middle classes of immigrant descent whose ancestors benefited from these policies while native Blacks were enslaved or segregated. Since significant parts of these constituencies have traditionally supported the Democratic party together with African-Americans, the conservative wing of the Republican party has won presidential power by backing ethnic White Democrats against Black Democrats in the conflict over affirmative action and quotas. As a result, there is now barely enough political support of affirmative action to prevent its elimination, while any national politician who mentions quotas without opposing them is committing political suicide.

A political realignment led by progressive Anglo-Saxons has altered this political dynamic by shifting from the politics of race and ethnicity to the politics of culture and class: the mosaic versus the melting pot, and economic fairness versus trickle-down economics. But since the politically dominant middle class is antiquota, quotas is still a forbidden issue. Nevertheless, it is important to explore this matter, because the combination of quotas for the minimally qualified and affirmative action for the highly qualified offers a constructive way out of the crisis into which melting-pot liberalism has driven higher education.

Most majority-White universities impose high qualifications on their applicants, and, therefore, most non-middle-class individuals of all races and national origins are automatically barred from acceptance. Affirmative action is to no avail here, since it applies only to those who can meet the high minimum entry requirements. Consequently, quotas must be applied to the most promising applicants who cannot meet those requirements.

At present, entry requirements vary significantly from university to university, so quotas would be more or less arbitrary. However, a uniform national standard which set the minimum qualification level for acceptance at a university significantly below current qualification levels could be based on the minimal entry skills necessary for a student to survive to graduation, rather than on attracting the most accomplished (but not necessarily the brightest) students. The quota program could then be restricted to promising students from low-income families and could guarantee ethnic and racial diversity in the same way that the affirmative-action program does.

The *combination* of an affirmative-action program, which now applies primarily to qualified middle-class native-Black and Hispanic students, with a quota program for underqualified non-middle-class students belonging to all ethnic and racial groups in proportion to their representation in the population would draw the working class and even part of the underclass into higher education. An important additional benefit provided by the quota program lies in the probability that the powerful motivation of the quota students would challenge the middle-class affirmative-action students to raise their academic sights, resulting in higher, rather than lower, academic standards.

But the most significant result of an ethnically and racially diverse *working-class* presence on university campuses would be the intensified challenge to the melting pot, since the real guardians of ethnic cultures are not the middle classes but the working classes. This is especially true of native Blacks among whom the working class still constitutes the great majority. So a significant native-Black working-class representation would severely undermine the fairly successful efforts of liberal education to negate the value of native-Black culture with its slave traditions.

Contrary to liberal dogma, native Blacks, despite the lack of a single national origin, possess an extraordinarily rich cultural heritage from the time of slavery—a set of traditions stemming from the multitude of ethnic groups who inhabit West and Central Africa. This heritage also incorporates elements of the melting-pot cultures and Anglo-Saxon culture which native Blacks have transformed and absorbed. So native-Black intellectuals are as comfortable with Aristotle and Shakespeare as they are with the African fables and Lao-Tze; as moved by Goethe and Burns as by Dumas and Pushkin; as interested in William Faulkner and Eugene O'Neill as in James Baldwin and August Wilson.

Such cultural flexibility reflects a non-Western way of thinking which emphasizes concrete symbols, people, spiritual factors, and metaphors, instead of assigning priority to abstract concepts, objects, rational factors, and literal expressions.

Process and means are not as important as behavior and result. Consequently, native Blacks exhibit some non-Western ways of learning, tending to view things as a whole with interconnected parts rather than as isolated pieces, and emphasizing nonverbal communication along with verbal facility.

These traits are not innately racial, since they were manifested by all ancient cultures and are part of today's Russian and Welsh cultures in the East and West, respectively, but they are useful in acquiring the varied skills required to succeed in the high-technology environment which is already upon us. A multicultural education could absorb native-Black and other non-Western modes of thought and convert them into universal educational assets, but liberal education belittles such approaches to learning because they derive from values unfamiliar to the melting pot and depart from the cultural outlook that underlies standard tests.

Thus, liberal education's apparently incurable Western ethnocentrism makes it imperative for America's universities to break the shackles of the melting pot and to focus on a future based on progressive multicultural education. The liberal tradition of Anglo-Saxon domination must give way to the progressive tradition of ethnic equality. Thomas Jefferson's comment that our government might be "more homogeneous, more peaceful, more durable" without large-scale immigration is an echo of the past, whereas Abraham Lincoln's belief that immigrants have the right to claim the American heritage "as though they were blood of the blood and flesh of the flesh of the men who wrote the Declaration of Independence" calls us to the future.

6

CULTURAL DIVERSITY
IN THE
WORKPLACE

ultural diversity in the American workplace during the 1990s is still influenced primarily by four factors: 1. the ability of non-Whites and women to gain employment; 2. their treatment after they have been hired; 3. the influence of the stereotypes of non-Whites and women that permeate American popular culture; and 4. the strength of the laws which outlaw discrimination in employment and the effectiveness of their enforcement.

The first two factors are heavily dependent on the third—that is, diversity hiring and diversity advancement are determined mainly by the degree to which personnel managers, hiring policies, and promotion opportunities are influenced by negative stereotypes of minorities. The fourth factor is the most powerful one, since antidiscrimination legislation provides the basis for going beyond mere rejection of antiminority stereotypes to mandating at least a minimum minority representation in the work force. And it is this legally-enforced affirmative action which has become highly politicized as the central dispute between liberals, who support it, and conservatives, who oppose it.

This political struggle over affirmative action pitted President Bush's conservative White male administration, with its almost exclusively White Republican constituency, against a Democratic Congress dominated by White male liberals whose constituency included a powerful Black component. Consequently, the broader implications of cultural diversity in the workplace were ignored as two White male elites polarized the electorate along racial lines in a manner which obscured the centrality of economic and gender issues.

A large part of White America accepts the Republican-inspired and media-fueled perception that affirmative action favors unqualified Blacks over qualified Whites. Actually, affirmative action is restricted to assuring the inclusion of a *minimum* number of *qualified* Blacks after generations of exclusion regardless of qualification. Moreover, the loose affirmative-action goals and targets, which differ significantly from the far more stringent constraints represented by quotas, assign Blacks only an adjustable portion of the broad minority classification encompassing all non-White groups and all women.

The chief beneficiaries, by far, of minority affirmative action have been White women of European and Hispanic descent who are the least controversial non-melting-pot additions to the work force. Black women come next as beneficiaries, since they meet the minority qualification according to *both* gender and race and are perceived as the least threat to White males. Black males are relegated to the very bottom of the scale because they are viewed as a threat by White males and are, therefore, the targets of most of the negative Black stereotypes. Moreover, Black men, including Black Hispanics, are subject to an added disadvantage when they compete with White Hispanic men who can claim minority status even though they are White.

Therefore, affirmative-action policies have had a disastrous effect on Black families. Black women are hired preferentially and often become the main hope for supporting the family, while Black men suffer hiring discrimination which results in an abnormally high unemployment rate. Since a disproportionately large number of Black men are prevented from providing for a family, and many Black women cannot afford to pay for child care because of their low wages, it is not surprising that these factors have produced an abnormally high Black presence on the welfare rolls.

The other non-White groups have been affected by affirmative action according to the hierarchy of conditional acceptability which the melting-pot culture has established for them. Non-White women are automatically given preference over non-White men because of their double minority status as women belonging to a racial minority. Asians receive preference over other non-Whites because of their generally higher average economic standing and stronger cultural cohesion. They also benefit from the fact that their smaller numbers in comparison with African-Americans and Hispanics make them less threatening to Whites. The brown groups (Indians, Filipinos et al., who are officially designated as "other") fall between East Asians and African-Americans, while the Native Americans (the "red" groups) and, to a lesser extent, native Blacks have suffered malign neglect.

Thus, affirmative action is ending the *exclusion* of women and non-Whites (except for Native Americans) from the national economy and is creating a universal melting pot called *cultural diversity* in the American workplace. However, the *hierarchy* of the melting pot is maintained in the job environment and is constantly reinforced through manipulation of affirmative-action hiring policies. White males remain at the top of the pyramid, above White women and non-Whites.

The underlying purpose of affirmative action was not to reward merit, or to pursue the imperative economic goal of improved labor productivity, or even to introduce greater fairness into employment and workplace practices. Affirmative action simply represented the political compromise arrived at between the conservative and liberal factions of the White male power elite in a political struggle for the loyalties of a variety of constituencies among which White males were viewed as the decisive group. Consequently, affirmative-action policies are based primarily on the melting-pot racial and gender divisions in American society.

Nevertheless, the changing demographics of the u.s. have created a new situation in which a culturally diverse work force is beginning to gain acceptance as a potential source of increased productivity and innovation.

A majority of new entrants into the workplace over the next decade will be women and racial minorities, including, by demographic necessity, a large number of Black males. This inevitability of a rapidly growing Black male presence in the workplace, combined with a growing recognition of common interest on the part of White and Black women, is starting to erode the effectiveness of racial politics. White women and Blacks, acting in concert in support of economic and social programs vital to both groups, can now prevail over the White male agenda.

Affirmative-action policies which produced widespread, though inequitable, cultural diversity in both the private and public sectors of our economy have had the unintended effect of dividing the political constituencies of both conservatives and liberals. By linking race and gender to *economic* issues, rather than to *social* issues, affirmative action created a work force whose cultural diversity fatally undermined the cultural uniformity and racial exclusion of the traditional melting pot. Today's culturally diverse melting pot is by nature unstable, since the very concept of the melting pot is based on an enforced cultural uniformity.

IN RECOGNITION OF THE FACT that the percentage of minorities in the employable population of the future will grow rapidly, all sectors of the U.S. economy have already introduced a new discipline called diversity management—the technique of getting the best job performance from a culturally diverse group of employees. As a consequence affirmative action is beginning to be viewed by employers as a matter of economic necessity, rather than as a matter of legal obligation or fairness.

This trend clashes with deeply entrenched melting-pot stereotypes of racial minorities and women, as well as with melting-pot ideology itself. The entire basis of the melting pot is the perceived necessity of eliminating all unassimilable cultural differences, while diversity management accepts such differences as potential assets and sets out to utilize them constructively. However, the national cultural ideology is still dominated by melting-pot values and perceptions, so the advocates of diversity management are compelled to make their case by modifying, rather than rejecting, the melting pot.

The January 1992 issue of *Training*, the human resources periodical, carried a lead article titled "Rethinking Diversity" by its editor, Jack Gordon, in which just such a position advocating a revised melting pot was staked out. Mr. Gordon avoids the multiculturalism controversy by presenting a definition of diversity management which accepts cultural diversity but projects the goal of unification: "How do we build systems and a culture that unite different people in a common pursuit without undermining their diversity? It's taking differences into account while developing a cohesive whole."

Then Mr. Gordon addresses the central issue of the melting pot and its insistence on a narrowly Anglo (i.e., WASP) national culture by referring to the traditional American motto "e pluribus unum" (out of many, one):

> Can we achieve *unum* without asking the *pluribus* in the melting pot to do quite so much melting? If that was ever the plan on college campuses, it doesn't seem to be working out. . . .
>
> Suppose, however, that we could go at this *pluribus* business without losing sight of the fact that *unum* is, indeed, our goal—a broader, more inclusive *unum,* to be sure. Might there not be payoffs for everybody?

What is particularly interesting about this approach of Mr. Gordon's is his muted call for basic change in the melting-pot concept. First, he suggests that there should be less melting in the pot, implying that those who are different from the WASP model can be allowed to preserve some of their cultural distinctiveness. This idea is of special importance to Blacks, since under such circumstances they would no longer have to be perceived as "White" by Whites in order to be integrated into American society. Second, the notion that "unum" (i.e., the melting pot) should be "more inclusive" suggests that native Blacks should no longer be excluded from it. Mr. Gordon, in effect, seems to be proposing a less demanding and less exclusive melting pot.

Further on in his article, Gordon quotes R. Roosevelt Thomas, Jr., president of the American Institute for Managing Diversity at Morehouse College, on the main goal of the melting pot—assimilation: "People don't know what management *is*. . . . Until recently, assimilation has made it unnecessary to learn to manage." Gordon then adds his own penetrating description of the stifling effect of melting-pot assimilation on the work force:

> The corporation dictated a mold for up-and-comers to fit: Always arrive early and work late, never turn down a transfer to another city, dress like so, talk like so, express the right opinions. "Managing" was largely a matter of enforcing the mold and rewarding those who fit it best.

Thus, American corporate policy has traditionally suppressed individuality in contradiction to the ideology of radical individualism proclaimed so loudly in the name of liberal democracy. For Black members of the work force in particular, the requirement that they must appear to be WASPs despite their color has made them especially vulnerable to the charge of failing to fit the prescribed mold. Moreover, any non-White can always be declared to manifest unassimilable differences from WASPs. However, by making unassimilable differences acceptable, the basis for employment and advancement discrimination against minorities is removed: merit and the management of *individuals* become the only valid issues.

Under these conditions, the workplace becomes, in a sense, color-blind by accepting color difference. But Mr. Gordon points out that even when an all-inclusive diversity is operative among the work force, affirmative-action programs must continue so as to guarantee fair entry of minorities into the workplace. The resulting implication is that the melting-pot fiction of color-blind laws operating in a color-prejudiced society should be replaced by the reality of color-conscious laws designed to produce an unprejudiced color-conscious society.

This profound change in ideology explains an important aspect of the widespread resistance to both cultural diversity and affirmative action. The most significant source of such opposition is to be found among the White-ethnic working class. Affirmative action combined with diversity management is stripping this group of the unfair advantage it acquired over non-Whites as a result of the exclusion of non-Whites from the melting pot and, therefore, from equal entry into American society. The basis on which White ethnics can look down upon non-Whites, and especially upon Blacks, is being eroded, and many White ethnics bitterly resent this development.

As Andrew Hacker wrote in his book *Two Nations,* Whiteness is the ultimate American privilege: "No matter how degraded their [White people's] lives, . . . they can never become 'black'."

White resentment of the new wave of self-interested corporate reduction of previous unfairness to non-White employees has been magnified by the prolonged economic recession, with its high unemployment and increased competition for job placement and advancement. In addition, the deliberate shrinkage of the public sector by the Reagan-Bush administrations heightened the disadvantage suffered by minorities, since affirmative action has been far more widespread in the public sector than in the private sector. The net result has been increased frustration and anger among both White ethnics and minorities, with the Republican party setting these two groups against each other for political gain.

For these reasons the issue of cultural diversity in the workplace and its inseparable companion affirmative action must be viewed within the broader context of the national economy and its impact on American society. It is the failure to do this—the failure to link economic policy with social consequences—which has contributed greatly to the sharp racial polarization of our country. As a consequence, the fact that the supply-side economics of 1980–1992 aimed at intensifying the impact of the melting pot by further empowering White males at the expense of everyone else (and not just at the expense of Black males) has been largely overlooked.

THE ECONOMIC REVOLUTION which took place in the United States during the decade 1980-1990 under the banner of Reaganomics benefited the very rich at the expense of the rest of the population.

A March 5, 1992, *New York Times* article reported that the richest one percent of American families reaped 60 percent of the growth in the average after-tax income of all American families from 1977 to 1989. Families in the top 20 percent accounted for 94 percent of after-tax income growth; families in the bottom 40 percent suffered a loss in income, and the middle 20 percent stayed in place.

Since the number of families grew from 55 million to 66 million while total income grew by $583 billion (adjusted for inflation) in the Carter-Reagan years, an enormous amount of wealth was transferred upward to the rich with profound economic and social consequences. The most significant consequence was the continued racial polarization of America into two nations, separate and unequal—one White and one Black.

In 1988, almost a quarter-century after the civil rights revolution, the median income of Black families was barely over half that of White families. At the bottom end of the economic spectrum, over 30 percent of Black families were below the poverty line, as opposed to about 14 percent of White families. Thus, an expanded but relatively small middle class, which is only about half the size of the White middle class, and an inordinately large poor class are the root causes of the crisis of the Black family.

There can be no solution to this crisis until employment discrimination against African-Americans is reduced at least to the extent that their family wage earners can lift their families out of poverty and then have a reasonable opportunity to rise from the working class into the middle class. This opportunity must be made roughly the same as it always has been for White ethnics, even though there will be predictable resistance from conservatives and from a significant segment of the White working class. Moreover, a significant part of the funding required to put such policies into practice must come from a progressive income tax that compels the rich to pay a fair share.

However, there is an additional and very important affirmative-action issue which is not directly related to fairness in employment—the matter of so-called set-aside contracts for minority (especially Black) businesses. Black businesses have far fewer connections and much less political clout than White businesses, and, therefore, they are virtually helpless in the face of the additional burden of racial bias. The inequitably small share of the market accounted for by Black business has led to an abnormally small Black business class and to large obstacles in the path of Black entrepreneurship. This leads to a stunted Black middle class, structural economic disability in African-American communities, and a lack of positive Black economic role-models.

Therefore, set-asides are designed to guarantee Black businesses a certain *minimum* number of private-sector and public-sector contracts. For those who consider this to be unfair special treatment, the following example should serve as a sobering rebuttal. In New York City, where African-Americans are about 40 percent of the total population, the Commission on Black New Yorkers reported in 1988 that Blacks "are relatively excluded from 130 of 192 industries in the private sector, . . . and black-owned businesses control just three-tenths of 1 percent of all private-sector jobs." The report added that, "although blacks are one-third of the city government work force, nearly half of all city agencies do not have a black senior manager." In 1992 New York City's first Black mayor, David Dinkins, reported that after three years in office he had achieved a level of only 7 percent in the number of city contracts awarded to minority businesses.

Hard facts such as those above demonstrate that the American economic system, especially as interpreted and manipulated by the Reagan-Bush administrations, is suffused with racial as well as class bias. However, the popular culture, led by the mass media, obscures this reality through omission and misrepresentation. For instance, the oft-repeated "big lie" that our poverty problem stems from poor people who allegedly don't work (code words for lazy Blacks) is refuted by statistics published by the Center for Budget and Policy Priorities showing that 8.7 million poor people worked full- or part-time in 1990. Their problem was that their families could not live on what they earned, and they could not find better-paying jobs.

The reason America tolerates such a high poverty rate and is willing to ignore the suffering of the poor and to blame the victims of poverty for their condition is that a disproportionately high percentage of America's poor is Black. The racially biased melting-pot culture not only justifies this neglect but perpetuates the discriminatory hiring of new White immigrants in preference to African-Americans. According to Professor Roger Wilkins of George Mason University in Virginia, a study conducted in 1991 at the University of Chicago showed that employers preferred White-immigrant male workers to African-American males even when the latter were willing to work for lower wages and had language skills superior to those of the immigrants.

Thus, in the broad economic and social context, the ending of racial discrimination in hiring and in business transactions is essential to the economic survival of the African-American community. It is this imperative that underlies Black insistence on universal enforcement of affirma tive action with compulsory numerical targets: African-Americans do not trust either the private or public sectors of the economy to cease the institutionalized practice of racial discrimination.

During the 1980s, the National Urban League provided annual documentation of the income losses suffered by Blacks as a result of racial bias in employment. Three types of discrimination were found to be the most damaging:

1. Exclusion of qualified Black workers from entry-level jobs by the preferential hiring of unqualified White workers.

2. Discrimination against Black workers which forces them to take lower-paying jobs despite their qualifications for higher-paying jobs reserved for Whites. As late as 1977, Black male college graduates of all age groups were still earning slightly less than White males who had only completed high school.

3. Lower income rate due to lower pay for the same work. In 1980, Black women had reached approximate parity with White men in years of schooling, yet the earnings of Black women were only about half those of White men. (White women suffer virtually the same disadvantage.)

Racial bias on such a large scale cannot be overcome without mandatory numerical standards for minority hiring and promotion. It bears repeating that these standards are *minimum* numbers which apply exclusively to *qualified individuals;* as such, they are definitely *not* quotas. A quota means a number of persons belonging to a particular group who are hired in direct proportion to their relative number in the total population, *regardless of qualification.* For example, a *quota* (as contrasted with affirmative action) for Blacks in New York City, where they account for over a third of the population, means that Blacks would automatically get over a third of the jobs, even if some of them were not qualified. India instituted such a policy to benefit the lowest, Untouchable caste and brought this group up to near-parity with the higher castes in just one generation. The former Soviet Union successfully used the same approach with workers and peasants in the field of higher education.

And it is precisely this quota policy, rather than merely affirmative action with mandatory numerical goals, that was instituted for White immigrants in the melting pot. *Unqualified* masses of these newcomers who could not yet speak English were hired in preference to English-speaking Blacks, and then they were melted into the work force. It is significant that the African-American community has *not* demanded the same treatment that benefited generations of White immigrants while Blacks were being excluded from the melting-pot economy. The *maximum* Black demand has been limited to the guaranteed employment of a *minimum* number of qualified Blacks, *even if a few better-qualified Whites are excluded.*

This unfair treatment of a relatively small number of Whites for the purpose of partially redressing the unfair treatment of most Blacks has led to two major political consequences.

First, since most Whites affected in this way are not WASPs, the quotas issue has been exploited by the Republican party for the purpose of driving a wedge between two major constituencies of the Democratic party—Blacks and ethnic Whites. The Reagan Democrats, who were the key factor in the Republican victories in the 1980, 1984, and 1988 presidential elections, consisted mostly of White-ethnic blue-collar voters who feared they would lose their jobs to Blacks because of affirmative action. Liberal Democrats fought to retain the loyalty of White ethnics in the face of Republican exploitation of racial issues, and in the process they all but abandoned their previous support of the Black civil rights agenda.

In this political context, the influence of the persistent Black stereotypes incorporated in the popular culture is a powerful factor in undermining the pursuit of equal economic opportunity by African-Americans. In 1978, for instance, an unpublished study by Louis Harris and Associates revealed that 49 percent of Whites felt that Blacks have less ambition than Whites; 36 percent felt that Blacks want to live off handouts; 37 percent felt that Blacks have tried to progress too fast, and 25 percent felt that Blacks have less native intelligence than Whites.

A comparison of these undoubtedly racist views with Alexis de Tocqueville's cruder racial stereotyping of free Blacks in the mid-nineteenth century (see "Black and White History") confirms the durability of the Black stereotypes created and nurtured by the melting-pot culture. Yet

America's White leadership, with few exceptions, still refuses to acknowledge what every Black schoolchild knows: half of White America is, to a significant extent, prejudiced against African-Americans. Therefore it is certain that the workplace, as well as every other area of American life, is rife with racial discrimination.

In addition to those White Americans who are prejudiced against Blacks, there are many Whites who are not prejudiced but have little or no experience with positive and authoritative images of Blacks in economic life, rather than in the fields of, say, sports and entertainment. This group is free of conscious bias against Blacks but cannot envision them in managerial positions or as successful entrepreneurs, bankers, etc. I have experienced this myself on the lecture circuit.

On several occasions when I was booked to lecture at major corporations, the limousine driver assigned to pick me up at the airport had difficulty finding me because he had not been told specifically to look for a Black man. The problem was definitely not racial prejudice on the part of the drivers, who invariably were appropriately polite, respectful, and gracious; rather, it arose from the culturally acquired inability of these well-meaning White men to conceive of a Black man lecturing to their highly placed White employers.

The modern melting-pot culture, by its very nature, filters out any such powerful roles for the Black male. Instead, it perpetuates an endless variety of subtle Sambo images. One can imagine the degree to which such images influence the hiring policies developed and practiced by the predominantly White male personnel managers of corporate America: no wonder the Black male is the most unfairly treated category in the U.S. work force.

Prior to the enactment of civil rights legislation in the 1960s, the American corporate establishment simply ignored the ghettoized Black entrepreneurial and managerial class—it was as if that class did not exist. Even today, the record of U.S. corporations with regard to the employment of Black males in managerial positions is abysmal. Although in 1991 African-Americans represented approximately 12 percent of the total population, they accounted for less than 5 percent of all managers and less than one percent of all middle- and upper-level executives. This inequity is magnified by the fact that Blacks are denied access to the informal connections, the networking opportunities, and the mentoring by White senior executives which their White counterparts take for granted.

For these reasons it is the corporate sector of the economy which holds the key to equal opportunity for minorities in the workplace. Yet this is the very sector of the economy where discrimination against minorities, and especially against African-Americans, is most prevalent. Therefore, only vigorous enforcement of the federal antidiscrimination laws and affirmative-action standards can provide a level playing field on which minorities can compete for jobs on an equal footing. Enforced, rather than voluntary, affirmative action is required on a massive scale to ensure even that *merit,* rather than race or gender, becomes the chief criterion for hiring and advancement. At present, as in the past, it is an undeniable fact that merely being White and male confers an advantage. It is this unfair advantage which must finally be eliminated.

THE RESISTANCE OF WHITE MALES to the loss of their traditional privileges in the workplace was exploited by the Republican party which deliberately politicized the issue of affirmative action and linked it to the racial stereotypes nurtured by the popular culture. Therefore, the struggle over cultural (racial) diversity in the workplace became central to a Republican conversion of the political divisions in the u.s. electorate from the traditional conservative vs. liberal and rich vs. poor to White vs. Black, male vs. female, and middle class vs. poor. As a result, decisive majorities of both the White middle class and the White working class formed a conservative coalition with the rich under the banner of White male dominance.

The liberal coalition, on the other hand, was left trying to unite upper-middle-class Whites with Blacks and women in support of a program of social liberalism combined with economic conservatism. The shift to the right on economic issues derived from the liberal establishment's adherence to a melting-pot tradition which tacitly accepted the dominance of White males and favored business interests over the interests of wage earners.

The unintended consequence of the liberal coupling of conservative economics with social liberalism was the alienation of all three groups in the ill-matched coalition of affluent Whites, Blacks, and women. Many affluent Whites, especially males, opposed liberal positions on racial issues, while Blacks and women deeply resented the new conservatism on economic issues. Liberal Whites, both male and female, supported the liberal positions on nonracial social issues, but most Blacks were, like the White working class, more socially conservative.

The abrupt end of the Cold War and the disappearance of the enemy superpower cleared the way for a new domestic political landscape dominated by the economic issues stemming from the deep and prolonged recession. Then the 1992 presidential primaries began the unraveling of the conservative coalition and the building of a new progressive coalition to replace the liberal one.

On the Republican side, ultra-conservative journalist Patrick Buchanan led a rebellion of the extreme right against President Bush's gestures toward a universal melting pot with limited affirmative action. His campaign was saturated with the symbolism and rhetoric of overt White supremacy and, thereby, forced President Bush to disavow the Republican policy of racial division based on obvious anti-Black appeals to White voters. Buchanan's resounding defeats by Bush in most primaries, combined with the strong rejection of former Klansman David Duke in Louisiana, demonstrated that the Republican party could not win with an overtly pro-White strategy in 1992 and that many conservative voters rejected *explicit* racial politics.

Thus, in retrospect it can be said that President Bush's nominations of Judge Clarence Thomas to the Supreme Court bench and General Colin Powell to the chairmanship of the Joint Chiefs of Staff signaled his abandonment of overtly racial code words. A more refined exploitation of racial divisions by the Bush administration appeared in the form of an emphasis on family values coupled with opposition to imagined quotas. Bush's new strategy also included an effort to divide Blacks along ideological and class lines by assigning Black conservatives the task of removing the racist label from Republican opposition to affirmative action. Both of these approaches failed to meet the challenge of the Clinton strategy.

In the Democratic primaries, Governor Bill Clinton of Arkansas forged a powerful *progressive* coalition which consistently defeated liberal opponents. His message focused on the tasks of pursuing economic fairness and ending racial division, and included essentially moderate positions on social issues. The overwhelming support given to Mr. Clinton by Black voters—60 to 80 percent in most primaries—was a decisive factor in his victories and was based both on the economic progressivism of his message and on his willingness to stress racial inclusion.

The other instructive lesson of the Clinton primary campaign was that active pursuit of Black votes on a platform of bringing the races together and of common, rather than racial, economic interests attracts the vast majority of Black voters without alienating White voters. On the other hand, the exploitation of racial division is a losing strategy for both White and Black candidates.

There is abundant proof that in 1992 Black voters were rejecting the politics of race in favor of coalition politics based on economic justice as embodied in a progressive economic program. Douglas Wilder, the first Black governor of Virginia, was forced to drop out of the race for the Democratic presidential nomination because his conservative economic message was rejected by the Black community. Black congressman Gus Savage of Illinois, who campaigned aggressively on themes of racial conflict, was resoundingly defeated by Black businessman Melvin Reynolds in the March 17 primary. Moreover, White candidates who tried to pander to Black voters on racial issues fared no better. Former California governor Jerry Brown failed in his attempts to win Black voters away from Bill Clinton by portraying Clinton as a kind of closet racist.

In such a context it becomes clear that the combined impact of cultural diversity in the workplace and the ascendancy of economic issues in presidential politics has forced the popular culture to become more inclusive and has begun to reduce the negative impact of race in the political arena.

THE LONG-TERM EFFECT of cultural diversity in the workplace on American society has been profound. The traditional melting-pot exclusion of non-Whites and women is ending along with the possibility of maintaining a color-blind system of laws. This development, combined with the cultural assertiveness of African-Americans and women, is finally producing a diverse, though divided, American society. The fact that modern economic necessity requires the unification of this society through abandonment of the melting pot is producing a political realignment by splintering the Republican and Democratic coalitions which have lingered on since the 1960s.

The Republican coalition is being split by a determined right wing which demands a return to an exclusively White melting pot with traditional family values stressing male superiority. *Both* multiculturalism *and* economic progressivism are anathema to these conservatives, while former President Bush's conservative constituency is similarly opposed to progressive economics but supports the inclusion of ethnic or middle-class non-Whites and women in the melting pot. However, the most important element in conservative disunity is the defection of the socially conservative blue-collar Reagan Democrats from the Bush version of Reaganomics to the perceived economic progressivism of Democrats like President Bill Clinton.

The Democratic coalition has been split along three lines: income, gender, and race.

First, the conservative economic policies of the liberal leadership have separated families with incomes above $50,000 per year from those with incomes below $50,000 per year. In the 1992 Democratic presidential primaries, the progressive candidate, Bill Clinton, consistently attracted a majority of the working-class vote, while former Massachusetts senator Paul Tsongas attracted a majority of affluent voters as the liberal candidate.

Second, women are coalescing to oppose the political dominance of both conservative and liberal White males. As the March 17, 1992, vote in the Illinois Democratic primary demonstrated, the Clarence Thomas nomination triggered a powerful political backlash by both women *and* Blacks against a liberal White senator, Alan J. Dixon, who had voted to confirm Thomas. Carol Moseley Braun, a Black woman who was Cook County recorder of deeds, won the Senate nomination in a three-way race on the strength of a coalition of White women and African-Americans. Her victory also confirms a stronger Black opposition to Judge Thomas's confirmation than was acknowledged by the media.

Third, Black voters abandoned Iowa's Senator Tom Harkin and

Paul Tsongas, the two liberal candidates, in order to support Bill Clinton's progressive message by large margins. The nationwide shift of Black voters toward an economic-justice agenda, combined with their movement toward coalition politics and away from liberal priorities and racially oriented politics, promises to end the long-standing liberal domination of the Democratic party.

The agenda of the newly ascendant progressive coalition in the Democratic party is clear. It consists of economic justice for all *individual* Americans, and equal opportunity for the diverse *groups* which make up the u.s. population.

Unlike the liberal establishment which shrinks from the pursuit of economic justice and avoids empowerment of the poor and disadvantaged, progressives appear to be determined not to abandon the ghettos of the inner cities with their suffering millions but to help them reclaim their own lives and enter America's mainstream. They also have the capacity, and I hope, the will, to use the vast powers of the federal government in compelling the wealthy and the corporate sector to pay a fair share of the cost of rebuilding our crumbling infrastructure.

Perhaps now, after more than a decade of self-protective avoidance and denial, an aroused American public will respond with a revived decency to the anguished cry of Rev. Martin Luther King, Jr. a quarter-century ago:

> I must confess to you today that not long after talking about that dream, I started seeing it turn into a night-mare as I moved through the ghettos of the nation and saw my black brothers and sisters perishing on a lonely island of poverty in the midst of a vast ocean of material prosperity.

I would like to believe that America's people still have enough heart to dispel the nightmare and to restore the dream.

7

GENDER AND THE MINORITY FIXATION

he designation of women as a minority, in blatant disregard of the fact that they are a 52 percent majority of the population and a 54 percent majority of the voters, serves the interests of the White male ruling elite at the expense of both women and racial minorities. First, the label reinforces the melting-pot image of women as the weaker sex who must defer to the stronger male members of the majority. Second, White women, through the sheer weight of their superior numbers, can be used to dominate racial minorities by combining all women and all non-Whites into a single minority category. Since Whites make up over 80 percent of the total population, White women outnumber the total non-White population by about two-to-one.

A typical large high-tech corporation at which I lectured on affirmative action boasted an impressive 36 percent minority representation among its employees. But when the minority category was broken down into subcategories, I found the representation to be: 28 percent White women; 2 percent Black women; 5 percent Asian (male and female);

1 percent Black males and Hispanic males and females. Racial minorities—Black men especially—had received short shrift as far as hiring went. And the White women who were hired so readily were given very little consideration when it came to promotion: there were hardly any in high-level jobs, and relatively few in middle-level positions.

However, the massive entry of White women into the workplace had profound social consequences which did not conform to the melting-pot cultural norms. Between 1960 and 1980, the number of White women in the work force soared from 37 percent to 51 percent—an increase of approximately 20 million. Women's incomes empowered them significantly, since their salaries became essential to the financial well-being of many families. Moreover, the large number of working White women and their growing alliance with non-White workers on the basis of common economic interests began to alter the power relationships within the American work force. Women came to exercise more influence than ever before over union policy, and more women were elected to positions of union leadership.

But the most significant influence of all has been the development of a growing solidarity of women across racial boundaries under the combined pressures of workplace discrimination and women's issues in the society at large. Concurrently, the average earned income of Black female high school and college graduates has reached virtual parity with the average earned income of their White counterparts. These changes have become especially important in Black-White relations, because Black and White women have been uniting even as the income gap and the hostility between Black and White men have been increasing.

The fact that women *as a group* have begun to overcome the racial exclusion which is a prerequisite of the melting-pot culture signals the demise of American liberal democracy with its tolerance of racism and sexism, its enshrinement of radical individualism, its acceptance of institutionalized economic injustice, and its rejection of group rights. It is fitting that after spending almost the entire twentieth century in the shadows of other movements, the women's movement in the 1990s is expanding the restricted individual rights established by the White male founding fathers into the universal human rights nurtured by two hundred years of struggle and sacrifice.

The issue of gender, even more than the issues of race and class, is therefore becoming the central issue of humanity's transition to the twenty-first century and its ultimate survival as a viable species. Life, individual liberty, and the pursuit of happiness cannot survive without a significant measure of equality and fraternity.

THE UNITY OF WOMEN across the boundaries of racial segregation was not possible prior to the massive and permanent entry of both White and Black women into the workplace, and both groups paid dearly for its absence.

For example, a majority of nineteenth-century White feminists who fought for women's suffrage did not support the abolition of slavery and opposed the Fourteenth and Fifteenth Amendments which established the political rights of Black men but ignored women. By contrast, Black feminists fought for the abolition of slavery and supported the Amendments at the same time they demanded women's suffrage. For them, racial solidarity transcended feminist issues.

In the 1920s, after women had won the right to vote, the Ku Klux Klan was at the height of its power and influence with a massive female representation among their national membership of approximately four million. In this case too, racial solidarity overrode feminist concerns.

The class-struggle ideology which helped to fuel the workers' movements of the 1930s and early 1940s unionized the American work force but failed to liberate women, while within the Black community a predominantly male leadership subordinated women's rights to the struggle for racial equality. It was not until the civil rights revolution of the 1960s legalized and institutionalized the principle of universal *individual* rights that women's *group* rights gradually grew to play a central role in U.S. politics.

Thus, both the melting-pot ideology of the liberal establishment and the class-struggle ideology of the socialist and communist left have failed to accommodate the central demands of women. In both cases, in the U.S. and abroad, the dominance of males belonging to the majority ethnic group has been imposed and maintained independently of the ideology of the male leadership elite.

Nevertheless, the liberal and left policies, programs, and style of leadership have traditionally provided far more opportunity for political action and advancement by minority groups and women than has been possible with conservatives in power. There could be no clearer evidence of this than the history of three successive conservative administrations under presidents Reagan and Bush.

Conservatives have attempted to shut down the advance of the women's movement with a three-pronged assault.

First, the conservative focus on family values is based on the melting-pot culture's principle of excluding White women from *public life* (i.e., from political power) as a group by restricting them to family life.

Second, conservatives insist on placing White women at a disadvantage in the workplace and in all other aspects of economic life so as to deny them *economic power* as a group.

Third, they have used the popular culture to blame feminism for White women's problems, just as they have blamed the civil rights movement for the problems of Blacks.

The Pulitzer Prize–winning journalist Susan Faludi has dealt ably with these issues in her book *Backlash: The Undeclared War against American Women.*

In a chapter titled, "Ms. Smith Leaves Washington: The Backlash in National Politics," Ms. Faludi cites compelling evidence to substantiate her claim that, "with Ronald Reagan's election, women began disappearing from federal office." New female judicial appointments fell from 15 percent under Carter to 8 percent. The number of women on the White House staff dropped from 122 in 1980 to 62 in 1981, and not a single woman ranked high enough to attend senior staff meetings. Even President Reagan's formidable United Nations ambassador Jeane Kirkpatrick left government saying that "sexism is alive."

Ms. Faludi makes clear the reason for Reagan's political purge of women in government by quoting Faith Whittlesey, assistant to the president for public liaison and the highest ranking woman in the first Reagan administration. According to Ms. Whittlesey, the federal government would aid women by ensuring that men earned a higher family wage so that "women can go home and look after their own children." This conservative policy seems to have been designed to reduce women's earning power and to drive large numbers of White women from the workplace, thus insulating the pervasive White male domination of the u.s. economy from challenge by White females. The assaults against women's political power prevent women from effectively defending their economic interests.

Ms. Faludi charges that women have been compelled to pay a heavy price for entering the work force on a permanent basis, while trend stories emanating from the mass media spread an inaccurate picture of an army of women who reportedly are being integrated into blue-collar, white-collar, professional, and management jobs. Actually, says Faludi, women, aside from a relatively few tokens who wield real authority, are for most part relegated to low-level jobs, paid less than men for the same work, denied earned opportunities for advancement, and harassed in the workplace. For White women, integration into the American labor market has turned out to be remarkably similar to the unfair treatment inflicted upon Blacks by the same melting-pot system.

For example, in 1988 a White woman's pay was an average of 59 cents of a White man's dollar, and in 1989 the average female manager received no income boost, whereas her male counterpart received a four percent increase. Women's status in public relations, a field in which the number of women employed doubled in the 1980s, is such that a woman is likely to lose a million dollars over a forty-year career due to the gender pay gap. According to one estimate cited by Ms. Faludi, Bureau of Labor statistics for the past decade reveal that the annual wage for an occupation drops by roughly $700 for every 10 percent rise in the number of women in that occupation.

Professional women, female entrepreneurs, and women who, by dint of enormous effort, get blue-collar jobs are all subjected to pervasive discrimination. Between 1972 and 1988, there was only a 2 percent increase in the number of working women in professional specialties, while in 1988 the majority of female-owned businesses had sales of less than $5,000 per year. Labor Department reports show that after 1983 there was no progress in the entry of women into the higher-paid blue-collar work force. Even the rapid female employment growth in the u.s. military was slowed substantially during the Reagan-Bush administrations.

The reports of the Equal Employment Opportunity Commission reveal that between 1981 and 1989 record highs of sex-discrimination and sexual-harassment complaints by both federal and private employees were reached. General-harassment complaints increased by a whopping 200 percent, while sexual-harassment complaints rose by 40 percent despite the well-known reluctance of women to file such charges.

It is against the background of her comprehensive statistical picture of sex discrimination throughout the American economic system that Ms. Faludi's indictment of the backlash unleashed against women's progress since the civil rights upheavals of the 1960s is especially telling. Faludi does not hesitate to brand the popular culture fostered by the melting-pot ideology of the ruling elite as the culprit. In chapter after chapter, she documents and condemns the roles of the national mass media, the consumer industries, corporate America, the national political leadership, and the academic elite in manipulating the popular culture against women. An early passage in her book aptly summarizes the politically correct line espoused by today's conservatives:

> Women are unhappy precisely *because* they are free. Women are enslaved by their own liberation. They have grabbed at the gold ring of independence, only to miss the one ring that really matters [i.e., their compatibility with men]. They have gained control of their fertility, only to destroy it. They have pursued their own professional dreams—and lost out on the greatest female adventure. The women's movement, as we are told time and time again, has proved [to be] women's own worst enemy [PAGE x].

However, because Ms. Faludi's feminism is strongly influenced by radical individualism, her reply to the conservative attack overlooks the common group interests shared by women and Blacks. With relatively minor modifications, Faludi's summary of the conservative attitude toward women echoes the arguments of the conservatives *and* liberals who opposed the abolition of slavery, or the arguments of the conservatives who opposed the Black civil rights movement of the 1960s. Moreover, the title of Ms. Faludi's book, *Backlash,* derives from the White backlash against Black progress. Yet Faludi ignores these linkages in her eloquent answer to the antifeminists:

> Feminism asks the world to recognize at long last that women aren't decorative ornaments, worthy vessels, members of a "special-interest group." They are half (in fact, now more than half) of the national population, and just as deserving of rights and opportunities, just as capable of participating in the world's events, as the other half. Feminism's agenda is basic: It asks that women not be forced to "choose" between public justice and private happiness. It asks that women be free to define themselves—instead of having their identity defined for them, time and again, by their culture and their men [PAGE XXIII].

Ms. Faludi claims that women do *not* want to be treated as members of a special-interest group despite the fact that feminist advances have been based on the civil rights won by Black Americans' *group* struggle. Such an approach tends to separate the feminist movement from the Black community which is potentially a powerful political ally, and this gulf tends to be widened by Faludi's failure to mention Black women in her repeated emphasis on the female majority in the national population. Black women, who constitute about 12 percent of the total female population, are no small minority of women and are the most consistent anticonservative voting block in the electorate. In the 1992 presidential election, the White woman's vote was split evenly between Bush and Clinton, whereas Black women gave Clinton 86 percent of their vote—the highest of any group.

In addition, even the abhorrent choice between public justice and private happiness which is available to White women is denied to Black women. The latter receive less public justice than White women because of their race, and are additionally burdened in the private realm by the racial stereotyping of the popular culture.

Finally, Ms. Faludi's insistence that women must be free "to define themselves," a principle which is unassailable when it stands alone, becomes, in my view, encumbered with radical individualism when Faludi rejects the idea that their identity should be "defined for them by *their* culture" [EMPHASIS MINE]. It seems to me that the identities of *all* individuals should *partially* be defined by a culture they can truly call their own. In this sense, Ms. Faludi appears to be demanding only the acceptance of women into the melting pot as equal *individuals,* instead of the recognition of a distinct and equal female *culture.* Apparently, she has not yet come to see that if the melting-pot culture abandoned its principle of White male domination, it would be replaced by a diversity of cultures.

Put another way, women's equality requires abolition of the melting pot, since the melting-pot culture cannot accommodate the *different* culture represented by feminism.

Both women and African-Americans require the institutionalization of multiculturalism with its inevitable companions—the recognition and enforcement of group rights—in order to enjoy full equality at long last. But it is African-American *women* who are by far the most advanced in their opposition to the melting-pot culture and in their rejection of radical individualism. White women are diverted by their acceptance of the melting-pot culture, while Black men are impeded by a reluctance to accept Black women as equals—a reluctance magnified by the inferior status of the Black male relative to the White male. Therefore, it is particularly appropriate to explore the role of the Black woman as the link between the White feminist movement and the Black community.

BLACK WOMEN HAVE ALREADY LINKED the feminist movement to the Black community by building majority Black support for a woman's right to an abortion as a civil right, despite strong opposition by a significant portion of the Black male leadership, including many members of the Black clergy and many Black nationalists. This has happened in part due to the high percentage of Black women living below the poverty line and the powerful economic pressures requiring Black working women to remain in the work force. The result is that Blacks account for 20 percent of all abortions although they constitute only 12 percent of the total population.

But the main reason Blacks support abortion rights is that a strong majority of them is committed to the stand that a woman's abortion right is included in her right to privacy. This commitment is especially strong among Black women and overrides the belief of a majority of African-Americans that abortion is morally wrong. Thus, it was Black women who converted Rev. Jesse Jackson from an ally of the right-to-life movement to a pro-choice position when he made his 1984 presidential bid. And today not a single Black congressman votes against women's reproductive rights.

However, Black participation in the pro-choice movement is minimal, and the feminist agenda is viewed by Black women as a program for middle-class Whites. For example, in *Backlash* Susan Faludi mentioned Black women only in passing and then failed to explore the significant Black-White disparities which she mentioned. For example, she revealed parenthetically that although equal percentages of Black and White women abused drugs and alcohol in the 1980s, Black women were ten times more likely than White women to be turned in to the state authorities. And there is the following arresting passage:

> These men [conservative spokesmen] were as anxious to stop single black women from procreating as they were for married white women to start. The rate of illegitimate births to black women, especially black teenage girls, was reaching "epidemic" proportions, conservative social scientists intoned repeatedly in speeches and press interviews. The pronatalists' use of the disease metaphor is unintentionally revealing: they considered it an "epidemic" when white women *didn't* reproduce or when black women *did.* In the case of black women, their claims were simply wrong. Illegitimate births to both black women and black teenagers were actually declining in the 1980s; the only increase in out-of-wedlock births was among white women [PAGE 34].

Ms. Faludi did not elaborate on the explosive racial implications of her claim that the conservative White establishment desired to: 1. reduce the size of the Black population by restricting Black births; 2. increase the number of White births by driving White women back out of the job market; and 3. scapegoat young Black women by means of racially divisive misinformation. Likewise, her book barely mentioned the extreme poverty of Black female-headed families whose median income is below 40 percent of the median income of male-headed Black families.

Ms. Faludi accompanied her reluctance to discuss the racial aspect of women's issues with a neglect of the pressing economic problems which burden women outside the workplace. For example, she did not even mention the fact that about two-thirds of the thirty to forty million Americans who lack medical insurance are women. The apparent reason for such an omission lies in Ms. Faludi's avoidance of the principle of rights for women *as a group* (and not merely as *individuals* belonging to a group), since it is this principle that would have to be invoked in order to address the economic roots of both female and Black poverty.

Faludi, like most liberals, is limited by the liberal credo of radical individualism to approval of equal *opportunity* for each individual of a group. This differs fundamentally from the *progressive* idea of a minimum guaranteed *result* (i.e., an entitlement) for all members of a group. Since such an approach would replace the melting pot with a multicultural society of groups and require a direct challenge to the liberal (and not merely to the conservative) leadership, Ms. Faludi does not go beyond the demand for female entry into the melting pot on an equal basis.

African-Americans, on the other hand, have always fought tenaciously for the progressive principle of group rights because of the exclusion of *Black males* from the melting pot. The main source of disparity between Black and White *families* has been this exclusion of Black men, and therefore, historically, the African-American struggle for family parity has been focused almost exclusively on the achievement of parity between Black and White males through admittance of *all* Black males (not just a selected few) into the melting pot.

In these circumstances, the imperatives of economic survival reinforced the patriarchal tendencies in African-American culture, and the pursuit of women's rights became a "luxury" that only highly educated and very courageous individual Black women could afford. Most Black women secured rights within their community by working at menial jobs to bring in additional income so that the family could survive, and so that their *male* children or close relatives could get a higher education. Similarly, the G.I. Bill, which guaranteed a higher education to the predominantly male World War II veterans if they were able to meet minimum college entrance requirements, benefited many Black men but very few Black women.

The opening up of the melting pot to middle-class Black *women* along with middle-class Black men rapidly raised Black women with skills to a level of parity with both White women and Black men. The dominant White male group attempted, with limited success, to pit these groups against one another—although tensions between Black men and women in the workplace increased, greater solidarity developed between White and Black women, and Black men tended to support them against the White male elite. But these tensions were reflected in a different way in the largely separate White and Black societies outside the workplace.

The traditionally acceptable levels of sexual harassment and abuse of women have been exceeded by a staggering margin in both communities. However, until recently, this state of affairs remained largely hidden because of the reluctance of both White and Black women to level public charges against their tormentors. White women have been deterred by the indifference and outright hostility of an administrative and judicial system that is overwhelmingly controlled by conservative White males. Black women have been inhibited by the fear that formal charges against a Black male would lead to his destruction by a racially biased system, as well as by the threat of being charged with race treason.

In these circumstances, Anita Hill's unquenchable dignity as a Black woman in publicly presenting her accusations of sexual harassment against Supreme Court nominee Clarence Thomas to an all-White, all-male Senate Judiciary Committee was inspiring and liberating for White and Black women alike. Moreover, the Thomas confirmation hearings exposed the gender bias of the present governmental system and its inability to deal effectively with matters of substance. Not surprisingly, women across the

nation responded with powerful and sustained resistance to sexual harassment and male domination.

For the first time, Black women raised their voices insistently against
the attempts of Black male leaders to sidestep the issue of sexual harassment
within the Black community. Over sixteen hundred Black women from all
parts of the country did so in an advertisement in the *New York Times* of
November 17, 1991, where they also denounced media misrepresentation
of the Black community:

> We speak here because we recognize that the media are
> now portraying the Black community as prepared to
> tolerate both the dismantling of affirmative action and
> the evil of sexual harassment in order to have any Black
> man on the Supreme Court. . . . We . . . understand that
> Clarence Thomas outrageously manipulated the legacy
> of lynching in order to shelter himself from Anita Hill's
> allegations. To deflect attention away from the reality of
> sexual abuse in African-American women's lives, he
> trivialized and misrepresented this painful part of
> African-American people's history.

Anita Hill herself had addressed the same issue at a news conference
several weeks earlier when she remarked that,

> I had a call from a male who identified himself by
> name, and also identified himself as associated with a
> national . . . civil rights organization, and he said to
> me that Clarence Thomas was only acting the way
> any man would act with a woman.

And several months later Ms. Karen Baker-Fletcher, an assistant professor
of theology and culture at Christian Theological Seminary, publicly
challenged the uncritical support given by the National Baptist Convention, the nation's largest Black denomination, to former world-champion
heavyweight boxer Mike Tyson after he had been convicted of raping a
young Black woman:

> In rallying around Mr. Tyson to the exclusion of Desiree Washington, the 18-year-old woman whom he was convicted of raping, the National Baptists sent a signal that the charge of injustice by one-half of the black community does not count.

This new willingness on the part of Black women to challenge the idea that they must postpone their quest for equality in the name of racial solidarity is of decisive importance in two ways. First, the political power of the Black community will be greatly expanded by the increased unity and mobilization resulting from the rejection of those who use Black women's commitment to the race as a means to control them. Second, the release of Black women from the demand that they choose loyalty to the race over the allegiance of gender will extend the growing alliance between Black and White women to an immensely powerful if loose political coalition between White women and the entire Black community.

In the aftermath of the Thomas confirmation hearings, Black male leaders moved quickly to close ranks in defense of their traditional dominance of Black political life. Those who opposed Judge Thomas's confirmation and those who supported it issued impassioned pleas for healing of the wounds resulting from the polarization of the Black community by the confirmation process. This language used the *process* to obscure the *issues* and placed the unification of the Black community in opposition to the interests of Black women.

The effective response of Black female leadership was to organize the expression of the majority support which Anita Hill enjoyed among Black women and White women alike. The success of this endeavor paved the way for progressive Black female candidates to run for political office, since their opposition to the White male melting-pot tradition appealed strongly to the entire Black community and to a majority of White women.

The results of this approach were manifested in the 1992 election, with overwhelming support from White women and Blacks, of Carol Moseley Braun from Illinois as the first Black female member of the United States Senate. However, there were also signs that White women could not win election without a progressive economic program and the strong support of Black voters.

The victory, over four male Democrats, of a relatively unknown White woman, Lynn H. Yeakel, in the April Pennsylvania senatorial primary was a major upset, but the weakness of her campaign lay in her virtually exclusive reliance on criticism of the Senate Judiciary Committee's mistreatment of Anita Hill. Ms. Yeakel lost the general election to incumbent Republican Arlen Specter, apparently because she failed to stress the economic issues that were the central concerns of most voters, and made no significant attempt to acknowledge the importance of the Black vote.

THE POLITICAL ALLIANCE between African-Americans and White women led to a conservative response aimed at neutralizing the rising political consciousness of White women by means of a technique strikingly similar to that used in efforts to divide the Black community. Just as Clarence Thomas's nomination to the Supreme Court symbolized the expansion of melting-pot opportunity for Blacks, highly successful White professional women have been used to sell the melting pot to other White women. In both cases, melting-pot individualism has been extolled, while group rights have been ridiculed and denounced.

A classic example of such a propaganda effort appeared in the form of an Op-Ed article in the *New York Times* of April 20, 1992, by Ms. Georgette Mosbacher, the former chief executive officer of a worldwide cosmetics business, under the title "The Backlash Myth." Presented as a thinly disguised reply to Susan Faludi's book *Backlash,* the article trivialized male domination of women by focusing on radical individualism in a melting pot which "celebrates" *individual* diversity.

Claiming that "there is no conspiracy against women," Ms. Mosbacher argued that:

> The successful women I know and meet do not find themselves at war with men.... They come from various economic, political, racial and religious backgrounds; they are all leading very different lives. ...
> They are the first to realize that the playing field isn't

even and that women have more obstacles to overcome than men do. But successful women find it more productive to concentrate on overcoming the obstacles, not on whining about them.

. . . If there's a backlash today, . . . it's the backlash of strong-minded women refusing to fit stereotypes of themselves.

. . . Instead of fearing diversity, let's celebrate it.

Ms. Mosbacher implies that "successful women" from different class, racial, and ethnic groups reached their positions by adopting two principles: 1. avoidance of any group "war" against the male-dominated melting pot which discriminates against them, and 2. exclusive concentration on individual advancement in spite of "obstacles," rather than on group opposition to discrimination against women. Then, in an appeal to women's individualism, she urges them to "celebrate" *individual* diversity in the name of combating *group* identification. ("If there's a backlash today, . . . it's the backlash of strong-minded women refusing to fit *stereotypes* of themselves.")

The debate between Ms. Mosbacher and Ms. Faludi over whether or not there is a White male backlash against White feminism mirrors the broader ideological conflict between White conservatives and White liberals primarily over social issues. At the same time, it reflects the agreement between the male leadership elites of these contending political groupings on preserving a melting pot based on the ideology of radical individualism.

In this context the position of Professor Elizabeth Fox-Genovese in her book *Feminism without Illusions: A Critique of Individualism* commands attention because it presents an alternative to the liberal and conservative views. In the introduction Professor Fox-Genovese argues convincingly that the ideology of radical individualism has served as the foundation for excluding minorities from the melting-pot culture and remains the Achilles heel of the feminist movement. However, she also speaks directly to the issue of class, as well as to the issue of group constraint of individual rights—issues which were ignored in the Mosbacher-Faludi debate.

Professor Fox-Genovese rejects the White middle-class bias of the feminist movement which insists that its own experience is the universal reference point for the experience of all women. She also criticizes current feminist politics for helping to perpetuate economic (class) and racial injustice. But her alternative to radical individualism, it seems to me, is flawed and undermines the principles of individual freedom.

By demanding that liberty be "grounded in the collectivity," Professor Fox-Geneovese negates the cardinal principle that liberty must be rooted in the *individual,* despite the necessity for a balance between collective interests and individual liberty. The progressive approach to this problem is based on the proposition that individual liberty must not be allowed to *cancel* collective rights, which is markedly different from basing liberty *in* "the collectivity."

Fox-Genovese's additional claim that individual freedom must be rooted in "community discipline" stands in contrast to the progressive view that individual freedom must be balanced by individual *responsibility* within the community. It should be remembered that a one-sided emphasis on community *discipline* has too often resulted, with tragic consequences, in the suppression of individual freedom.

Finally, it seems to me that Professor Fox-Genovese fails to tackle the central issue of practical action aimed at altering the present cultural environment. It remained for Ms. Faludi, the liberal, to suggest a progressive program of action. Near the end of her book, Faludi wrote:

> That women have in their possession a vast and untapped vitality also explains . . . the seeming "overreaction" with which some men have greeted even the tiniest steps toward women's advancement. Maybe these men weren't overreacting after all. In the '80s, male politicians saw the widening gender-gap figures. Male policymakers saw the polls indicating huge and rising majorities of women demanding economic equality, reproductive freedom, a real participation in the political process, as well as a real governmental investment in social services and a real commitment to peace [PAGE 459].

Here we have a progressive agenda and a clear understanding of the potential political power of women *as a group*. What a difference there is between a White female liberal and a White male liberal! Given this reality, it is vital for the nascent progressive coalition to avoid ideological litmus tests. If the coalition is based on a program, rather than on a "progressively correct" ideology, its breadth and unity will be vastly easier to achieve.

Therefore, progressives should not be constrained by the often arbitrary labels which have gained political currency, such as liberal, conservative, right, left, centrist, moderate. A fine example of this can be found in the ringing call to progressive action the nominally liberal Ms. Faludi issues in the closing paragraph of her book. It is a passage in which we hear echoes of both President John F. Kennedy and the Reverend Martin Luther King, Jr.:

> Women can act. Because there really is no reason why the '90s can't be their decade. Because the demographics and the opinion polls are on women's side. Because women's hour on the stage is long, long overdue. Because, whatever new obstacles are mounted against the future march toward equality, whatever new myths invented, penalties levied, opportunities rescinded, or degradations imposed, no one can ever take from the American woman the justness of her cause.

8

JEWS
AND
BLACKS

ver eight years have elapsed since Rev. Jesse Jackson referred to New York City as "Hymietown" during the 1984 presidential campaign, but the Black-Jewish tension symbolized by that remark is still with us. During those years, Black Muslim Minister Louis Farrakhan made several overtly anti-Jewish public statements, and some Jewish leaders interpreted the failure of many Black politicians to repudiate him as proof that rising Black anti-Semitism threatened two centuries of friendship between Jews and Blacks. The mass media almost eagerly announced a "war" between the two communities; some self-styled Black nationalists and Black community activists climbed on Minister Farrakhan's bandwagon, and some Jewish leaders tried to depict Blacks as the main threat to Jews.

By contrast, the collaborative relationship between the majority of Jewish and Black elected officials continued unaltered: both consistently joined in support of liberal and progressive legislation; both remained reliable supporters of the liberal coalition within the Democratic party; and both led their voting constituencies in continued reciprocal support of Jewish and Black candidates for political office.

Yet these same politically allied Black and Jewish politicians usually adopted harshly opposed public positions on the issue of Black anti-Semitism. Jewish politicians refused to accept Rev. Jackson's apologies and fanned Jewish hostility toward him despite his political importance to the Black community, whereas Black politicians defended Jackson unreservedly and often accused his Jewish critics of a racial double standard. Jewish politicians attacked Minister Farrakhan as an anti-Semite comparable to Hitler's Nazis, while many Black politicians refused even to criticize Farrakhan, let alone repudiate him. Jewish politicians expressed fears of a rising Black hatred of Jews, whereas Black politicians either denied the existence of Black anti-Semitism or underestimated its significance.

The reasons for Black-Jewish collaboration derived from overriding common interests: a common fear, a long history of mutually beneficial alliance, and similar religious outlooks. The election of a conservative Republican over a liberal Democrat was viewed as damaging to the perceived interests of both Blacks and Jews, so they voted together against Republicans. Both Jews and Blacks feared the hostility of the majority WASPs and of the non-Jewish ethnic Whites more than they feared each other, so they were united by a common threat. And a history of alliance in common struggles which included the building of the labor movement in the 1930s and the civil rights movement in the 1960s was reinforced by similar Judeo-Christian religious traditions.

The recent sharpening of Jewish-Black conflict is the result of a gradually intensifying clash between Jewish and Black economic interests—a clash that became inevitable when the Black middle class was admitted to the melting pot. Consequently, today's high level of Black-Jewish tension can be traced to four principal developments which have pitted the Black and Jewish communities directly against one another.

1. The Black middle class which had been admitted to the melting pot found itself in fierce competition with the predominantly middle-class Jews for the economic benefits that could be extracted from the melting-pot system. This direct Black-White clash of vital economic interests led

inevitably to racial and ethnic tensions between the relatively poor Black community with its large underclass excluded from the melting pot, and the relatively affluent Jewish community with its much larger middle class.

2. Many, and perhaps most, Jews opposed affirmative action and the admission of the Black underclass to the melting pot—two demands that Blacks viewed as central to their economic progress as a people. Blacks viewed affirmative action as a life-and-death economic necessity; Jews opposed affirmative action because it gave Blacks leverage in their competition with Jews and other Whites. And while Blacks demanded the right of the entire underclass to enter the melting pot as a matter of principle, Jews, as well as other middle-class Whites, objected to the entry of the *Black* underclass because they feared the negative Black stereotypes which saturate the mass media.

3. Since both Blacks and Jews vote heavily Democratic, the Black-Jewish conflict was reflected in the political alignments within the Democratic party. The progressives, who backed underclass advancement through elimination of the melting pot and favored an intensification of affirmative action, supported the Black position in alliance with the traditional liberals who favored admission of the underclass to the melting pot. The modern liberals, who rejected underclass entry into the melting pot and were willing to weaken affirmative action, supported the Jewish position in alliance with conservative Democrats. By 1984 Black Democrats had closed ranks behind Jesse Jackson to form a coalition with traditional liberals and progressives, while Jewish Democrats had joined with the more powerful modern-liberal and conservative Democrats who opposed Jesse Jackson.

4. The insertion of the Black-Jewish conflict into Democratic party politics made it an issue in Democratic primary elections and led to powerful attacks by self-styled Black-militant spokesmen for the underclass on Black Democrats who supported Jewish candidates.

Rev. Jesse Jackson's 1984 and 1988 campaigns in the Democratic party presidential primary registered multitudes of voters from the underclass and compelled virtually all Black Democrats to back Jackson and his progressive economic justice program against the opposition of the modern-liberal Dukakis faction of the Democratic party. This political environment neutralized the nationalists and militants within a Black constituency which was united behind Jackson's Rainbow Coalition.

Then came the April 1988 New York Democratic presidential primary. With Jesse Jackson riding high as the progressive candidate after a spectacular victory in the Michigan primary, the White modern-liberal leadership of the Democratic party backed Michael Dukakis and set out to isolate Jackson. I was told by a reliable source that New York City's Jewish voters were quietly urged by pro-Dukakis Jewish leaders to abandon Senator Albert Gore's candidacy even though his position on the Middle East was the most supportive of Israel, because it was said that a vote for Gore was a vote for Jackson. Jewish Mayor Edward Koch was much blunter, publicly proclaiming that "Jews would have to be crazy to vote for Jesse Jackson."

This maneuver by the modern-liberal wing of the Democratic party produced a near-unanimous Jewish vote that propelled Dukakis to victory, but it resulted in a nasty public controversy which polarized Democratic primary voters by race and revitalized the Black-separatist movement in the Black community. The race card played so effectively by the modern liberals in the Democratic party had won them a hollow presidential nomination at the expense of splitting their party's loyal Black constituency and poisoning the atmosphere between Blacks and Jews for years to come.

BECAUSE OF ITS LONG TENURE inside the traditional melting pot, the Jewish middle class benefited far more from the economic opportunities created for minorities by the civil rights laws than did the Black middle class which was just beginning to enter the new melting pot. As Albert Vorspan, senior vice-president of the Union of American Hebrew Congregations (Reform) said in a May 7, 1989, speech at a dinner sponsored by the progressive Jewish monthly magazine *Jewish Currents*:

> When laws were passed against discrimination in housing, we benefited too. When laws were passed against discrimination in employment, we benefited too. And the very schools which once had quotas against Jews

today are schools in which the president of the university may very well be Jewish, a majority of the faculty may very well be Jewish, and a large segment of the student body is also Jewish. In fact we now have some Jewish organizations *kvetching* [complaining] on the other side, saying, "Look, there's too much affirmative action for women or for blacks and it's discommoding *us.*"

This vivid description of how Jews used their long experience in the traditional melting pot and their advantage of having a far larger middle class than Blacks in today's melting pot reveals the source of the hostility of some middle-class Blacks toward Jews: after Blacks had carried the main burden in the struggle to kick open the doors for everyone, others, Jews included, reaped more of the benefits.

Nevertheless, polls show that although almost twice as many Blacks as Whites subscribe to *economic* stereotyping of Jews, a significant majority of Blacks are less hostile toward Jews than toward other Whites, with only a small minority feeling angrier at Jews than at other Whites. The rest are equally hostile to Jewish and non-Jewish Whites. Understandably, Jews take small comfort from this mixed but less negative attitude of Blacks toward them.

Polls likewise show that, despite Black-Jewish conflict, Jews are far less prejudiced against Blacks than non-Jewish Whites and subscribe much more rarely to anti-Black stereotypes. Jewish hostility toward Blacks is expressed more indirectly through criticism of the Black underclass ("why can't *they* pull themselves up by their bootstraps like we did") and through exaggeration of Black anti-Semitism ("neo-Nazism in its most virulent form").

Jewish Democrats can condemn White racism with little risk of losing the votes of middle-class Whites and with the certainty of gaining Black votes. On the other hand, Black Democrats who condemn Black anti-Semitism risk losing Black votes and fear that the anti-Black stereotypes still harbored by many White voters will prevent them from gaining sufficient White votes to offset the risk. Adding to this danger is the stark contrast between the significant advancement of the Black middle class during the twelve Reagan-Bush years and the precipitous rise of Black poverty, which has made mainstream Black leaders vulnerable to the charge that they have sold out to White (often spelled Jewish) interests.

The decline in the authority of this leadership since the 1968 assassination of Rev. Martin Luther King, Jr. has opened the gates to a rise in the influence of a Black nationalism that is based on a *religious* racial solidarity.

Minister Louis Farrakhan's Nation of Islam is primarily a racial religious group which combines racial solidarity with religious purity for the purpose of replacing the pursuit of group integration *into* American society with group separation *from* American society. Although a large majority of Blacks reject Farrakhan's separatist program, his message of aggressive racial solidarity falls on more receptive ears.

So when Black politicians are confronted by Jewish charges of Black nationalist anti-Semitism they are reluctant to risk having their racial loyalty challenged for criticizing the Black nationalists. (A similar reluctance is exhibited by many Jewish leaders when they are confronted with Black charges of Jewish racism.) On the other hand, it is natural that the combination of Black racial and religious hostility arouses the deepest fears among Jews because of their tragic encounters with religious hatred (the Spanish Inquisition) and race hate (the Nazi Holocaust).

What needs to be explained here, not just to Jews but to all Americans, is that the isolationist *racial-religious* solidarity of a small Black minority is in ideological and programmatic conflict with the multiethnic, coalition-oriented *racial* solidarity of the large majority of Blacks whom Rev. Martin Luther King represented. The true nature of this conflict is obscured by the separation of race from ethnicity which has been ingrained in American culture by melting-pot ideology.

Because the melting pot has pitted White ethnic identification against Black racial identification, the majority of Blacks are compelled to use *racial* solidarity as the means of achieving their goal of *integrating* into American society as an *ethnic group* with equal status (ethnic integration). The significance of the separatist Black-nationalist movement lies not in its ideology, or even in its program, but rather in its embodiment of a reaction to the melting pot's denial of ethnic status to African-Americans. Black nationalism counters the artificial *separation* of race from ethnicity with the equally artificial *substitution* of race for ethnicity. The use of ethnicity against race is opposed by the use of race against ethnicity.

A small separatist minority of the Black middle class has abandoned the struggle for entry of Blacks as a group into the melting pot and has attempted to convert underclass anger at the WASP melting-pot system into what I see as misdirected grievances against "the Jews"—an appellation which invokes race against *ethnicity,* since Jews form an *ethnic group* that is distinct from other Whites. Note that it is the ethnic term, rather than the racial one, that is hostile and threatening: "the Whites" could not imply any threat to Jews, since this appellation includes them as part of a large racial majority instead of isolating them as a small ethnic minority.

The response of the culturally militant section of Jewish leadership to this use of race against ethnicity has been, in effect, to substitute ethnicity for race, making Jewish nationalists the mirror images of Black nationalists.

In an article titled "Black Demagogues and Pseudo-Scholars" appearing on the Op-Ed page of the July 20, 1992, issue of the *New York Times,* Professor Henry Louis Gates, Jr., chairman of the Afro-American studies department at Harvard University, described the use of anti-Semitism "as a weapon in the raging battle of who will speak for Black America":

> The strategy of these apostles of hate, I believe, is best understood as ethnic isolationism—they know that the more isolated black America becomes, the greater their power. And what's the most efficient way to begin to sever black America from its allies? Bash the Jews, these demagogues apparently calculate, and you're halfway there.

Note Professor Gates's use of the melting-pot phrase "*ethnic* isolationism" to describe the *racial* isolationism of the separatists. Yet, only a sentence earlier, Gates had recognized Black isolationism as racial by referring to "those who preach a barricaded withdrawal into *racial* authenticity" [EMPHASIS MINE]. I believe that Professor Gates knowingly substituted ethnicity for race in order to counter the racial-isolationist Black stereotype among Whites. Apparently, this is why he wrote that the separatist strategy is "best *understood*" (by Whites) as ethnic isolationism.

Be that as it may, it is the melting-pot culture that substitutes ethnicity for race, in the case of Whites, and race for ethnicity, in the case of Blacks. The Black nationalists unknowingly act out the racial role assigned to them by melting-pot ideology, whereas Professor Gates knowingly combats this stereotype.

Because Jews form the most ethnically distinct White group, and are relatively small in number, they serve as an ideal target for Black nationalists who counterpose Black racial authenticity to White ethnic authenticity. This explains why some members of the isolationist minority of the Black middle class promote Black anti-Semitism in an attempt to advance their status in the Black community.

Professor Gates left no doubt as to his belief that the recent Black anti-Semitism emanated from the Black middle class:

> Make no mistake: this is anti-Semitism from the top down, engineered and promoted by leaders who affect to be speaking for a larger resentment. This top-down anti-Semitism, in large part the province of the better educated classes, can thus be contrasted with the anti-Semitism from below common among African-American communities in the 1930s and 1940s which followed . . . a familiar pattern of clientilistic hostility toward the neighborhood vendor or landlord.

The point Gates makes here and elsewhere in his article is that anti-Semitism of this kind is all the more dangerous because it is purveyed by educated people who are consciously promoting the vicious and blatantly racist slander that accuses *all* Jews not only of historical misdeeds but also of having an essential nature that is evil.

Finally, Professor Gates touched on the failure of so many Black leaders to challenge Black anti-Semitism:

> For decent and principled reasons, many black intellec-

tuals are loath to criticize "oppositional" black leaders. Yet it has become apparent that to continue to maintain a comradely silence may be, in effect, to capitulate to the isolationist agenda, to betray our charge and trust.

Yet Gates did not mention Minister Farrakhan's implied avowal of Black supremacy through his claim that Blacks are God's "Chosen People." This claim heightened Jewish-Black tensions because it touched all too many members of the new, post–civil rights Black middle class in that secret personal place where everyone's individual share, no matter how small, of reactive racism and intolerance resides. But apparently the ultimate target of this call to Black separatism was not the Jews, despite the provocative insults Farrakhan hurled at the Jewish people. ("Jews, I am your last chance. If you kill me, the ovens were as nothing—the scriptures charge you with killing the prophets of God.") Farrakhan's real aim was to discredit the mainstream Black leadership, and he made no bones about it.

In a speech delivered in Washington, D.C., on August 18, 1984, Minister Farrakhan asked the audience: "What should be done to Black leaders who seek Jewish support?" When the audience shouted—"Kill them," Farrakhan responded: "I didn't say it, but I second the motion." And in a speech at New York City's Madison Square Garden on October 7, 1985, he said that Black leaders like David Dinkins (now New York City's mayor) were finished because they stood with the Jews who were the enemies of Black people. Then Minister Farrakhan indirectly threatened Dinkins:

> The reason David Dinkins would do that is because they [Black leaders] don't fear us. They fear white people. . . . When the leader sells out the people, he should pay a price for that. . . . Do you think the leader should sell you out and then live?

Thus it is clear that Jews have far less to fear from Minister Farrakhan than does the present Black leadership. Nevertheless, the Jewish and Black constituencies remain sufficiently misled so that the respective leaderships are unable or unwilling to break the racial circle of fear and suspicion

within which vested ethnic, economic, and political interests have imprisoned them. However, intellectuals on both sides have been raising their
voices to demand an end to hostilities. Professor Gates's forthright
indictment of Black anti-Semitism could be viewed as a belated reply to the
eloquent plea issued by a Jewish colleague six years earlier.

A JEWISH SCHOLAR, DR. LEONARD FEIN, wrote the following impassioned
lines in the January-February 1986 issue of the magazine *Moment* at the
height of a period of acute tension between Jews and African-Americans:

> Considering the disparity in circumstances that separates
> us, is our dream of alliance merely idle fantasy? For look
> about: we, the Jews, came from Europe's oppression to
> America's freedom; you, the Blacks, came from Africa's
> freedom to America's slavery. . . . We are decisively
> among the haves; you are decisively among the have-
> nots. Our children worry about which college to attend,
> yours worry about how to deal with joblessness. So what
> is it that impels us to persist in searching for common
> ground? First, we have both known Egypt. Second, we
> share not only the memory of Egypt but the dream of
> Jordan. And third, far from memory and far from faith is
> the common understanding that if America's Jews and
> America's Blacks cannot repair their own alliance, then
> all of America is in trouble.

After describing the immense gulf of race and class which separates
African-Americans and Jews, Dr. Fein used vivid biblical metaphors—
Egypt (slavery) and Jordan (freedom)—having deep emotional meanings
to both Blacks and Jews in order to emphasize the long-standing bond
between the two groups.

Jews and African-Americans are bound together in two fundamental
ways—first by a link between their cultural traditions, and second by their
common rejection of melting-pot *assimilation*. The cultural link stems from
biblical epics, like those of Moses and Joshua, that provide some of the
imagery found in the traditional Negro spirituals. The rejection of melting-

pot assimilation lies in the refusal of both groups to abandon the centrality of their *cultural* self-identification, the diversity and universality of their cultural traditions, and their continued identification with the land and people of their foreign ancestors.

Jews center their cultural self-identification in their ethnicity, whereas their color is of relatively minor significance to them, because they consider themselves to be different from other Whites (i.e., from gentiles). Therefore, whatever race consciousness Jews have tends to be associated mainly with their *ethnicity* instead of with their *color*. Moreover, since both the Jewish religion and the overall Jewish culture are in principle *multiracial as well as multinational,* only ethnicity and its derived culture can provide common ground for all Jews.

By contrast, slavery imposed on African-Americans a cultural self-identification centered in their race, since they were denied any *group right* to claim or to express their *ethnic self-identification.* Consequently, the *ethnic* status sought by the integrationist majority of African-Americans offers the common *ethnic* ground for Black-Jewish reconciliation, *provided that Jews are prepared to treat Blacks as ethnic equals.* A mosaic of equally recognized groups in which race is of minor significance would reduce Black-Jewish tensions dramatically.

In view of the cultural miscommunication that is prevalent between Jews and Blacks, it is of special interest to explore the implications of the third factor Dr. Fein sees as uniting Blacks and Jews: "the common understanding that if America's Jews and America's Blacks cannot repair their own alliance, then all of America is in trouble."

First, it is important to preserve an alliance between two major ethnic groups across the boundaries of *both* race *and* class at a time when American society is fractured along precisely those lines.

Second, Black-Jewish political collaboration remains central to the continued viability of the anticonservative congressional coalition which prevents conservative domination of the federal government.

Third, an irrevocable split between Jews and Blacks, combined with the collapse of the anticonservative coalition in Congress, would invite an upsurge in WASP expressions of bigotry against Jews and Blacks alike. Racial and ethnic discrimination would then tend toward a dangerous merger as the suppressed WASP "master-race" instincts, revealed during the Manifest Destiny period of the nineteenth century, returned. And Dr. Fein knew well that he did not have to remind either his Jewish readers or his Black readers of the parallels between U.S. Manifest Destiny and Hitler's Third Reich.

THE DEEP DISTRUST OF WASPS by both Jews and Blacks—the distrust that was not mentioned explicitly by Dr. Fein—was revealed openly in two articles which appeared on the Op-Ed page of the *New York Times* on September 2, 1989, and March 9, 1990.

The first piece was written by twenty-four-year-old African-American businessman, Devin Standard, a graduate of an elite White college; it speaks for itself:

> I cannot walk throughout the city in which I was born without fearing for my safety—just because I am an African-American. . . .
>
> . . . Apparently there are gangs of white people just waiting to kill me. . . .
>
> . . . Do white people secretly aspire to intern us all in jails or concentration camps—to permanently do away with us? . . .
>
> . . . African-Americans will not be led quietly to their deaths, interned, or just disappear. Those murderers among you better realize that because I am an American, I will defend myself.

The second article was written by well-known Jewish sociologist Seymour Martin Lipset and referred to a dinner-party conversation with three of his prominent Jewish acquaintances:

> They were all extremely successful members of the Jewish intelligentsia who mingle easily and frequently with gentile colleagues. Yet at one point one publisher said: "I believe that when gentiles go home at night, they dream of killing Jews.". . .

> ... Every Jew learns that ... Jewish communities, no
> matter how rich and powerful, wound up persecuted,
> expelled, the victims of pogroms. The murder of one out
> of every three Jews in the world, the Holocaust, occurred
> in our lifetime or that of our parents.

The bottom line in both of these articles is a deep fear of the WASP
majority—a fear that raises the ultimate specter of genocide in the minds
of African-Americans and Jews alike. Yet, curiously, neither Mr. Standard
nor Mr. Lipset chooses to recognize, even in passing, the fear of the same
potentially hostile majority expressed by the other minority group.

Mr. Standard makes no distinction between the majority WASPs and
the unassimilated Jewish Whites who share common interests with Blacks.
Mr. Lipset goes so far as to imply that Blacks are *more* threatening than the
ethnic Whites who form the gangs that *actually* kill individual Blacks and
beat up individual Jews, but do not remotely threaten either group with
genocide. That danger comes from the WASPs only.

In a passage that ignores the racial factor by treating Blacks *merely* as
an "ethnic community," Mr. Lipset writes:

> In America, blacks are the only major ethnic community
> in which some spokesmen voice anti-Semitic stereo-
> types. There are, of course, overt white anti-Semites. But
> they are on the fringe: David Duke, Lyndon LaRouche,
> the Liberty Lobby and marginal radical grouplets.
>
> When most mainstream black politicians hesitate
> before repudiating apparent anti-Semites like [Black
> Muslim minister] Louis Farrakhan, . . . they frighten Jews,
> even though the Jews think they are not anti-Semitic
> themselves.
>
> . . . While a plurality of blacks support Israel and are
> not anti-Semitic, a larger minority among them than may
> be found among whites back the Palestinians *or* agree
> with various anti-Jewish statements [EMPHASIS MINE].

Although Lipset's recognition of the ethnic aspect of the Black community is insightful and transcends the confines of melting-pot ideology, his failure to appreciate the racial aspect blinds him to the Black nationalists' substitution of race for ethnicity. It is precisely the importance of *racial* unity in the Black community that enables them to deter many Black spokesmen from condemning Black anti-Semitism.

Moreover, Mr. Lipset's claim that the Black community is "the only major *ethnic* community in which *some* spokesmen voice anti-Semitic stereotypes" has some validity only if one excludes *the* major ethnic community—WASPS—and recognizes that "some spokesmen" does not include any with significant economic or political power. By contrast, the "overt anti-Semites" whom Lipset dismisses as being "on the fringe" *are* politically and economically significant WASPS: David Duke won 55 percent of the White vote in a Louisiana gubernatorial election in which a huge Black vote defeated him. Lyndon LaRouche is a multimillionaire who was able to fund an independent political party. The Liberty Lobby is a well-funded, far-right lobbying organization.

The statement that "most mainstream black politicians hesitate before repudiating [*black*] *apparent* anti-Semites like Louis Farrakhan" is true, but here the words "apparent" and "repudiating" reveal the weakness of Mr. Lipset's point: given the trend in the Black community toward racial solidarity at almost all costs, a "mainstream" Black politician with a predominantly Black constituency would have to be not only courageous but foolhardy to "repudiate" (rather than merely to criticize) an "apparent" Black anti-Semite. The facts are that many Black elected officials did criticize Minister Farrakhan but refused to repudiate him as a person.

And, finally, the statement that although "a plurality of Blacks support Israel and are not anti-Semitic, a larger minority among them than may be found among Whites back the Palestinians *or* agree with various anti-Semitic statements" is true but is misleading in three ways:

1. Supporting Israel and not being anti-Semitic are two different things which are not necessarily related. Not only a "larger minority" of Blacks, but also many Whites, including many Jews in America and in Israel, have publicly opposed Israeli foreign and domestic policies without in any sense being anti-Semitic.

2. The great majority of Blacks who support Palestinian human

rights and the implementation of the United Nations resolutions on the Palestinian question *also* support secure borders and peace for the state of Israel. A greater proportion of Blacks than of Whites take this position rather than uncritical support of Israel, but they do not simply "back the Palestinians." Therefore, the issue of Israel is not divisive enough to produce a break between Jews and Blacks.

3. Thus, the word *or* which inappropriately links agreement with various anti-Jewish statements to support for the Palestinians is misleading. Many Blacks who support Palestinian *rights* do not agree with anti-Semitic statements, and, therefore, these two issues cannot legitimately be lumped together. When they are separated, statistical data and personal experience appear to demonstrate that Blacks are *less hostile* to Jews than ethnic Whites are.

This is not to say that tensions between Jews and African-Americans have not risen since the 1960s, but this rise stems primarily from the fact that the twelve Reagan-Bush years brought major economic advances to the Jewish community and an economic disaster to the majority in the Black community. The current Black-Jewish conflict arose more from class and economics than from anti-Semitism, and it was for the purpose of avoiding this reality that the Black and Jewish middle classes who benefited from the melting pot tended to conceal class issues in the murky waters of race and ethnicity.

Abetting this avoidance was a behind-the-scenes struggle between Jewish and Black middle-class liberal leaders for political power within the Democratic party, and in this context it is hardly surprising that many White liberal intellectuals chose to support the Jewish side.

TAYLOR BRANCH, WHITE LIBERAL AUTHOR of the book *Parting the Waters,* which is an epic treatment of the civil rights movement, wrote an article titled, "Blacks and Jews: The Uncivil War" for the May 1989 issue of the magazine *Esquire.* Mr. Branch, by vastly exaggerating Black Muslim Minister Farrakhan's stature in the Black community, implied that Blacks were mainly responsible for the Black-Jewish "war":

In the beginning, there was Moses. Now there is

> Farrakhan. All along, there's been an epic struggle of
> power and of pride. . . .
>   . . . Jews . . . look with both longing and horror upon
> the last generation's procession of black prophets:
> Malcolm X, Martin Luther King Jr., Louis Farrakhan,
> and Jesse Jackson. Depending on one's prediction of the
> outcome, blacks and Jews are either intimate enemies or
> quarrelsome cousins. . . .
>   . . . Although Jackson gathers hosannas from coast to
> coast, hailed as the new black Moses, it is Farrakhan who
> for better or for worse is more closely modeled on the
> prophet.

Minister Farrakhan is no Moses. In fact, he has never wielded nearly as much power or influence in the African-American community as any one of hundreds of Black elected officials, business leaders, ministers, and institutional figures. Moreover, the Black middle class and working class, who together make up about 63 percent of the African-American population, gave up looking for a Moses after the assassinations of President John Kennedy, Malcolm X, Rev. Martin Luther King, Jr., and Robert Kennedy. Only the powerless Black underclass still longs for a Moses.

Furthermore, it makes no sense to lump Rev. Martin Luther King, Jr., Malcolm X, Minister Louis Farrakhan, and Rev. Jesse Jackson together indiscriminately. King, who led the largest and most effective mass movement in African-American history and achieved worldwide influence, far outranks Malcolm X who was assassinated just as he was beginning to reach his full potential. And Rev. Jesse Jackson, who has already played a major role in the realignment of American politics, far outranks Minister Farrakhan.

A 1985 poll of African-Americans by the Simon Wiesenthal Center revealed a more than eight-to-one (59% to 7%) preference for Jackson over Farrakhan when it came to choosing a top leader. But even Jackson does not wield the direct political and economic power wielded by an army of Black elected officials, business people, and civic leaders who are independent of any individual leader.

As for Mr. Branch's view of Blacks and Jews as "either intimate enemies or quarrelsome cousins," it seems to me that a more apt description of the relationship between the two groups might be something like: "close political allies and neutral neighbors at best; quarrelsome political allies and quarrelsome neighbors at worst."

Like most White liberals, Mr. Branch apparently accepts melting-pot ideology's view of Blacks as a racial minority and not an ethnic one. Yet his claim that Blacks and Jews "have suddenly become both the victims and the perpetrators of racial hatred" is contradicted several paragraphs later by his acknowledgment that the Black-Jewish conflict is exaggerated and is actually more ethnic than racial:

> The leaders masquerade as peacemakers, but the fight is almost exclusively theirs. It is confined not just to the articulate but to those whose chosen role is to speak of power, pride, and religion. Waged between two peoples who have practically no daily contact, this war continues precisely because they are peoples for whom such abstractions reach deeper than pocketbooks or parking spaces.

Note that Mr. Branch speaks of power, pride, and *religion,* rather than power, pride, and *race.* Moreover, I think he is wrong when he refers to *"two* peoples . . . for whom . . . abstractions reach deeper than pocketbooks or parking spaces," because for most Blacks the opposite is true. Furthermore, tolerance of other religions and beliefs is central to the religious beliefs of the great majority of African-Americans, including the majority of Black followers of the Islamic religion; only the small minority constituting the Shiite-oriented Black Muslim group led by Minister Farrakhan manifests intolerance.

Mr. Branch's undue emphasis on this group apparently leads him to demean African-American culture in comparison with Jewish culture despite his description of the Black-Jewish cultural relationship as "a historic creative collaboration between America's foremost outsider cultures":

> The ancient Jews forged religious and historical ideas so

> powerful that they blended into *a distinctive race*. . . .
> Working in the opposite direction, some blacks have
> struggled to fit a religion to race. Even so, they often find
> themselves borrowing their symbols from Judaism.
> Farrakhan, for instance, appropriates the Hebrew proph-
> ets along with their concepts of Moses, Exodus, and the
> chosen people. More than any people on earth, includ-
> ing the Jews, American blacks have adopted the Mosaic
> model of social organization [EMPHASIS MINE].

Branch's basis for the comparison is the melting-pot precept that a set
of ideas and institutions can produce a "new" or a superiorly endowed
"*chosen race*," as in the case of the "new American race" which the original
melting pot was to have created. This notion is not only wrong, since
"races" (i.e., people) create ideas and institutions, rather than the other way
around; it is also racist in the sense of Hitler's master race or Farrakhan's
chosen Black race. The marriage of *ideology to race* is always and without
exception reactionary and dehumanizing in the extreme. So when Mr.
Branch claims that "ancient Jews forged religious and historical ideas so
powerful that they blended into a distinctive race," he is on dangerous
ground.

Mr. Branch then makes a demeaning comparison between these
ancient Jews and Blacks who "worked in the opposite direction . . . to fit
a religion to race." But the "opposite direction" is in fact the only direction
in which human culture is produced: a race produces a wide variety of ideas
and religions (cultures) via a broad spectrum of ethnic groups.

Interestingly, in his devaluation of Black culture in comparison with
Jewish culture, Branch has acknowledged that Black religion (i.e., culture)
is racially derived. Thus he flatly contradicts the melting-pot claim that
Black (or any other) racial traits are culturally derived.

In the preface of his book *Parting the Waters,* Branch makes the same
point with exquisite perception:

> Almost as color defines vision itself, race shapes the
> cultural eye—what we do and do not notice, the reach of
> empathy and the alignment of response. This subliminal

force recommends care in choosing a point of view for a history grounded in race. . . .

. . . Truth requires a maximum effort to see through the eyes of strangers, foreigners, and enemies.

But, in his *Esquire* article Mr. Branch sees Black culture through his own eyes and implies that the Black church—the core of a Black culture which survived slavery and produced a civil rights movement with leaders like Rev. Martin Luther King, Jr.—is merely an imitation of Jewish religion.

Mr. Branch's article goes on to compare the unrepresentative culture of Black nationalism with the highest level of the Jewish cultural tradition:

> Against the backdrop of the Six-Day War, black nationalism was but a dreary shadow. The Israeli's had a real army that had just whipped the surrounding hosts; the guns of the few u.s. black nationalists never amounted to more than media props. . . . Black nationalists had no ready-made psalms, no private comfort or accumulated wisdom of four thousand years. Their own heritage remained largely to be discovered, let alone evaluated and tested. Jews already had the Torah; blacks waited for Alex Haley to write *Roots.*

The juxtaposition of Black nationalists to Israel's "real army that had just whipped the surrounding [non-European] hosts" strikes an ethnic-nationalist tone that insults Blacks and is probably embarrassing to many American Jews. Mr. Branch compounds this insensitivity when he uses the Black-nationalist obsession with the Mosaic model to caricature the Black underclass using still another Black-Jewish comparison. Near the end of his article, Branch writes:

> For Blacks . . . the Mosaic model may not serve to raise the underclass from suffering—that great march now may lead to a blind door rather than the land of milk and honey. The historic model of uplift by politics, in a mass march behind a great Moses figure, may have no application to the modern dispossessed. This possibility,

together with the realization that American Jews themselves did not reach prosperity by such a path, presents
dilemmas of nearly unbearable sensitivity.

Here Mr. Branch equates "uplift by politics" to a "mass march behind
a great Moses figure," but surely there are other forms of political action.
Then he warns Blacks that even "the American Jews themselves did not
reach prosperity by such a path." Apparently, he believes that since the Jews
did not adopt uplift by politics, it should not be used by the Black middle
class to win entry to the melting pot ("the land of milk and honey") for the
Black underclass.

Finally, Mr. Branch adds that:

American public life is accustomed to the faces and
words of tormented Black prophets, but none of them
dares tell their people that they may have to become
more like Jews—rising from the rubble family by family,
shop by shop. They summon the rest of America to help
them avoid this awesome chore rather than to join it, and
most of the lesser black prophets speak for those who
would rather picket a business than run one.

No less than four classic anti-Black stereotypes appear in these two
sentences: 1. "tormented Black prophets" are popular-culture caricatures
who are afraid to tell their constituency to imitate the Jews; 2. Blacks are too
lazy to pull themselves up by their bootstraps as Jews did in the melting pot;
3. Blacks want a handout from "the rest of America" so they won't have to
earn their way to success; and 4. the underclass "would rather picket a
business than run one." All in all, this list is worthy of an "old-style"
conservative.

These stereotypes fit the pattern of Mr. Branch's disparagement of
Black culture, his caricaturing of the Black underclass, his exaggeration of
Black anti-Semitism, and his mockery of "a chirpy Jesse Jackson urging
listeners to register . . . , sounding at once Pollyannaish and impossibly
brave." This openly anti-Black stance offers a revealing look at the racial
attitudes of liberal defenders of the melting pot.

GOVERNOR CLINTON'S STRONG CAMPAIGN in the 1992 Democratic presidential primary and his success in winning the presidency derived from his progressive challenge to the melting-pot system. He shattered the conservative-liberal melting-pot consensus by speaking directly to the American people across the divisions of gender, race, ethnicity, and class, and his progressive program was augmented by an ideological clarity with which the artificial melting-pot concepts could not compete. Consequently, Clinton was able to win the overwhelming electoral support of both Blacks and Jews despite the tensions between them: 82 percent of the Black vote and 78 percent of the Jewish vote provided him with most of his margin of victory.

The effect of this progressive revitalization of the Democratic party on the Jewish-Black conflict was profound and was manifested in at least five positive ways.

1. Just before the Democratic convention, Jesse Jackson accepted an invitation to the World Jewish Congress in Brussels where he delivered an address which was well received and in which he declared Zionism to be a liberation movement. By this single act, Jackson established an unbridgeable ideological gulf between himself and Minister Louis Farrakhan, for whom Zionism is anathema, and thereby intensified his personal challenge to Black anti-Semitism.

2. The loss of power by the liberal faction in the Democratic party removed the reason for the power struggle between Black and Jewish liberals in the party.

3. The selection of Al Gore as the vice-presidential nominee was unanimously hailed by Jewish leaders as positive from the standpoint of Gore's Middle East positions.

4. Clinton's blunt criticism of rap singer Sister Souljah's racially inflammatory lyrics when he addressed a June conference of Jesse Jackson's Rainbow Coalition signaled the future president's determination to challenge *all* manifestations of racism and bigotry, including those emanating from racial or ethnic minorities. It also rejected the liberal paternalism which became fashionable in the 1960s and lingers on in the 1990s. In this sense, Clinton was indirectly warning *both* Black *and* Jewish leaders to clean up their racial acts.

5. Despite the strident and often hypocritical condemnations of Governor Clinton by Black separatists and by some mainstream Black leaders, many Black voters, if not a majority, privately welcomed Clinton's criticism of Sister Souljah. Moreover, Jesse Jackson, after initially expressing some outrage, undermined the anti-Clinton movement in the Black community by announcing that he had put this minor matter behind him, and by publicly distancing himself from Sister Souljah's remarks.

The cumulative effect of all these developments is a political climate in which Jews can look to a friendly White House; Blacks can take heart from the fact that after twelve cruel years under the Reagan-Bush heel the new president is a familiar southern WASP who apparently cares about economic and social justice; and the intimidation power of the separatists among Blacks is sufficiently reduced so that Black intellectuals like Professor Henry Louis Gates, Jr. can raise their voices effectively. In these new circumstances, any continuation of the present hostility between Jews and Blacks is not only irrational but inadmissible from both the pragmatic and moral standpoints.

So it is past time for Jews and Blacks to end a war which was phony to begin with and has benefited only those opportunists on both sides who furthered selfish agendas at the expense of the true interests of their people. The progressive agenda coupled with the cultural mosaic offers not only Blacks and Jews but the entire nation a new beginning. Let both groups set aside old habits and old thinking; let them break free from stereotypes and from bigotry's shackles; let them reach out to one another in friendship across the divide of different cultures; let them share each other's pain; and yes, let them once more bear each other's burden in the heat of the day.

9

THE
BLACK
MIDDLE
CLASS

he admission of the native-Black middle class and of
immigrant-descended Blacks into the melting pot has
placed the Black middle class in an ambivalent position,
since the native-Black working class and underclass
remain as the only excluded groups. Moreover, the native-
Black middle class does not enjoy the full ethnic status of all other melting-
pot groups, so it is still a second-class group within American society. This
inferior ethnic status explains the insecurity and anger of the Black middle
class despite its success inside the melting pot. Moreover, it has produced
a sharp racial division between the White and Black middle classes over
cultural values.

Most middle-class Whites are inspired as they recite the line in the
Pledge of Allegiance which proclaims "one nation, under God, indivisible,
with liberty and justice for all," whereas many middle-class Blacks choke
on it because their personal experience has demonstrated the opposite.

Most Whites insist that the civil rights laws have eliminated institutional racism, while most Blacks not only denounce such racism as pervasive but occasionally demonstrate against it. Most Whites angrily condemn the Black underclass for rioting, whereas most Blacks condemn the violence and looting but identify partially with the rioters.

But the sharpest division between the Black and White middle classes concerns law enforcement. The melting pot employs the police to maintain law and order by suppressing the underclass as a *class,* not just as individuals. The White middle class, which is entitled to liberty, is guaranteed individual freedoms which are respected by the police. But the Black underclass in the inner cities is not deemed worthy of individual rights by the melting pot, and, therefore, the predominantly White urban police forces are at liberty to violate the civil rights of Blacks whom *they* judge to be members of the underclass. Since few White members of urban police forces live in communities like the ones they work in, they often treat members of the Black middle class the way they treat the underclass. The result is distrust of the predominantly White police by virtually the entire Black community.

The remainder of the criminal justice system is likewise dominated by the White middle class, and the cultural affinity of predominantly White juries for melting-pot values usually result in verdicts favorable to Whites in general and to the police in police-brutality cases in particular. This perception of a racially biased criminal justice system is one of the main causes of underclass riots and cripples the authority of the Black middle-class leadership in its efforts to reduce crime in the Black community. The predominantly White police are a significant part of the Black crime problem and present one of the obstacles to its solution.

In these bleak circumstances, the Black middle class has all but given up on moral and political leadership and has concentrated on its economic survival as a class in an increasingly harsh economic environment. The disillusionment that has set in after the failure of twenty-five years of civil rights laws to produce racial integration or even to end institutional racism is expressed in the widespread belief among Blacks that racism is a permanent feature of u.s. society. Derrick Bell, a professor at New York University Law School and author of a recent book titled *The Permanence of*

Racism, believes that Blacks are in a worse position now than at any time since slavery, the only difference being that "a more effective, more sophisticated means of domination" is used.

In any case, virtually no African-American today believes that assimilation as individuals with the liberties promised by American liberal democracy will *ever* be made possible for Blacks by the White majority. Therefore, the African-American population, from top to bottom, demands *group rights* and refuses to trust any combination of *individual rights* as adequate protection even for *physical survival.* However, Black leadership, which is overwhelmingly middle-class, is divided into two main groupings and a third, smaller one over how to secure stable *group security.* Each group has its radicals, moderates, and conservatives, but the three differ fundamentally on the overall strategy for Black group survival and progress.

The first and by far the largest group is made up of ethnic integrationists who advocate *economic* and *cultural* integration into American society as a cohesive *ethnic group* with a distinct culture. This amounts to demanding an ethnic mosaic instead of an ethnic melting pot. In comparison with other ethnic groups, the Black status sought by the ethnic integrationists is comparable to that of the Jewish-American minority. Their core constituency is the majority of native Blacks. Their legacy derives from the traditional Black churches and civic organizations; from the Black trade-union caucuses; from Rev. Martin Luther King, Jr., Paul Robeson, W.E.B. Du Bois, Booker T. Washington, and Frederick Douglass.

The radicals and moderates (Douglass, Robeson, Du Bois, King) *demanded* Black group entry into an ethnic mosaic; the conservatives (Washington) *appealed* for entry of the Black middle class into the melting pot.

The second, much smaller group consists of ethnic nationalists who advocate *economic* integration but oppose *cultural* integration; they demand a status comparable to that of the Chinese-American or Japanese-American minorities. The Black Power movement of the late 1960s, the cultural nationalism of the 1970s, and the Afrocentrism of the 1990s are the ideological signatures of this grouping, and their constituency centers among African-Americans of immigrant ancestry and new Black immigrants, young native Blacks from the underclass in northern cities, and Black students on majority-White campuses.

The ethnic nationalists reject European culture as alien to African-Americans and, therefore, espouse cultural separatism, but they also reject both economic and political separatism. Malcolm X, as opposed to Martin Luther King, is the current symbol for the younger members of this constituency, while the older generation reflects the legacies of such figures as A. Philip Randolph, labor leader, socialist, and civil rights leader from World War I into the 1970s; of Harlem Renaissance writers such as Claude McKay; of Black-history bibliophile and curator Arthur Schomburg, as well as of W.E.B. Du Bois and Paul Robeson whose radical brand of ethnic integrationism appealed to ethnic nationalists.

The third group, which is insignificantly small in number but is important because of its message and its ability to influence the ethnic nationalists, consists of racial nationalists who reject all forms of integration with Whites and advocate a separatism based on a racial interpretation of the Shiite Muslim religion. Known as the Nation of Islam and led by Minister Louis Farrakhan, this group is a minority of Black followers of the Islamic religion; the majority are Sunni Muslims, and they reject racial exclusivity.

The racial nationalists inherit the legacies of Marcus Garvey's nonreligious mass movement for universal Black solidarity and emigration to Africa which failed in the 1920s, and of Elijah Muhammad's Nation of Islam which followed in the 1930s as a Black religious sect. Today's racial-nationalist constituency is confined to a relatively small number of religiously devoted, highly disciplined followers, to supporters among the northern Black urban underclass, and to groups of Black college students on northern university campuses.

The Black mass movements that have benefited all African-Americans, such as the civil rights movement of the 1960s, were always the result of a strong alliance between the ethnic integrationists and the ethnic nationalists, whereas the racial nationalists have traditionally boycotted these movements because they aimed at integration. The ideological distinction between the ethnic integrationists and the ethnic nationalists is subtly reflected in the two names, Black and African-American, while the distinction between ethnic nationalists and racial nationalists is blurred by their common color identity despite religious difference. Therefore, outsiders have difficulty sorting out ideological differences among Blacks.

The term Black, which according to national polls is favored by a 72 percent majority of the Black population, emphasizes the native-Black, slave heritage and is preferred by ethnic integrationists. By contrast, the term African-American, which is favored by 28 percent, emphasizes the ethnic, immigrant heritage while downplaying the slave heritage and is preferred by ethnic nationalists. Black is preferred by the working class which is excluded from the melting pot on racial grounds and is, therefore, concerned with racial, rather than ethnic, entry requirements. On the other hand, the mainly middle-class ethnic nationalists are inside the melting pot and prefer African-American which confirms their ethnic status.

The racial nationalists, despite the fact that they are far more alienated ideologically from the ethnic integrationists than from the ethnic nationalists, prefer the term Black because of its racial focus.

But all of these distinctions are blurred by the interchangeable use of both terms by all three groups, since Black and African-American imply the interrelated concepts of racial and ethnic solidarity.

Successful Black politicians, Rev. Jesse Jackson and Mayor David Dinkins among them, use the term African-American while pursuing ethnic-integrationist policies. Their assumption has been that this is the way to win the allegiance of the two main groups in the Black community while minimizing the hostility of the racial nationalists—symbolism for the ethnic nationalists, policy substance for the ethnic integrationists, and reduced ideological conflict with the racial nationalists.

However, this strategy was already beginning to unravel in the middle 1980s. Reaganomics and the decline of the manufacturing unions brought about a decline in the numerical weight and political clout of Black trade unionists, thus weakening the ethnic integrationists. The inability of integrationist policies to halt the deterioration in the economic status of all non-middle-class Blacks, combined with the contrast of a significant rise in the fortunes of the Black middle class, dramatically strengthened the ethnic nationalists at the expense of the ethnic integrationists and simultaneously increased the leverage of the racial nationalists and of militants representing the Black underclass. The net result of these developments produced a kind of gridlock among Black leaders.

IN THE HEADY DAYS of civil rights triumphs and Rev. Martin Luther King's unchallenged moral leadership of Black America, the ethnic integrationists, including Rev. King himself, placed primary emphasis on racial integration and downplayed the issue of ethnicity on the assumption that the melting pot would at last admit Blacks as a group. Then the struggle for the mosaic could be launched from inside the melting pot with numerous ethnic-White allies. King's famous "I Have a Dream" speech at the 1963 March on Washington epitomized this approach. However, he never contemplated giving up Black cultural distinctiveness or ethnic cohesiveness. In his 1964 book *Why We Can't Wait,* he answers those who "shudder" at the notion of a "Negro political bloc" because it supposedly smacks of "racial exclusiveness":

> The Negro minority will unite for political action for the same reason that it will seek to function in alliance with other groups—in this way it can compel the majority to listen.

Rev. King clearly had in mind a Black minority functioning as an *ethnic group* "in alliance with other [minority] groups." In other words, since native Blacks are a distinct ethnic group with a distinct culture, they can choose to function as an *ethnic* group and not exclusively as a racial group. It is this option to act as an ethnic group that the melting pot seeks to deny to Blacks by restricting their entry.

The melting pot refused to admit Blacks as a group; the ethnic-nationalist advocates of Black power said "we told you so"; King's White liberal allies abandoned him when it came to the acceptance of non-middle-class Blacks into American society, and Rev. King embraced the radical view that the entire structure of American society would have to be altered in order to secure the rights of Blacks as a group. By 1967–1968, King was saying that

> the black revolution is . . . more than a struggle for the rights of Negroes. . . . It reveals systemic . . . flaws and suggests that radical reconstruction of society itself is the real issue. . . . We're dealing with the problem of the gulf between the haves and the have-nots.

The 1968 assassinations of Rev. King and of Senator Robert Kennedy during his potentially successful quest for the presidency, compounded with the effects of the earlier assassinations of President John F. Kennedy in 1963 and of Malcolm X in 1965, shifted the political and ideological momentum away from the ethnic integrationists. As a result, the preeminent Black politician of the 1980s emerged in the person of Rev. Jesse Jackson whose Rainbow Coalition presaged the progressive mosaic of the 1990s; who placed primary emphasis on the ethnic aspect of ethnic integration, and who won back the allegiance of the ethnic nationalists.

The ethnic nationalists of the 1980s and 1990s, like the cultural nationalists of the 1970s, have had a profound impact on American culture because they express the searing contradictions which the Black middle class faces from within today's melting pot. Spike Lee's films and August Wilson's plays are two examples of this influence.

Mr. Lee's films offer perceptive and vivid juxtapositions of the Black underclass to the contradictions that plague today's young, upwardly-mobile, Black middle class, but his own apparent personal ambivalence underlies both the strengths and weaknesses of his work. *Do the Right Thing* and *Jungle Fever* are about Black male antiheroes from the fringe of the underclass and from the "striver's row" upper-middle class, respectively. What they have in common is a profound self-alienation and lack of dignity.

Because, in their different ways, they are torn between a craving for a strong ethnic self-image and a desire to be an *accepted* part of the White melting pot, their attempts to be ethnic appear pitiful in contrast with the genuine and powerful ethnicity of the Italian-American characters with whom they interact. At the same time, the gulf between Black and White ethnics is portrayed as so wide that sharing a mosaic on the basis of equality would hardly seem possible.

Both films metaphorically imply the guilt of the Black middle class over its abandonment of the Black underclass and reflect the preference for Malcolm X over Martin Luther King among the ethnic nationalists. *Do the Right Thing* romanticizes the underclass world by omitting the drug addiction and violence that ravage it, while *Jungle Fever* depicts it as an unrelieved hell populated by lost souls. The Malcolm-King opposition is made explicit at the end of *Do the Right Thing* with contrasting statements from the two against the background of a Black riot; and Mr. Lee leaves little doubt that he prefers Malcolm.

Malcolm X, Mr. Lee's most important film so far, has made a major cultural contribution by portraying the evolution of a Black male from a street-hustler, who fits many of the melting-pot culture's *racial* stereotypes, to a powerful and dignified *ethnic nationalist* with a broad cultural world-view. This evolution, combined with Mr. Lee's treatment of Malcolm's intermediate stage of development as a leader of the Nation of Islam, dramatizes the interplay between race and ethnicity in the Black community in a way that is effective for a mass audience. In my view, these accomplishments far outweigh its flaws, which some Black reviewers have seized upon to denounce Mr. Lee's work for ideological reasons.

Mr. Wilson's insightful and moving plays are about past family and individual conflicts of the Black lower-middle class, rather than about group struggle or the native-Black heritage dating back to slavery. In a thoughtful address to a 1992 Black Theater Conference, Wilson revealed the ethnic-nationalist ideology which apparently affects his artistic choices:

> We are only the victims of our own inability to resolve our relationship with the society in which we live. If the African who arrived on the shores of North America chained and malnourished . . . is still chained and malnourished after 373 years, can it be anybody's fault but ours? . . .

> We work for somebody else. We have doctors, but we
> do not have hospitals. We are accountants, but we do not
> have banks. We are bricklayers, but we do not build
> houses for ourselves. . . .
>
> And we have failed . . . to put our economic muscle to
> use to make some boots with whose straps we might pull
> ourselves up.

Since Mr. Wilson believes native Blacks themselves to be responsible for their failure to overcome the effects of slavery, oppression, and exclusion from the melting pot, it is not surprising that he avoids the cultural heritage of slavery and the tradition of common struggle. Moreover, he underscores the traces of economic and cultural separatism which form the ideological link between the ethnic and racial nationalists.

A detailed presentation of ethnic-nationalist ideology appears in *Afrocentricity* by Professor Molefi Asante, chairperson of the Department of African American Studies at Temple University. Professor Asante's Afrocentrism, like Eurocentrism, is a broad cultural trend, and, like Black Power, it means different things to different constituencies. Superficially, it means the study of Black people "from the inside out, rather than from the outside in." However, it blurs the significant distinctions between ethnic integrationists, ethnic nationalists, and racial nationalists by lumping together figures as diverse as Marcus Garvey, W.E.B. Du Bois, Elijah Muhammad, Martin Luther King, Malcolm X, and Booker T. Washington while omitting such a seminal cultural figure as Paul Robeson.

The Afrocentrist, according to Professor Asante, eliminates from consideration everything that is not in African culture and history, "not because we have something against someone else's culture; it is just not ours." Then Asante goes on to express the view that "victory will surely come as we carry out the Afrocentric mission to humanize the Universe."

His ethnocentric world outlook blends with the racial nationalism of Dr. Leonard Jeffries, the controversial former head of the black studies department at the City University of New York. In an interview published in the December 2, 1991, issue of *The Final Call,* the official newspaper of Minister Louis Farrakhan's Nation of Islam, Dr. Jeffries claims that Africans "are the mothers and fathers of the human family" and that multiculturalism is a "tactic" invented by "those who don't want to deal with the African center":

> The African center begets physical humanity. The African center begets cultural humanity in its multi-dimensions. . . .
>
> . . . The genius of the Hon. Elijah Muhammad . . . was this . . . spirit that [he] had. . . . Marcus Garvey and Elijah Muhammad are the same tradition of spirituality coming from the root source. . . .
>
> Elijah Muhammad structured the Nation of Islam with a strengthened male/warrior principle, the Fruit of Islam. He also had the female develop a sense of purpose. The strength of the female is in bringing forth life and nurturing life. That is not a weakness.

Here we have the essence of racial-nationalist ideology: world racial supremacy, cultural exclusivity, male supremacy. It offers the mirror image of Anglo-Saxon Manifest Destiny. In this context, Malcolm X looms large as a leader who broke decisively with racial nationalism in order to cross over to the common ground of progressive ethnic nationalism. Tragically, this ideological break, which consisted of the repudiation of Elijah Muhammad along with the Nation of Islam and its racialist ideology, cost Malcolm X his life.

In an article which appeared in the August 25, 1964, issue of the *Egyptian Gazette*, Malcolm wrote:

> In the past I permitted myself to be used by Elijah Muhammad, the leader of the sect known as the Black Muslims, to make sweeping indictments of all white people, the entire white race, and these generalizations have caused injuries to some whites who perhaps did not deserve to be hurt. Because of the spiritual enlightenment which I was blessed to receive as the result of my recent pilgrimage to the Holy City of Mecca, I no longer subscribe to sweeping indictments of any one race.

> . . . I am now striving to live the life of a true Sunni
> Muslim. In the future I intend to be careful not to
> sentence anyone who has not first been proven
> guilty. I must repeat that I am not a racist nor do I
> subscribe to the tenets of racism. I can state in all
> sincerity that I wish nothing but freedom, justice, and
> equality; life, liberty, and the pursuit of happiness for
> all people.

Malcolm X also reached out to leading ethnic-integrationist figures, including Rev. Martin Luther King and Paul Robeson. In my father's case, Malcolm X spoke to me at Lorraine Hansberry's funeral service in January 1965 and asked me to arrange for him to visit my father privately. To our deep sorrow, Malcolm was brutally assassinated only weeks later at Manhattan's Audubon Ballroom, a few blocks from my parents' home. Nevertheless, my brief conversation with him left me with the indelible impression of a man who possessed immense strength and dignity—a man who was spiritually at peace with himself despite the danger that stalked him hourly.

That danger stemmed from the violent rhetoric of the Nation of Islam's leaders who set out to destroy Malcolm X for his "heresy." Minister Louis Farrakhan was prominent among those leaders and helped set the tone for the ensuing attacks on Malcolm when he wrote in the December 4, 1964, issue of *Muhammad Speaks* that Malcolm was doomed: "Only those who wish to be led to hell, or to their doom, will follow Malcolm. . . . Malcolm shall not escape. . . . Such a man is worthy of death."

It was in a political atmosphere created by statements such as this one that Malcolm was gunned down by Black Muslim assassins two months later, so it is not surprising that voices in the Black community were raised in protest twenty years afterward when Minister Farrakhan used similar rhetoric to threaten Black leaders with whom he disagreed. However, the silence of many top Black leaders was both surprising and shameful.

As the preceding chapter mentioned, in a speech on October 2, 1985, in New York City, Minister Farrakhan accused David Dinkins, now mayor of New York, of "selling out to the Jews," adding: "Do you think the leader should sell you out and then live?" The collective Black political leadership of New York City left this threat against the life of one of its colleagues publicly unanswered, limiting themselves to *private* sympathy phone calls.

Rep. Charles Rangel, arguably the most powerful Black member of the House of Representatives, finally yielded up the grudging comment that "the First Amendment requires that we defend the right to speak even when we despise the message." Ms. Hazel Dukes, then president of the New York State Conference of the NAACP, said: "The man [Farrakhan] has a right to free speech, just like anyone else." And Rev. Calvin Butts, now pastor of Harlem's famous Abyssinia Baptist Church, explained in the *New York Post* of October 9 that Farrakhan had not really threatened Dinkins's life but was merely saying that Dinkins "doesn't deserve to be a leader because he denounced Farrakhan at the behest of the Jewish community."

On December 1 and 8, 1985, I had the following exchanges with Rev. Butts on the subject of Minister Farrakhan's threat against Dinkins during panel discussions about Farrakhan on Gil Noble's WABC/TV program "Like It Is":

> *Robeson:* There was a true threat against him [Dinkins], I think, implied in Mr. Farrakhan's remarks. . . . I think that's out of bounds. Political threats, that's one thing. Shouldn't reelect him. But to talk about death, and he shouldn't live, and that kind of thing—even rhetorically—is a mistake. . . . And certainly the Malcolm X example should be enough to dramatize that.
>
> *Butts:* . . . The Dave Dinkins that I knew was not a man who of his own volition would have stood up and denounced . . . Farrakhan. He was a man who, perhaps, I believe, did that as a result of pressure. Because Dave Dinkins knew first of all, and knows, that Farrakhan is not anti-Semitic. . . .
>
> *Robeson:* . . . Some of Minister Farrakhan's statements were clearly anti-Jewish. There's no question about that

in my mind. I don't need to be pressed by any outside forces to say that. I don't think Mr. Dinkins needed to be pressured by anyone to say that, because indeed they [the statements] were [anti-Semitic] . . . .

. . . And the statements about Black leaders did come in a context; let me quote for you from Minister Farrakhan's Washington, D.C., speech [July 22, 1985], from the tape . . . : "I say Black people, whenever you put a Black man in office and that Black man betrays the best interests of those who put him there, I say take him out and if he does not repent, well then, . . . we will tar and feather them; we will hang them from the highest limb; we will chop off their heads and roll them down the street . . . ." I think that's dangerous.

Butts: I would like to just point out again that Farrakhan is not the issue. . . . I do think that . . . the ways he makes some of his statements are more divisive than they are unifying, even for the Black community. . . . And I think that his criticism can be better informed . . . as it relates to the Black community and some of its institutions. . . . I think he needs to be somewhat more responsible in his statements. I think some statements are irresponsible. . . . I think he would improve his leadership if he would tailor his rhetoric just a bit. I'm not saying change the truth. But I'm saying the presentation of the truth has to be in such a way that you bring people together rather than keeping certain people back.

What is striking about Rev. Butts's remarks is that he refuses to condemn the *content* of Minister Farrakhan's death threats against Mr. Dinkins and against any Black leaders whom he accuses of "selling out." Instead, he offers fairly mild criticism of Farrakhan's style ("irresponsible"), even implying that Farrakhan had presented "the truth." What is at play here is the refusal of African-American leadership to take positions based on moral principle even if they violate the popular custom of refraining

from Black-on-Black public criticism. Of course, this tendency is reinforced by the efforts of Minister Farrakhan and other racial-nationalist
leaders to create a climate of intimidation in the African-American
community, but it commands widespread support within African-
American leadership and media circles.

Thus, the racial correctness of Black leadership combines with the
melting-pot correctness of the White media and the political correctness of
much of the organized Left to produce a political dialogue of maximum
opportunism and minimum principle. Moreover, racial correctness only
reinforces White stereotypes of Black people and sharply increases the
vulnerability of Black leadership to manipulation by the White melting-
pot media.

THE RACIAL ATTITUDES of the American people have been shaped by
decades of bombardment with media images of Black stereotypes without
countervailing experience with real African-Americans. Today's media
images, especially those on television, substitute new counterfeit characters
for the old Sambo ones—characters who conform to the individualist
melting-pot ideology.

The popular Black television shows, including the record-breaking
"Cosby Show," primarily present artificial images of relatively affluent
Blacks whose values duplicate those of the average middle-class White
American and reinforce the melting-pot status quo. Images of the real
Black middle class are carefully filtered out because they contradict the
racial preconceptions of most Whites.

The Hollywood film industry follows similar melting-pot "rules"
under which Black characters are stereotyped into familiar underclass or
middle-class roles, with the women often Whitened up to be more
appealing to the White male audience, or else they are portrayed as noble
victims. Characterizations smacking of true history, real life, or the need to
alter traditional melting-pot thinking and social customs are shunned as
being too controversial.

A *New York Times* article by Neal Gabler on September 2, 1990,
exposed the sophisticated racism of the melting pot when it argued that
Black exclusion from Hollywood decision making stems from "a set of

traditions, misconceptions, fears, and prevarications which have the unfortunate effect of racism without its motive." According to Gabler, the real problem is that the largest film constituency is the White middle class and that Hollywood "reflects" the "social realities" of America: "The big-budget American movies are made by young white males because they are for young white males. . . . The ideology of pluralism pulls one way and the muscle of the implacable market pulls the other [way]."

In order to combat this monopoly of the image culture by the White middle class, Black producers and artists have begun to unleash the market muscle not only of the Black middle class but also of the entire African-American community by presenting realistic Black images reflecting African-American values rather than White imitations reflecting melting-pot values. And as a result of this growing cultural assertiveness on the part of the Black middle class and the strong support it has received from the entire Black population, a degree of racial diversity has been forced upon American popular culture.

The response of the mass media has been to intensify the portrayal of the Black middle class as cloned from the White middle class, to ignore the Black working class entirely, and to perpetuate an exaggerated focus on the social pathology of the Black underclass.

◆ ABC television's David Brinkley news-analysis program revealed on April 4, 1992, that the majority of welfare recipients are White, live in the suburbs, want to work, and stay on welfare for less than two years. Yet most news-media reports present an opposite picture of Black, inner-city welfare recipients who refuse to work, have too many children, and stay on welfare permanently.

◆ An Op-Ed piece by Evan Stark in the *New York Times* of July 18, 1990, titled "The Myth of Black Violence," finally exposed the central myth purveyed by the mass media on this topic, a myth based on biased statistics. Mr. Stark points out that the primary source of Black crime data—*arrests and imprisonment*—is tainted by the thoroughly documented racial bias of the local, state, and federal criminal justice systems. According to Stark,

> a far more accurate source of information about crimes
> committed . . . is the National Crime Survey based on

victim interviews. . . . The actual proportion of blacks
and whites committing aggravated assault in 1987 was
virtually identical: 32 per thousand for blacks; 31 per
thousand for whites. Similarly, the National Youth
Survey . . . reported that "no significant race differences
were found in any of the violent or serious offense
scales."

Only two years later, in the wake of the Los Angeles riots, did the
liberal leaders of the print media admit the truth of Mr. Stark's charges. A
New York Times editorial on May 7, 1992, stated flatly:

There's nothing inherently criminal in young black men
of the 1990s any more than there was in young immigrant men of the 1890s. What is criminal is to write them
off, fearfully, blind to the knowledge that thousands can
be saved from lives of crime and for lives of dignity.

◆ The May 29, 1989, issue of the up-scale liberal magazine *New York*
carried a feature article by Joe Klein, titled "Race: The Issue," in which the
melting-pot line was recycled in the form of a question: "Why, after 25
years of equal rights—indeed, of special remedial treatment under law—
do so many [Blacks] remain outside the bounds of middle-class society?"
Here Mr. Klein ignored the undeniable fact that all immigrant ethnic
groups moved up into the middle class through the *working class* with the
aid of communitarian efforts and trade unions. Moreover, his characterization of affirmative action for the *fully qualified* as "special remedial treatment"
was inaccurate in the sense that affirmative action applies only to those who
do not require remedial treatment.

Mr. Klein then quoted numerous conservative sources to argue that
1. the Black underclass must be "middle-classified"; 2. since recent Asian
immigrants have practiced economic *integration* while maintaining "a
fierce" ethnic identification, Blacks ought to be able to do the same; 3.
Blacks must *assimilate* into the middle-class economy while abandoning
"racially divisive" affirmative action and rejecting ethnic "diversity or
pluralism" in favor of "commonality." Klein made no attempt to resolve the

obvious contradictions between two and three: although Asian immigrants could only practice *economic integration* on the foundation of strong ethnic identification *plus* affirmative action, Blacks are required to achieve *economic assimilation* while being denied *both* affirmative action *and* ethnic identification.

Thus, it is hardly surprising that the Black middle class has rejected these melting-pot rules, as Mr. Klein acknowledged in quoting an unidentified pollster to the effect that the rapid growth of the Black middle class has greatly increased the divergence between its views on issues and the views of "middle-class America." This latter formulation implies that the Black *middle class* is not fully a part of America and explains why middle-class Black leadership rejects the melting-pot ideology of a White-only American society.

The mass media carefully conceal this alienation of the Black middle class from both melting-pot ideology and American society, and, therefore, the real spokespeople for the Black middle class are mainly bypassed in favor of those unrepresentative Blacks, most of them conservatives, who undeviatingly support the melting pot. The other Black group that has media access ahead of genuine Black middle-class leaders are spokespeople for the Black underclass and racial-nationalist leaders. This bias establishes the myth of two camps in the Black community—one favoring the unrealistic goal of middle-class assimilation without ethnic identification, and the other favoring violent direct action or racial separation. The majority of Blacks, who favor ethnically based economic integration and consist of the combined ethnic-integrationist and ethnic-nationalist constituencies, are virtually ignored by the mainstream media.

Black middle-class leadership abets this concealment because it has not been able to win any significant economic benefits for the underclass which has been excluded from the same melting pot that is so beneficial to the Black middle class. Consequently, since race is what bridges the conflicting interests of the Black underclass, working class, and middle class, *all* Black leaders are compelled to seek mass political support in the name of *racial* solidarity rather than on behalf of the *ethnic* cohesion required for success in the melting pot.

The mass media trap Black middle-class leaders in their racial-solidarity line by limiting the alternatives to the unacceptable melting-pot line requiring the abandonment of racial identification, while racial nationalists attack these leaders effectively by demanding that they follow the logic of racial solidarity and leave the "White man's" melting pot. Then the mass media give maximum publicity to the racial nationalists and militants while simultaneously demanding that the ethnic integrationists and ethnic nationalists repudiate them.

The result of these contradictions, which have been created by the melting pot and exacerbated by the mass media, has been a crisis—even a paralysis—of Black leadership. The only Black remedy for this grim situation is to address its cause by acknowledging the profound contradictions which have matured within the Black community and by debating them openly. The attitude that we should not wash our dirty laundry in full view of White America is rapidly becoming economically and socially suicidal despite its political usefulness.

The only White remedy is to abandon the melting pot along with all its trappings and to replace it with a multicultural ethnic mosaic which includes both native Blacks and WASPs as ethnic groups. But change of this magnitude can be achieved only by a decisive majority within White America, and its pursuit cannot count on rallying the support of the Black middle class or of any other major segment of Black America until such a majority is a reasonable possibility. After fighting for generations to gain entry to the melting pot so as to benefit from its middle-class entitlements, African-Americans could hardly be expected to welcome its demise.

This background indicates that the efforts of the mass media to racialize ethnic, economic, and political issues have succeeded to the extent that the beleaguered Black middle-class leadership and most of the Black media which it controls have lapsed into a racial correctness which distorts reality in a way that protects Black middle-class interests within the Black community while simultaneously preserving those interests inside the melting pot. Any attempt to expose the contradictions inherent in such a posture is usually ignored by the Black media and the White media alike. Here racial correctness meets melting-pot correctness. Examples of this abound.

Prof. Anita Hill, the Black lawyer who accused Judge Clarence Thomas of sexual harassment during the Senate hearings on his confirmation as the second Black man nominated to the United States Supreme Court, has become an admired symbol for millions of American women of all races. Her stand was responsible for a powerful surge of both Black and White women into the political arena on a scale that has altered the political arithmetic to the detriment of conservatives. On the other hand, Justice Thomas has voted against Black interests on every occasion since his confirmation and has lost his credibility among Blacks and Whites alike. But the Black middle-class leaders who supported Judge Thomas on the ground of racial solidarity and trivialized the issue of sexual harassment have yet to be held accountable by the Black or White media.

During the 1992 Democratic presidential primary campaign, a strong majority of participating Black voters backed Arkansas governor Bill Clinton, while a minority coalition of militants and racial nationalists campaigned for the rejection of both major parties in favor of supporting an independent Black candidate. But just before the Democratic convention in New York City, a large delegation of Black Democratic luminaries, accompanied by their liberal White allies, attended a Jesse Jackson tribute sponsored by this opposition minority at Harlem's Apollo Theater where they listened respectfully to varied denunciations of Bill Clinton and the Democratic party.

Not one of these leaders had the political courage to defend either the party or its nominee. They simply delivered neutral remarks about Black uplift and the need to vote, and then went to the Democratic party convention to endorse the ticket of Bill Clinton and Al Gore with varying degrees of enthusiasm.

This behavior of Black and White liberals demonstrates that they are hostage to racially correct politics. By contrast, the Black and White Democratic *progressives,* led by then-Governor Clinton, pointedly failed to come to the Apollo meeting despite the fact that they were conspicuously invited, one might even say summoned, to attend. The progressive message was clear: "We are not liberals, so we are not hostage to racial correctness."

On June 13, 1992, the presumptive Democratic presidential nominee

Bill Clinton chose to criticize some racially inflammatory remarks by Black rap singer Sister Souljah. Presented at a meeting of Rev. Jesse Jackson's Rainbow Coalition, Clinton's comments incurred the public wrath of many Black leaders across the nation on the questionable ground that he had embarrassed Rev. Jackson in order to appeal to conservative Whites. But it seems to me that their outrage stemmed from the fact that, as a White man speaking at a Black event, Clinton had violated the unwritten Black rule forbidding public criticism of Blacks. It also appears that Clinton was, in a calculated way, urging Blacks to abandon this rule by appealing to them over the heads of their leaders.

The Black media accepted Black criticism of Clinton at face value, along with Sister Souljah's claim that she had been misquoted, and provided a platform for a one-sided barrage directed against the Democratic party and its Black supporters by racial-nationalist, ethnic-nationalist, and militant spokespersons. Black dissenters from this line were attacked for racial disloyalty, and even some ethnic integrationists joined in the attack on Clinton.

Because reality was quite different from the picture presented by the Black media, Rev. Jackson and other Black Democrats who had been publicly critical of Governor Clinton quickly backed off from the confrontation when Clinton stood his ground, leaving the rest of the critics politically isolated. But much of the Black media continued on a biased course and even resorted to direct censorship. I had the unusual experience of being invited to provide commentary on the Democratic convention on a popular Black radio station, only to be taken off the air suddenly after what the producer described as two highly successful broadcasts. Apparently too successful, he said in embarrassment; top management had ordered the immediate restoration of better balance to the program—that is, a return to the standard racially correct line.

The reason for such sensitivity on the part of the Black media resides in three aspects of the Sister Souljah controversy which were underplayed or suppressed by *both* the White mass media *and* the Black media.

First, vehement denials by Sister Souljah and attempts by the Black media to sow confusion could not alter the impression that Souljah's remarks to a *Washington Post* interviewer were, even if considered in the broader context of an extensive interview, still inflammatory and irresponsible in their delivery:

> *Washington Post:* But even the people themselves who were perpetrating that violence [i.e., gang members during the Los Angeles riots], did they think it was wise? Was that wise, reasoned action?
>
> *Souljah:* Yeah, it was wise. I mean, if black people kill black people every day, why not have a week and kill white people? You understand what I'm saying? In other words, white people, this government, and that mayor were well aware of the fact that black people were dying every day in Los Angeles under gang violence. So if you're a gang member and you would normally be killing somebody, why not kill a white person? Do you think that somebody thinks that white people are better, or above and beyond dying, when they would kill their own kind?

It is clear from the above that Ms. Souljah, in response to the question: "Was that wise . . . ?" expressed her own opinion that the violence by the gang members was wise ("Yeah, it was wise"). Moreover, Souljah did not put the idea of killing White people in the mouths of the gang members but chose to express the idea herself without explicitly disavowing it.

Second, the context of Clinton's criticism of Sister Souljah at the Rainbow Coalition meeting shows that his remarks were addressed to a broad interracial constituency of liberals and progressives, rather than to White conservatives. He praised Jesse Jackson's Rebuild America economic program and said that he respected the Rainbow Coalition's determination to "come together across racial lines." Only then did he add the comment that Sister Souljah's remarks about Black people killing White people because Black people kill each other daily ran counter to racial reconciliation.

Governor Clinton called the remark a mistake similar to his decision to play golf at a country club with no Black members, adding: "We can't get anywhere in this country pointing the finger at one another across racial lines. If we do that, we're dead." His approach was clearly tailored to resonate with a *multiracial constituency* (coming together across racial lines) that rejects racial politics ("pointing the finger at one another across racial lines"). And his comparison of Sister Souljah's "mistake" with his golfing at an all-White country club could hardly have been addressed to White conservatives.

Third, and most important, Governor Clinton was sending clear messages to the liberal wing of the Democratic party and to the entire Black community. To White liberals he was saying that he was not hostage to racial correctness and would criticize *them* if they continued to appease it. To the Black community he offered a choice between racial politics and progressive, multiculturalist politics while simultaneously challenging Black leaders to oppose racial nationalists publicly. Clinton succeeded in winning the overwhelming support of both White liberal voters and Black voters, since both of these constituencies were tired of racial politics and of rhetoric like Sister Souljah's.

However, since an end to racial politics would undermine the melting pot, the mass media were happy to play off Sister Souljah and her racially correct backers against Clinton with banner front-page headlines such as, "SISTER SOULJAH: DON'T TRY TO MAKE ME WILLIE HORTON" (*New York Newsday*, June 17, 1992).

Governor Clinton calculated that much of the Black political leadership had lost touch with the true interests and feelings of Black voters, so he refused to back down. The September 1992 New York state Democratic primary proved him right: Rev. Al Sharpton, a militant Black outsider candidate with virtually no campaign money, ran third by focusing on ethnic-integrationist issues, rather than on racial or ethnic nationalism, in a campaign against three well-known, heavily financed, and widely endorsed White establishment candidates. But the most significant result was that Rev. Sharpton received 67 percent of the Black vote despite the fact that not a single Black elected official and virtually no members of the Black establishment had endorsed him.

THE MASS MEDIA USE the individualistic precepts of melting-pot ideology to construct an endless variety of role models that reinforce melting-pot cultural values. The values inculcated by the personifications of these role models are ideological rather than moral: *success* through individual effort, loyalty to the *American state,* and belief in the *Protestant* religious ethic are established as the litmus tests for a good American, rather than *human fulfillment* through a balance of individual and community needs, loyalty to *one's own convictions,* and practice of the *ecumenical* principle of love thy neighbor.

The idea of a role model is essentially value-free, since its dictionary definition is someone whose conduct in a specific role is copied by others. Melting-pot role models, from the founding fathers to today's athletes and entertainers, are presented as trivialized success icons who serve as advertisements for American individualism, but their personal values are buried under an exclusive emphasis on achievements and on attitudes that conform to melting-pot ideals.

Since the mass media insist that in America limitless opportunity is open to all, role models have tended to decrease, rather than to increase, the self-esteem of the underclass. True heroes and heroines, on the other hand, teach universal values like courage, nobility, self-sacrifice, and the importance of personal achievements that contribute to the common good and not merely to one's personal advancement. They inspire others to adopt similar values and to set their own positive goals.

This is why melting-pot ideology suppresses heroic stories, especially those of the so-called minorities—heroism evokes independent thinking and common action, both of which contradict the melting-pot ideal of uniform thinking and individual action. The role models that the mass media of today's melting pot have crafted for non-Whites and White women serve as new stereotypes having middle-class WASP values—stereotypes that are all the more credible because they contradict the previous crude racist and sexist stereotypes that the same mass media institutionalized for generations.

The Black middle class, thriving in the melting pot, has absorbed the obsession with role models while losing touch with the values nurtured by the rich cultural inheritance from the time of slavery. The notion that substitution of Black role models for White ones can provide an adequate set of cultural values has permeated the thinking of the Black middle class to an alarming extent and underlies its current lack of vision, its failure to lead the Black community adequately, and its lack of accountability to the great majority of African-Americans. A sure sign of the moral debilitation which has overtaken the Black middle class is its failure to reject racial correctness in favor of moral leadership, and its refusal to take moral responsibility for Black behavior.

The cure for this malaise lies close at hand in the native-Black value system which was tempered in the suffering of slavery and enriched by the unconquerable spirit, wise courage, and perceptive vision of the many generations of Black working people who have served as the able and dedicated guardians of our native-Black culture. It is from the value system of this culture that the Black middle class must draw its power.

The individuals, some of them just successful and some of them great, who serve as past and present role models are inevitably *originals* who cannot be imitated. Real achievement and greatness can come only from within—from a positive self-image. Role models can serve as inspirational examples, but values are the tools with which any ordinary person can succeed and become great. So it is worthwhile to review the essential values of native-Black culture, values that my father, as the son of a slave, passed on to me, not only by example but as part of my rite of passage to manhood.

First: Strive for excellence; try to be the best that you can possibly be. Aim for perfection instead of merely trying to "beat" others.

Second: Success without advancing the interests of our people as a whole, without helping those who have fallen behind, is worthless.

Third: The human race is one family with diverse but equal members having different cultures, and a deeper understanding of one's own culture will inevitably lead to a better understanding of other cultures.

Fourth: Personal growth is the mother of greatness, but its price is pain and perseverance.

Fifth: Temper strength and power with gentleness and compassion; balance courage with wisdom.

Sixth: Don't go along to get along. Be willing to sacrifice to do what you know is right.

These values are universal values and not merely values for Black people. They illuminate the road of popular, progressive democracy which leads to an ethnic mosaic and a multicultural society, whereas melting-pot liberal democracy leads to the dead-end conflict between ethnic and racial nationalisms. They offer the ultimate transition from ethnic integration to a universal cultural humanism, while the melting pot offers the continued fragmentation of society by ethnicity, race, gender, and class. They form a part of our hard-earned national birthright, and those who learn them will serve themselves and our country well.

At a time when so many Americans look back with nostalgia or look forward having forgotten the past, we must, together, face our future with clear vision and firm knowledge of our history. Then, remembering that only the crucible of struggle will endow us with the power to reach our goal, we shall march with resolute step to secure a true government "of the people, by the people, and for the people." And then we shall be able to cry out as one people: "Great God Almighty, *America* is free at last."

10

THE BIRTH
OF A NEW
AMERICAN CULTURE

T oday's fracturing melting pot was designed to maintain a monocultural America which tolerates only *individual* cultural diversity devoid of *group* ethnic identification, whereas the mosaic alternative encourages the assertion of *group* ethnic identity. The melting pot pits ethnic groups against racial groups in a splintered society, whereas the multiculturalist mosaic offers the common cultural ground of an ethnic parity capable of starting the transformation from a *single* culture dominated by one ethnic group to a *diverse* culture shared equally by all ethnic groups. In the 1990s, America's traditional melting-pot motto, "out of many—one," is under challenge from the mosaic credo which could be described roughly by the motto: "out of many—a team."

The melting pot, burdened by its ethnic and racial biases, is in deep crisis as it tries desperately to maintain the status quo in the face of both an internal shift of power from White men to White women and non-Whites and external pressure from progressive Anglo-Saxons to end its exclusion of the Black underclass. In addition, the dominant Anglo-Saxons, whose

WASP elite used the melting pot so successfully to perpetuate its control of American society, are beginning to rebel against the melting-pot system because of its failure to address any of the vital problems besetting our country.

American culture is degenerating within the constraints of individualist melting-pot ideology; the growing barrenness of the cultural landscape is causing a progressive loss of freedom; and the continual narrowing of our cultural heritage is jeopardizing America's future. The greatest American myth is the illusion that freedom is automatically guaranteed by radical individualism, liberal democracy, and free enterprise.

Evidence of a national malaise is all around us. A federal government which spends hundreds of billions of dollars on the defense budget and on bailing out failed savings and loan associations cannot find a way to assist the tens of millions of American children who are living in poverty. The mass media are obsessed with the private excesses of the rich and powerful while they neglect or trivialize burning social issues. The highest levels of national authority are willing to risk war and to subvert the foundations of democratic government and rational foreign policy in pursuit of sole-superpower status.

Yet the influence of the melting pot remains profound, since it has shaped the social stratification of America through the opportunities it provided those who entered it and denied those who were excluded from it. The advantages it offers today's new entrants from the previously excluded groups are a powerful attraction which has temporarily moderated overt opposition to the melting pot. Moreover, President Bush showed both sophistication and flexibility in the three years from January 1989 to January 1992 by further opening the melting pot to non-Whites of immigrant descent and to the native-Black middle class *as groups,* thereby shifting attention from their exclusion to their new opportunities.

However, the massive entry of non-Whites into the melting pot undermined one of its main reasons for existence, since White males lost many of their previously automatic advantages over non-Whites. A further weakening of the melting-pot system's power resulted from its failure to suppress the group identifications of many Americans, while many new immigrants chose to exploit the advantages of the melting pot without melting. At the same time, the assertion of group cultural identity by

African-Americans and their search for ancestral cultural roots led many apparently melted Whites to reclaim their own ethnic roots.

This process of melting-pot disintegration within a degenerating American culture is the source of the current multiculturalism debate in which a traditional cultural elite is being challenged by both the culturally subordinated minorities and disaffected members of the so-called majority. But the decisive struggle is a long-term one between a pro-melting-pot alliance of conservative Anglo-Saxons and ethnic Whites and a loose coalition of progressive Anglo-Saxons and ethnic Whites which has challenged the conservative-liberal cultural consensus on which the melting pot rests. In the 1990s, the issue of our civic culture and its values has surpassed the ethnicity-versus-race division in national importance as the conflicts generated by the divisions of culture, gender, and class begin to overtake ethnic and racial strife.

The civic culture of American liberal democracy arose from John Locke's seventeenth-century "civil society" governed according to a "civic religion" in which the individual members accepted by that society were divinely endowed with universal "natural" rights and were equal under the law. American liberal democracy filtered this basic idea through the melting pot in order to restrict the membership in this civil society to the Anglo-Saxon ethnic group and those other White ethnic groups chosen by the WASP elite. The "civic religion" was used to sanctify the melting-pot system.

As we enter the twenty-first century, the inherent tension between the universalist principles of Locke's civil society and the ethnocentrism of the melting-pot culture has generated the present cultural crisis in American society. The partial ethnic inclusion forced upon the melting pot by the cultural revolutions of the 1960s and 1970s survived the conservative backlash of the 1980s to help empower the *ethnic mosaic* as an alternative to permanent melting-pot hostilities between ethnic and racial groups.

THE COVER OF THE JULY 8, 1991, issue of *Time* magazine highlighted the themes: "Who Are We?" and "Whose America?" Significantly, the opening section of the story sounds the alarm about the mounting resistance to the individualist civil society and the growing manifestation of ethnic, gender, and class identification: "The customs, beliefs and principles that have unified the u.s., however imperfectly, for over two centuries are being challenged with a ferocity not seen since the Civil War." Here the alternative that the emerging cultural mosaic poses to the homogenizing melting pot is interpreted as a challenge to the traditional American civic culture ("customs, beliefs, and principles") comparable in magnitude to the Civil War.

Today's intense clash between individual liberties and civil rights, between local sovereignty and federal authority, is indeed a continuation of the struggle between the Confederacy's defense of states' rights and the Union's exercise of federal power. Moreover, the current tension between the monoculturalism of the melting pot and the multiculturalism of the mosaic reflects the tension between Thomas Jefferson's tilt toward *individual* rights and *liberties* and Abraham Lincoln's unyielding commitment to *civil* rights and individual *freedoms*.

The Thirteenth and Fourteenth Amendments to the Constitution, which resulted from the unconditional victory of the Union in the Civil War, guaranteed the rights of *both* former slaves *and* immigrants, thereby permanently establishing the rights of both racial and ethnic *groups*. The melting pot has always tried to circumvent these rights on behalf of the White male tradition expressed most assertively by the Confederacy, whereas the mosaic upholds them. President Lincoln, who made full use of his Constitutional right to exercise extraordinary presidential war powers, freed the slaves by decree, and then laid the philosophical basis for a new civil society in his Gettysburg Address of November 19, 1863.

Lincoln linked "a new nation *conceived in liberty* and dedicated to the proposition that all men are created equal" with "a new *birth of freedom*" ushered in for that nation by the Civil War. His Union "government of the people, by the people, for the people" opposed the Confederate government of the states, by the states, for the individual. This is why Lincoln called the war the Civil War, meaning a people's war, whereas the Confederate leaders called it the War between the States.

After the Civil War, the wasp elite used the melting pot to harness the economic resources of a unified nation. According to historian Howard Zinn in *A People's History of the United States,* the leaders of this elite created the melting-pot society which launched "the greatest march of economic growth in human history." They accomplished it

> with the aid of, and at the expense of, black labor, white labor, Chinese labor, European immigrant labor, female labor, rewarding them differently by race, sex, national origin, and social class, in such a way as to create separate levels of oppression—a skillful terracing to stabilize the pyramid of wealth.

Thus, the WASP elite's "pyramid of wealth" rested on the ethnic, racial, gender, and class divisions imposed by the melting pot and anchored by an institutionalized conflict between ethnic and racial groups. Retired journalist Joseph Alsop, who is descended from this elite which he calls the "WASP ascendancy," recalled how President Franklin D. Roosevelt defeated the "ascendancy" and provided the opening for the labor movement to win *group* economic rights during the 1930s and 1940s (*New York Review of Books*, November 9, 1989). In his view, Roosevelt's victory made possible the winning of the economic, political, and social rights that have so drastically weakened the melting-pot civil society over the past sixty years—rights that Alsop feels are America's greatest achievement: "If the ascendancy had hung on to anything like its old leverage, I cannot imagine this country achieving . . . its greatest . . . feat in the twentieth century."

Whereas President Franklin D. Roosevelt undermined the economic foundations of the melting-pot culture without significantly curbing its ability to use ethnicity against race, President John F. Kennedy opened the way for the color-blind civil rights legislation of the 1960s which terminated the melting-pot superiority of ethnicity over race in *law* but not yet in the color-prejudiced *civil society*. It remained for the subsequent cultural revolutions and the mosaic movement of today to begin the enforcement of *equal opportunity* in our society, which explains the insistence of conservatives that civil society is in the protected *private* realm rather than in the public realm where it is subject to legislation.

In this sense one could paraphrase President Lincoln by saying that the civil rights movement of the 1960s brought forth a new civil society conceived in liberty, so that our culture shall have a new birth of freedom.

The civil rights *laws,* interpreted by a liberal Supreme Court, served as midwife to the multiculturalist movement of the 1990s and proved to be decisive in promoting the decay of the melting pot. The civil rights *movement* forced African-American culture into the melting-pot mainstream by compelling American society to deal with African-Americans as a *group,* rather than merely as individuals.

Symbolism and personalities likewise contributed heavily to the weakening of the melting pot during the 1960s. The core melting-pot principle of encouraging the hostility of White ethnic groups toward non-White racial groups was severely impaired by the visible empathy and collaboration between President John F. Kennedy, an Irish Catholic who overcame strong anti-Catholic bigotry during his presidential campaign, and Rev. Martin Luther King, Jr., the charismatic and widely respected leader of the Black crusade for equal rights. Later, the widespread mood of tragedy and trauma surrounding the successive assassinations of President Kennedy, Malcolm X, Rev. King, and Senator Robert Kennedy tended to bridge the ethnicity-race divide despite the controversy associated with each of these victims of hate.

But John F. Kennedy's greatest contributions to the fight against melting-pot ideology resided in the powerful statements on civil rights that he made from the presidential bully-pulpit. On the critical day in the spring of 1963 when Alabama governor George Wallace tried to prevent two Black students from entering the University of Alabama, President Kennedy addressed a national television audience in words that signaled his determination to uproot the foundations of the melting-pot caste system:

> This nation was founded . . . on the principle that all men are created equal and that the rights of every man are diminished when the rights of one man are threatened.
> . . . One hundred years of delay have passed since President Lincoln freed the slaves, yet their heirs, their grandsons, are not fully free. They are not yet freed from the bonds of injustice. They are not yet freed from social and economic oppression.
> . . . Are we to say to the world, and much more

importantly, to each other that this is a land of the free except for the Negroes; that we have no second-class citizens except Negroes; that we have no class or caste system, no ghettos, no master race except with respect to Negroes?

What is unusual in this excerpt is its flat denunciation of the racial, social, and economic oppression perpetuated by the class and caste stratification in the melting pot, as well as its association of melting-pot ethnocentrism with the Nazi ghettos and master race. Strong stuff for 1963, yet President Kennedy did not stop there; he warned directly of civil strife and indirectly of federal intervention:

We are confronted primarily with a moral issue. It is as old as the Scriptures and is as clear as the American Constitution. The heart of the question is whether all Americans are to be afforded equal rights *and equal opportunities*. . . .

Now the time has come for this *nation* to fulfill its promise. . . .

. . . We face therefore a moral crisis as a country and as a people. *It cannot be met by repressive police action. It cannot be left to increased demonstrations in the streets. It cannot be quieted by token moves or talk.* It is a time to act in the Congress, in your state and local legislative body and, above all, in all of our daily lives. . . . In too many communities, in too many parts of the country, wrongs are inflicted on Negro citizens as there are no remedies at law. *Unless the Congress acts, their only remedy is in the street* [EMPHASIS MINE].

Three things stand out in this passage:

1. The "Scriptures" and the "American Constitution" are invoked in support of the proposition that all Americans are entitled to *equal opportunity*, and not just equal rights.

2. The imperative of "a moral issue" is backed by the pledge that *the*

nation must fulfill its promise, implying that the *military force* of the federal government will be used if necessary.

3. Unconditional surrender of the South on the civil rights issue is being demanded. If the "moral crisis" cannot be met by "police repression" and cannot be left to "demonstrations in the streets," while at the same time concessions and negotiations are precluded by eliminating the admissibility of "token moves or talk," the only alternatives remaining are the granting of full Constitutional rights or military occupation. And in case anyone misses that point, President Kennedy adds that since Blacks have no "remedies at law," "their only remedy is in the street," implying that federal troops will guarantee Blacks' right to demonstrate in the streets.

One could arguably claim that this speech of Kennedy's was the toughest speech on a domestic issue by any president since Abraham Lincoln's speeches during the Civil War.

THE TWELVE REAGAN-BUSH YEARS represented an attempt to nullify the Kennedy-Johnson legacy but turned out to be the last gasp of the WASP male elite in defense of its melting pot. Ronald Reagan's presidency rested upon a cultural symbolism that emanated from an ethnicity and religious affiliation that were ideally suited to attract disaffected WASP and ethnic-White males in the 1980s: English, Scottish, and Irish ancestry, combined with membership in the Episcopalian Church that has traditionally been the preferred denomination of the WASP elite.

President Reagan's main priority was to replace the more equitable society which resulted from enforcement of the Kennedy-Johnson civil rights laws with a revival of the individualist and ethnocentric civil society of the 1920s melting-pot heyday of the WASP ascendancy. Reagan achieved part of his purpose by undermining the public sector of the national economy with massive tax cuts for the upper income levels. The result was a crushing federal deficit that crippled federal programs and led to a massive increase in the number of poor, but the new civil society never did emerge. Instead, the people's society deteriorated, primarily because of the Reagan administration's irresponsible, ideologically driven fiscal policies.

David Stockman, President Reagan's budget director at the time of the fateful tax cuts during Reagan's first term, resigned from the Cabinet and wrote a book in 1986 titled *The Triumph of Politics*. There he pinned the blame for the present paralyzing federal deficit squarely on the shoulders of Ronald Reagan and the Republican conservatives:

> Having enacted a generous tax cut for all Americans, . . . we couldn't win support for the spending cuts needed to balance the equation. . . . Reagan had one real option: to retreat and give back part of the huge tax cut we couldn't afford. But he wouldn't. Ronald Reagan chose not to be a leader but a politician.

So it turns out that conservative Republicans, and not "tax and spend" Democrats, created the deficit monster.

Fortunately, however, a majority of the American people rejected the Reagan administration's attempts to launch a cultural counterrevolution, and many members of the WASP elite, especially women, began to work actively against the trend toward cultural uniformity. For example, the WASP-led feminist movement, despite the fierce attacks leveled against it, expanded its horizons to include broad social issues. Feminist historian Elizabeth Fox-Genovese tapped this tradition when she wrote in *Feminism without Illusions*:

> When feminism fails to defend social and economic changes that can ensure decent lives for all people, the rights of women collapse into privilege for the few and exploitation for the many.

The women of the WASP elite played a decisive role in defense of feminism's responsibility to remain committed to social transformation, and in the process they firmly resisted the male-centered individualism foisted upon America during three conservative Republican administrations.

In Joseph Alsop's memoir about the WASP elite ("The Wasp Ascendancy," *New York Review of Books*, November 9, 1989), he described a culture in which women were not expected to have careers but could wield formidable political clout because of their great wealth. Alsop told how the 1933 repeal of the Eighteenth Amendment to the Constitution prohibiting intoxicating beverages was due largely to the efforts of "the mobilized womanhood of the WASP ascendancy." Today, the struggles of WASP working-class and middle-class women for women's rights have quietly been joined by their enormously wealthy sisters from the WASP elite.

Consequently, today's conflict within the top level of WASP society—the cultural advance of the mosaic against the melting pot—is a challenge spearheaded by all classes of WASP women which has fragmented the WASP culture and elevated the mosaic to the status of a viable cultural alternative.

Paralleling this development, most women belonging to ethnic and racial minorities, including some native-Black women belonging to the underclass, have an enhanced mobility within the melting pot because the gender category is distinct from the ethnic-minority and racial-minority categories and affords minority women a second affirmative-action credential. As a result, women of many different backgrounds have acquired new skills in the melting pot and are encountering strong male resistance to their professional advancement.

At the same time, all women continue to suffer from an inferior cultural status. Women in the workplace are encouraged to be individuals in their own image and to embrace the ideology of radical individualism, but their efforts to claim *group rights* in order to counter the discrimination they experience are rejected. Whenever women express their own cultural values and their own individualism, the melting-pot establishment "just doesn't get it."

This combination of rising empowerment and inferior status fuels the anger and militancy of many women in their struggles against the unfairness of the same melting pot that has ended their exclusion. WASP women and ethnic-White women have become an especially serious threat to the status quo inside the melting pot because of their large combined numerical weight. If they win their just demands for equal opportunity for *all* women, the male advantage which serves as the foundation of the melting pot would vanish. Similarly, the ethnic advantage and the ethnicity-race conflict which are the core of the melting-pot system would be undermined fatally by the equal status of women from all ethnic and racial groups.

Precisely because American feminism has developed primarily as a

White, predominantly Anglo-Saxon, middle-class movement, rather than as a coalition of women across racial, ethnic, and class divisions, individual rights have always been the movement's primary goal. Consequently, the inevitable incompatibility between female individualism and the discriminatory individualism of the melting pot has led the most perceptive feminist writers to reject the individualist foundation of melting-pot ideology.

In her book *Feminism without Illusions,* Professor Fox-Genovese presented one such challenge by accusing "modern Western society" of unleashing "the specter of a radical individualism that overrides the claims of society itself." However, I believe she was on questionable ground when she concluded that the cure for radical individualism is the insistence that individual rights must "derive from society." This would permit society to repress the individual.

According to Professor Fox-Genovese,

> Feminism, as the daughter of individualism, carries the potential of bringing individualism back to its social moorings by insisting that the rights of individuals derive from society rather than from their innate nature.

However, if individual rights are not "innate," they can, theoretically, be denied either by government or by society. And this is exactly what happened to Native Americans, to African-Americans, and, in a lesser degree, to other American minorities.

Historically, the ideology of radical individualism used the notion of divinely bestowed natural individual *liberties* to establish a civil society of Anglo-Saxon male property-owning individuals that was upheld by a civic religion and stood above the people's society consisting of all U.S. citizens. These liberties (liberties of individuals *to do things*) overrode the people's society's claim to individual *rights* (freedoms *from things done to* individuals).

To correct this injustice, individual rights (freedoms *from*) must be seen as innate and natural as human rights, whereas individual liberties (liberties *to*) must derive from society. This stands in opposition to the traditional American idea that liberties are innate and rights (i.e., freedoms) are derived from society. Thus, the melting-pot motto "life, *liberty,* and the pursuit of happiness" must be replaced by the mosaic motto "life, *freedom,* and the pursuit of happiness."

Professor Fox-Genovese did not make this distinction between liberty and freedom, between liberties and rights. And by denying the innate nature of individual *rights,* she left the door open to society's domination of the individual. Nevertheless, I think her basic idea that feminism has the capacity to merge the elitist civil society of preferred individuals with the people's society is sound.

In social practice, such a merger would mean joining the dominant WASP society with both the melting-pot society and the underclass society which is still excluded from the melting pot. The result would inevitably be the mosaic society. The year 1992—the year of the woman—marked the beginning of this feminist crusade. The *individual liberty* of male middle-class WASPs is to be superseded by universal *human freedom;* divine *natural law,* protecting individual liberty, is to be transferred to the protection of individual freedom; and nondivine *legislative law,* protecting freedom, is to be transferred to the protection of individual liberty.

The journey along this road began, in my opinion, with Bill Clinton's election to the presidency, and the harbingers of profound cultural change surfaced in his Cabinet choices, in his culturally diverse inauguration pageantry, and in his clear signals that he will use the awesome power of the presidency to its fullest extent in the quest to expand the civil rights of the American people.

SUPPRESSION OF HUMAN FREEDOM in the name of individual liberty is the hallmark of melting-pot individualism and pervades American economic life. Conservative demands that government stay out of the way of private business reflect the individualist belief that civil society is part of the private realm rather than a public responsibility, and Republican efforts to dismantle the public sector of the national economy and to deregulate the private sector represent the political expressions of this ideology.

By contrast, the communitarian logic of the universalist mosaic requires a judicious match between human freedom and individual liberty, which is reflected in a mutual reinforcement of the public and private economies and is accompanied by a careful balance between economic profit and human needs. Current political conflicts over the American economy—especially over the basic issues of public-versus-private investment and tax policy—are driven by the tension between the individualist and communitarian ideologies expressed in the melting pot and mosaic metaphors.

Today's American conservatives attempt to sanctify their profit-is-everything principle by invoking the traditional individualist civic religion that governs civil society. However, many religious leaders here and abroad have rejected this view. A significant example surfaced in a May 2, 1991, encyclical issued by Pope John Paul II which spoke directly to the concept of property as a natural right:

> In *Rerum Novarum,* Leo VIII strongly affirmed the natural character of the right to private property.... The Church teaches that the possession of material goods is not an absolute right, and that its limits are inscribed in its very nature as a human right....
>
> ... Profit is a regulator of the life of a business, but it is not the only one; other human and moral factors must also be considered.

In Pope Paul's view as I interpret it, the right to property is not an absolute right but a *human,* universal right, and as such it is a *freedom* rather than a liberty. As Pope Paul puts it, "its very nature as a human *right*" (i.e., a freedom *from*) imposes limitations on it. It appears to me that this approach implies that 1. nobody should be propertyless, since owning property is a human right; 2. natural rights are by nature limited as freedoms *from;* and 3. since natural rights are limited, *liberties to,* which are individually *not* limited, should *not* be treated as natural or divine *rights.*

It is worth noting that this viewpoint contradicts a central tenet of the Declaration of Independence—the idea that *liberty* is a natural, divine *right.* Moreover, another outlook similar to Pope Paul's underlies the economic-fairness rallying cry of the successful progressive challenge to the neoliberal Democratic leadership in the 1992 presidential campaign.

As a result, Democrats united around the slogan of economic fairness against the Republicans who united behind the idea of unlimited profit;

thus, on the main economic issues the partisan political division became clear. But on the key issue of culture—the melting pot versus the mosaic— the politicians of both main political parties reflected the divisions within their constituencies and did not unite along party lines.

Right-wing Republicans favored a return to the traditional melting pot with its outright exclusion of non-Whites and women. Moderate and liberal Republicans supported retention of today's melting pot which includes all immigrants without regard to ethnicity or race, as well as those native Blacks who can meet the middle-class family-values requirement.

Conservative and neoliberal Democrats joined moderate and liberal Republicans in support of today's melting pot. Traditional liberal Democrats, like Senators Ted Kennedy of Massachusetts and Tom Harkin of Iowa, favored a universal melting pot open to everyone, including the underclass, but they added the requirement that Blacks shed their racial identification without being accorded ethnic equality.

Progressive Democrats (Rev. Jesse Jackson and Governor Bill Clinton, for example), whose positions were overwhelmingly adopted by the 1992 Democratic National Convention, implicitly backed a mosaic of ethnic, racial, and social groups with equal cultural status in order to heal the ethnicity-race, male-female, straight-gay, and middle class-underclass rifts in our society. The last, middle class-underclass division was sidestepped by the convention, and this provoked spirited but futile resistance from some traditional liberals and a small but vocal minority of the Black delegates who felt that the issue of Black exclusion from the melting pot had been sidetracked.

These dissidents' failure to win significant support from the convention despite the validity of their complaint was due to the hard political reality of 1992: the White middle class which would determine the outcome of the presidential election was determined to keep the melting pot as a buffer against the Black underclass, and a sitting Democratic president was far more likely to overcome that determination than a mere Democratic candidate. The resistance and anger of some Black leaders, including Rev. Jackson, were aimed at retaining credibility with a Black underclass that perceived a betrayal of its interests by the Democratic leadership.

By contrast, the Republican platform appealed to the traditional melting-pot constituencies consisting of WASPs and White ethnic groups.

First, the unsettling ethnicity-race conflict was skillfully covered up by combining an exclusive focus on immigrants with the pretense that all ethnic and racial groups were treated equally and the myth that all groups are now joined in a common culture. At the same time, the Republican leadership appealed to the Black middle class on ethnic grounds by offering it ethnic status:

> Our Nation of *immigrants* continues to welcome those seeking a better life. This reflects our past, when some newcomers fled intolerance; some sought prosperity; *some came as slaves.* All suffered and sacrificed but hoped their children would have a better life. All searched for a shared vision—and found one in America. Today we are stronger for our diversity [EMPHASIS MINE].

Here the bizarre classification of *slaves* as immigrants accepts the ethnic parity of native Blacks with all other immigrant groups and legitimizes the name African-American on the basis of immigrant status. By appealing to the *ethnic* and class interests of the African-American middle class against the *racial* and class interests of the Black underclass, Republican moderates hoped to undermine the racially based political unity of Black voters.

However, the Republican misrepresentations of history—the reference to slaves as immigrants; the implication that all immigrants, regardless of ethnicity, race, or religion, received equal treatment; the omission of the Native-American *nations* whom our nation has at various times subjected to government policies titled "extermination," "Indian removal," and "tribal termination"—minimized the effectiveness of the offer within the African-American community.

Elsewhere in the Republican platform one finds a clear espousal of radical individualism which extols America's traditional civic religion:

> We believe our *laws* should reflect what makes our Nation prosperous and wholesome: faith in God, hard work, service to others, and limited government. . . .

> ... The protection of individual rights is the founda-
> tion for opportunity and security. . . . We believe the
> unborn child has a fundamental individual right to life.
> . . . We . . . support a human life amendment to the
> Constitution, and we endorse legislation to make clear
> that the Fourteenth Amendment's protections apply to
> unborn children [EMPHASIS MINE].

The demand for *laws* to reflect "faith in God" is in clear contradiction to the principle of separation of church and state, since the Constitution and the Bill of Rights guarantee the right *not* to have "faith in God." In addition, it is clear that the Republican platform demands a double legal barrier to *all* abortions: a "human life" Constitutional amendment and legislation to apply the protections of the Fourteenth Amendment to unborn children.

The platform of the Democratic party used anti-individualist cultural code words to signal a progressive commitment to the mosaic cultural alternative while omitting the code words that are essential to the preservation of melting-pot ideology. It coupled *individual responsibility* with *restoring community,* instead of stressing the centrality of individual rights. Emphasis was placed on *civil rights for groups,* on *equal rights for individuals,* and on a woman's right to choose abortion, in contrast with the Republicans' exclusive emphasis on *individual rights* and on the right to life of an unborn child. In addition, the strong need for the federal government to guarantee equal opportunity was implied, and an economic agenda incorporating the priorities of working-class families was presented. Moreover, these coded messages were sent in the context of rejecting the ethnicity-race and gender conflicts inherent in the melting pot and countering the individualism of Republican leaders who elevate private interests above public responsibilities:

> Republican leaders have urged Americans to turn in-
> ward, to pursue private interests without regard to public
> responsibilities. By playing racial, ethnic and gender-
> based politics, they have divided us against each other. . . .
> . . . We take special pride in our country's emergence

> as the world's largest and most successful *multiethnic,*
> *multiracial republic* [EMPHASIS MINE].

Note the difference between the Democratic "multiethnic, multiracial republic" (the mosaic), and the Republican "nation of immigrants" (the melting pot).

Yet the Democratic-versus-Republican cultural battle that pitted the incipient mosaic against the decaying melting pot, and the old individualism against the new communitarianism, did not completely dominate cultural politics during the 1992 presidential campaign. A new cultural phenomenon masked as a political movement swept across the White middle-class suburban enclaves of America. Millions of relatively affluent voters, alienated from the two-party system, demoralized by the failing economy, and fearful of the inner-city underclass, flocked to support Ross Perot, a WASP Texas multibillionaire who promised radical change in an individualist melting pot that would make no distinction by race or religion.

Mr. Perot's cultural message resided in his call for preservation of the melting pot and its values. He presented his main ideas for change in a "Meet the Press" television interview on May 3, 1992, and in a speech to a rally of his supporters in California on June 18, 1992. His prescriptions for the declining economy amounted mostly to a repackaging of proposals already offered in detail by former senator Paul Tsongas of Massachusetts who had been Governor Clinton's most serious challenger for the Democratic presidential nomination; however, his cultural platform presented some new ideas in carefully coded phrases.

Perot wove together the issues of saving the melting pot; "family values" and "God-training"; "business ownership" and not "just jobs"; and the "outsider" liberty of local government versus the corrupt power of the "insider" federal government. The centerpiece of Mr. Perot's ideological rhetoric was a plea to save the "fragile melting pot," coupled with a warning that it is "all we have" and must be repaired as "the only feasible framework" for our society:

> We're a nation of many races and many creeds. We are a
> melting pot. That is a strength, not a weakness. . . . Every

time we have an election we turn it into a weakness. . . .
We split the melting pot into all kinds of special pieces,
pandering to everybody's fears and special interests.

By indirectly attacking the multicultural mosaic ("all kinds of special pieces") Mr. Perot was appealing to modern liberals like historian Arthur Schlesinger, Jr., as well as to modern conservatives. He was also signaling that he was not going to court Black voters, women, or labor ("special interests"). In this context, Perot's repeated contention that the problems of poverty and race were exacerbated by "failed" federal programs and required *exclusive* local initiative invited a retreat from affirmative action. His statement that he was "uncomfortable" with "racial-preference" programs buttressed this perception.

Perot was trying to take away the individualist ethnic coalition from Bush by offering a reorganized melting pot welcoming all "races and creeds" from the working class and underclass; this radically different melting-pot society would be subordinate to a *suburban* middle-class society consisting of *all ethnic groups,* including both the WASPs and those among the native-Black *suburban* middle class who have WASP values.

However, his reorganized melting pot was eliminated as a viable cultural alternative by the Democratic platform which united the Democratic party behind a robust communitarian (mosaic) alternative to the "fragile" individualist melting pot. Immediately after the Democratic convention nominated a ticket of two southern WASP males who were far closer in age (forty-ish) to the majority of suburban voters than either Mr. Perot or President Bush (late sixties), Ross Perot withdrew his presidential candidacy because, as I see it, he had lost his *cultural* battle with Bill Clinton.

When Clinton confidently mounted the rostrum as the presidential nominee of a united and revitalized Democratic party, he used the occasion to send a progressive, mosaic message to the American people—a cultural message that drew on the progressive traditions of Presidents Abraham Lincoln, Franklin D. Roosevelt, and John F. Kennedy, rather than on the liberal traditions of Presidents Thomas Jefferson, Harry Truman, and Jimmy Carter.

Governor Clinton introduced the cultural issue on a personal note:

> When I think about opportunity for all Americans, I think about my grandfather. He ran a country store in our little town of Hope. There were no food stamps back then, so when his customers—whether they were white or black—who worked hard and did the best they could came in with no money, well, he gave them food anyway. Just made a note of it. So did I. . . .
>
> . . . If you want to know where I come by the passionate commitment that I have to bringing people together without regard to race, it all started with my grandfather.

Subtly linking the issue of family values to the issues of cultural and class bias, Governor Clinton launched a direct attack on the way in which family values were being discussed by conservatives and liberals alike:

> Frankly, I'm fed up with politicians in Washington lecturing the rest of us about family values. Our families have values. But our Government doesn't.
>
> I want an America where family values live in our actions, not just in our speeches. An America that includes every family. Every traditional family and every extended family. Every two-parent family, every single-parent family, and every foster family. . . .
>
> . . . I want to say something to every child in America who's out there trying to grow up without a father or a mother: I know how you feel. You're special too. You matter to America. And don't you ever let anybody tell you you can't become whatever you want to be. And if other politicians make you feel like you're not a part of their family, come on and be a part of ours.

Here the open invitation to the *underclass* children who have been written off by most of American society carried an especially pointed message, yet the most powerful passages of the speech explicitly addressed federal intervention in local affairs and the sharp divisions in American society.

Clinton, a southerner, evoked President Lincoln's uncompromising prosecution of the Civil War to signal that he would use his presidential powers to the fullest extent of Constitutional law, instead of deferring to state and local rights:

> A President ought to be a powerful force for progress. But right now I know how President Lincoln felt when General McClellan wouldn't attack in the Civil War. He asked him, "If you're not going to use your army, may I borrow it?" And so I say, George Bush, if you won't use your power to help America, step aside. I will.

Finally, Governor Clinton took dead aim at the individualist melting-pot ideology, its racial code words, and its central precept of ethnic, racial, and class hierarchies by discussing what he called "our common community":

> Tonight, every one of you knows deep in your heart that we are too divided.
> It is time to heal America.
> And so we must say to every American: Look beyond the stereotypes that blind us. We need each other. All of us—we need each other. We don't have a person to waste. And yet for too long politicians have told the most of us that are doing all right that what's really wrong with America is the rest of us. Them. Them, the minorities. Them, the liberals. Them, the poor. Them, the homeless. Them, the people with disabilities. Them, the gays. We've gotten to where we've nearly themed ourselves to death. Them and them and them. But this is America. There is no them; there's only us. One nation, under God, indivisible, with liberty and justice for all.

Rarely has there been a more eloquent call for cleansing the American body politic of the lingering stench of the slave market; rarely has a politician delivered a heavier indictment of the pervasive expression of racism, bigotry, and intolerance by those in high places; rarely has American society as a whole been called to account so skillfully for its unpardonable acquiescence to the suffering of so many of its people; and rarely has a presidential nominee replied more effectively to ethnocentric and racialist demagogues, both White and Black.

IN THE AMERICA OF THE 1990S, human rights and community responsibility contend with individual liberty and radical individualism, while community values challenge family values. Those Americans who do not conform to the strictures of melting-pot culture can no longer be marginalized within our society, nor can the rest be molded as readily as in the past into a uniformly thinking mass of "one-hundred-percent-Americans" with middle-class aspirations.

As the wide discrepancy between present-day reality and melting-pot ideology disintegrates our political infrastructure and social fabric, the central issue facing our people is whether the melting pot is to be replaced by the mosaic. A growing fragmentation of American society, so-called political gridlock, and great public distrust of professional politicians have produced dialogues of the deaf across gender, racial, ethnic, and class divisions, while group stereotypes have become the rule rather than the exception. Hostile references to an amorphous "them" have become all too common in place of the inclusive and tolerant "us."

The unacknowledged source of this pervasive corrosion of our public life is the melting-pot culture which must now be dismantled in its entirety so that the health of our nation can be restored, just as one-hundred-thirty years ago slavery had to be abolished in order to save the Union.

The multiculturalist, mosaic vision of America is the natural complement of a progressive economic program from the standpoint of the social issues that American society must confront. Truly equal economic opportunity and the universal right to a job that pays a living wage would alter fundamentally the present distribution of economic and political power, resulting in new and more realistic expressions of the gender, racial, ethnic, and class aspects of culture. Consequently, the varied racial and ethnic groups which form our society would be able to replace the inherently deep divisions imposed by the melting pot with the potentially nonantagonistic diversity of the mosaic.

A nationwide community spirit generated by a national leadership having the courage to define the real problems besetting our country and to act decisively in the national interest regardless of political expediency can never take root without a rejection of the individualist traditions of melting-pot culture.

It is the mosaic that can offer the principled equality of multicultural universalism combined with freedom of individual development within an interdependent community.

Diverse groups differing widely in their expressions of the gender, racial, ethnic, and class aspects of culture would then be able to share equitably in a common culture that would nourish its varied sources instead of suppressing them. Even Anglo-American culture would recover the rich diversity of its ancient Anglo-Saxon traditions.

Although multiculturalism cannot eliminate genuine differences between the outlooks and perceived interests of different racial and ethnic groups, it can provide an environment in which those differences can be dealt with more honestly and fairly. And it is certain that the negative centrality of race, with which the twin legacies of slavery and the melting pot have burdened American society for over two centuries, can be eliminated by multiculturalism. This alone would represent a giant step toward the purification of our national soul.

BIBLIOGRAPHY

Asante, Molefi Kete. *Afrocentricity*. Trenton, N.J.: Africa World Press, 1988.

Bell, Derrick. *The Permanence of Racism*. New York: Basic Books, 1992.

Branch, Taylor. *Parting the Waters: America in the King Years 1954–1963*. New York: Simon and Schuster, 1988.

Clarke, John Henrik, ed. *William Styron's Nat Turner: Ten Black Writers Respond*. Boston: Beacon Press, 1968.

Cross, Theodore. *The Black Power Imperative: Racial Inequality and the Politics of Nonviolence*. New York: Faulkner, 1984.

Cummings, Scott, ed. *Self-Help in Urban America: Patterns of Minority Economic Development*. Port Washington, N.Y.: Kennikat Press, 1980.

D'Souza, Dinesh. *Illiberal Education: The Politics of Race and Sex on Campus*. New York: The Free Press, 1991.

Duberman, Martin B. *Paul Robeson: A Biography*. New York: Ballantine Books, 1990.

————. *The Uncompleted Past*. New York: E. P. Dutton, 1971.

Edsall, Thomas B., and Mary D. Edsall. *Chain Reaction: The Impact of Race, Rights, and Taxes on American Politics*. New York: W. W. Norton, 1991.

Elkins, Stanley M. *Slavery: A Problem in American Institutional and Intellectual Life*. Chicago: The University of Chicago Press, 1968.

Faludi, Susan. *Backlash: The Undeclared War against American Women*. New York: Crown, 1991.

Foner, Philip, ed. *Paul Robeson Speaks: Writings, Speeches, Interviews 1918–1974*. Secaucus, N.J.: Citadel Press, 1982.

Fox-Genovese, Elizabeth. *Feminism without Illusions: A Critique of Individualism*. Chapel Hill: The University of North Carolina Press, 1991.

Fuchs, Lawrence H. *The American Kaleidoscope: Race, Ethnicity, and the Civic Culture.* Hanover, N.H.: Wesleyan University Press, 1990.

Garrow, David. *Bearing the Cross: Martin Luther King, Jr., and the Southern Christian Leadership Conference.* New York: William Morrow, 1986.

Gates, Henry Louis Jr. *Loose Canons: Notes on the Culture Wars.* New York: Oxford University Press, 1992.

Gerberg, Mort. *U.S. Constitution for Everyone.* New York: Perigee Books, 1987.

Glazer, Nathan. *Ethnic Dilemmas 1964–1982.* Cambridge, Mass.: Harvard University Press, 1983.

Glazer, Nathan, and Daniel P. Moynihan. *Beyond the Melting Pot: The Negroes, Puerto Ricans, Jews, Italians, and Irish of New York City.* Cambridge, Mass.: The M.I.T. Press, 1970.

Hacker, Andrew. *Two Nations: Black and White, Separate, Hostile, Unequal.* New York: Scribners, 1992.

Hitler, Adolph. *Mein Kampf.* Boston: Houghton Mifflin, 1971.

Hofstadter, Richard, ed. *Great Issues in American History.* Vol. 2, *From the Revolution to the Civil War, 1765–1865.* New York: Vintage Books, 1958.

Horsman, Reginald. *Race and Manifest Destiny: The Origins of American Racial Anglo-Saxonism.* Cambridge, Mass.: Harvard University Press, 1981.

King, Martin Luther Jr. *Why We Can't Wait.* New York: Signet Books, 1964.

Lehmann, Nicholas. *The Promised Land: The Great Black Migration and How It Changed America.* New York: Vintage Books, 1991.

McPherson, James M. *Abraham Lincoln and the Second American Revolution.* New York: Oxford University Press, 1992.

Oates, Stephen B. *Let the Trumpet Sound: The Life of Martin Luther King, Jr.* New York: Mentor, 1985.

Phillips, Ulrich B. *American Negro Slavery: A Survey of the Supply, Employment, and Control of Negro Labor as Determined by the Plantation Regime.* Baton Rouge: Louisiana State University Press, 1969.

Pinkney, Alphonso. *The Myth of Black Progress.* Cambridge: Cambridge University Press, 1984.

Robeson, Paul. *Here I Stand.* Boston: Beacon Press, 1988.

Scott, Joan Wallach. *Gender and the Politics of History.* New York: Columbia University Press, 1988.

Sowell, Thomas. *The Economics and Politics of Race: An International Perspective.* New York: William Morrow, 1983.

———. *Ethnic America: A History.* New York: Basic Books, 1981.

Stampp, Kenneth M. *The Peculiar Institution: Slavery in the Ante-Bellum South.* New York: Vintage Books, 1989.

Steinberg, Stephen. *The Ethnic Myth: Race, Ethnicity, and Class in America.* Boston: Beacon Press, 1982.

Stuckey, Sterling. *Slave Culture: Nationalist Theory and the Foundations of Black America.* New York: Oxford University Press, 1987.

Styron, William. *The Confessions of Nat Turner.* New York: Random House, 1966.

Tocqueville, Alexis de. *On Democracy, Revolution and Society.* Edited by John Stone and Stephen Mennell. Chicago: The University of Chicago Press, 1980.

Toynbee, Arnold. *A Study of History.* Vol. 8. Oxford: Oxford University Press, 1954.

Wheeler, Thomas C., ed. *The Immigrant Experience: The Anguish of Becoming American.* New York: Penguin Books, 1971.

Whitman, Walt. *Leaves of Grass.* New York: Aventine Press, 1931.

Wilson, John Dover. *Othello.* Cambridge: Cambridge University Press, 1957.

Wilson, William Julius. *The Declining Significance of Race: Blacks and Changing American Institutions.* Chicago: The University of Chicago Press, 1978.

Woollcott, Alexander. *While Rome Burns.* New York: The Viking Press, 1934.

Zinn, Howard. *Declarations of Independence: Cross-Examining American Ideology.* New York: Harper Perennial, 1991.

———. *A People's History of the United States.* New York: Harper Perennial, 1990.

INDEX